The Void of Ethics

AGM STUDIES

AVANT-GARDE & MODERNISM

The Void of Ethics

Robert Musil and the Experience of Modernity

PATRIZIA C. McBRIDE

Northwestern
University Press
Evanston
Illinois

Northwestern University Press
Evanston, Illinois 60208-4170

Printed in the United States of America

10 9 8 7 6 5 4 3 2 1

ISBN 0-8101-2108-5 (cloth)
ISBN 0-8101-2109-3 (paper)

Library of Congress Cataloging-in-Publication Data

McBride, Patrizia C.
The void of ethics : Robert Musil and the experience of modernity / Patrizia C. McBride.
p. cm. — (Avant-garde & modernism studies)
Includes bibliographical references.
ISBN 0-8101-2108-5 (cloth text : alk. paper) — ISBN 0-8101-2109-3 (paper text : alk. paper)
1. Musil, Robert, 1880–1942—Ethics. 2. Musil, Robert, 1880–1942—Criticism and interpretation. I. Title. II. Series.
PT2625.U8Z982 2005
833′.912–dc22

2004029866

♾ The paper used in this publication meets the minimum requirements of the American National Standard for Information Sciences—Permanence of Paper for Printed Library Materials, ANSI Z39.48-1992.

For Salvatore Carollo (1930–2001)

Questo libro è per te

Contents

Acknowledgments

I benefited from the help and support of many individuals while working on this book. In particular, I would like to thank Bill Rasch, Marc Weiner, and Andreas Michel for their exceptional engagement in the early stages of the project. Jack Zipes generously read various drafts of the manuscript and provided critical feedback. I owe a great deal to Leslie Morris and Rick McCormick, on whose expert opinion and friendship I have come to depend. Peter Sprengel offered invaluable help and criticism during my yearlong research leave at the Free University in Berlin. I also wish to thank the Alexander von Humboldt Foundation for the generous research grant that enabled me to complete this project while in Berlin; I especially appreciated Cäcilia Nauderer's help and good humor at the Foundation. Grants from the Office of International Programs and the McKnight Foundation at the University of Minnesota supported research at Vienna's National Library. Finally, none of this would have happened without Brent.

Abbreviations

Only a selection of Musil's nonfictional writings have been translated into English (by Burton Pike and David Luft in *Precision and Soul,* by Philip Payne in *Diaries,* and by Burton Pike in volume 2 of *The Man without Qualities*). Where no English translation was available, I have provided my own translation with page reference to the German original. Frequently cited works by Robert Musil are abbreviated as follows:

D	*Diaries 1899–1941.* Trans. Philip Payne. Ed. Mark Mirsky. New York: Basic Books, 1998.
GW	*Gesammelte Werke in neun Bänden.* Ed. Adolf Frisé. 9 vols. Reinbek bei Hamburg: Rowohlt, 1978.
MoE	*Der Mann ohne Eigenschaften.* Vol. 1–5. *Gesammelte Werke in neun Bänden.* Ed. Adolf Frisé. 9 vols. Reinbek bei Hamburg: Rowohlt, 1978.
MwQ	*The Man without Qualities.* Trans. Sophie Wilkins and Burton Pike. 2 vols. New York: Knopf, 1995.
P	*Precision and Soul: Essays and Addresses.* Ed. and trans. Burton Pike and David S. Luft. Chicago: University of Chicago Press, 1990.
T	*The Confusions of Young Törless.* Trans. Shaun Whiteside. New York: Penguin, 2001.
TB	*Tagebücher.* Ed. Adolf Frisé. 2 vols. Second, revised edition. Reinbek bei Hamburg: Rowohlt, 1983.

The Void of Ethics

> "And yet it seems very important to me," she said, "that there's something impossible in every one of us. It explains so many things. While I was listening to you both, it seemed to me that if we could be cut open our entire life might look like a ring, just something that goes around something." She had already, earlier on, pulled off her wedding ring, and now she peered through it at the lamplit wall. "There's nothing inside, and yet it looks as though that were precisely what matters most."
>
> —Musil, *The Man without Qualities*

Introduction: An Unfashionable Modernist

At the end of one of the numerous verbal showdowns that oppose Ulrich, the protagonist in *The Man without Qualities,* to his boyhood friend Walter, Walter's wife Clarisse pulls off her wedding ring and comments on its round shape in what seems an attempt at changing the topic of a conversation that is going nowhere. What follows, however, is not one of those allusive and vaguely disturbing statements so typical for her character, a Nietzsche convert whose recurrent Nietzsche paraphrases indicate not so much her philosophical appreciation as her mental imbalance and impending insanity. What at first appears as one more incident testifying at once to the young woman's lurking disease and to the dangers of a Nietzsche reception gone awry turns into perhaps the most incisive diagnosis of the plight that confronts virtually all the main actors in Musil's imaginative chronicle of life in the Austro-Hungarian monarchy in 1913. Irritated by her husband's narrow-mindedness and display of petty-bourgeois aspirations, as they once again surface in the conversation with Ulrich, Clarisse finds herself musing on what she calls the impossibility of human existence, which she suddenly sees strikingly symbolized in her wedding ring. What she has in mind is not her rocky marriage to the frustrated and resentful Walter, though. It is the ring's shape that fires her imagination, its fact of being "just something that goes around something." In peering through the ring as through a telescope of sorts, Clarisse begins to see it as a perplexing cipher for "our entire life." As she explains, "There's nothing inside, and yet it looks as though that were precisely what matters most." Clarisse's representation of life as a ring, a thin band of precious metal encircling a hollow space, would not seem to rise above the sentimental stock images so dear to her husband if it were not for its peculiar twist. Contrary to what one would expect, it is not the ring's gold or silver that make up its value, but rather what is inside it. That inside, however, is nothing but a hollow space, a void. What matters most in life, Clarisse shrewdly suggests, is its structural void, the hollow space around which life's events congeal.

In Musil's narrative, that void stands for ethics. Ethical experience, as the ineffable promise of unconditional happiness and a fulfilled life glimpsed in fleeting moments of illumination, is presented in the novel as an "Other Condition," which is destined to remain a black hole for language and thought. It thus appears as a void delimited by life's inessential, inherently meaningless circumstances.[1] As the man without qualities later puts it to his sister, reproposing and modulating the image of a ring: "there's a whole circle of questions here, which has a large circumference and no center, and all these questions are: 'How should I live?'" (*MwQ* II, 972). In choosing the image of a centerless circle, Ulrich too seeks to clarify the paradox inherent in the modern quest for moral coordinates. In his characterization, the circle's circumference, though very extended, is reasonably well defined by the myriad of individual questions revolving around the quest for the good life. And yet the space inside the circle, that middle space from which all these queries are to be addressed, amounts to a logical impossibility. The circle as a geometric figure suggests a class of objects that are structurally endowed with a center. In this case, however, the particular circle whose perimeter is formed by the quest for moral coordinates actually lacks a center, in patent defiance of the logical properties one would expect from it. These images of a centerless circle or of a ring whose most precious attribute is the hollow space it encloses are so ostensibly fraught with contradictions that they immediately evoke a whole array of questions: Is the void normal, or is it an anomaly? Has it always been this way, or was there once something taking the place of the present nothing? And, if the circle was once replete with a lost ethical substance, where has this substance gone and what caused its disappearance? Should the void be filled again and is this still a viable proposition? If not, what is next? These questions capture the experience of modernity as it surfaces in aesthetic modernism. The idea of dysfunction and malformation suggested by the trope of a centerless circle clearly resonates with the analysis of cultural and ethical crisis that became an article of faith within German-speaking culture at the turn of the twentieth century and maintained this status throughout the upheavals of World War I, the troubled Weimar period, and the triumph of totalitarianism in both Germany and Austria. Musil's answer to these questions is, however, quite uncharacteristic of the modernist response staked out by contemporaries like Thomas Mann, Hugo von Hofmannsthal, Hermann Broch, and Rainer Maria Rilke. To be sure, Musil's characters in *The Man without Qualities* are primarily confronted with that "withdrawal of the real" that Jean-François Lyotard placed at the heart of the experience of modernity.[2] Robbed of its traditional metaphysical braces—the century-old notions of self, subject, history, community, God—life recoils from the human gaze that seeks to grasp and interpret it and falls apart in a heap of fragments. The inner core of human existence, its very center and substance, becomes a void, an unpresentable idea, as Diotima, another of Musil's protagonists, discovers in her quest for a symbol that will make manifest the world-historical meaning of the Habsburg monarchy in the twentieth century. All that is presentable are life's shattered pieces, as the experts summoned to Diotima's salon demonstrate. Entrusted with the task of articulating that elusive 'Austrian idea,' each is hopelessly trapped in the cage of his or her specialized knowledge, like asteroids orbiting a black hole of meaning. But Musil's novel offers more than this stock diagnosis of the modern condition. It sets out to interrogate the nature of the void, following a path that approximates what Lyotard described as the postmodern sensibility, which, far from representing a qualitatively different successor to modernism, reaches into modernism's very heart, as it were, and makes it beat faster.

Modernism's most familiar German narratives—exemplified in paradigmatic texts such as Hofmannsthal's "Chandos Letter," Rilke's *Malte Laurids Brigge,* Mann's *The Magic Mountain,* and Broch's *The Sleepwalkers*—tend to regard this void as resulting from the collapse of age-old certainties that provided the foundations for knowledge and morality, for politics and science, in Western civilization. This collapse, which had been prepared by epochal processes of rationalization, secularization, and specialization at work in Western societies at least since the Renaissance, was the ultimate trigger of the historical cataclysms of the twentieth century: two world wars, the rise of totalitarianism, the Shoah. In the second half of the twentieth century, other evils have come to bolster this narrative: the atomic threat, the economic rape of so-called emerging countries, the destruction of the environment, the manipulation of genetic technology. In order to counter these sinister developments, the narrative explains, society must either reinstate the old systems of coordinates (an option that seems ever more implausible given the dizzying speed of advances and innovations that unceasingly alter the physiognomy of postindustrial societies) or formulate new reference points and binding visions that will replace the old ones (to reconceptualize the "project of modernity," to speak with Jürgen Habermas).[3] Otherwise Western civilization—a worldwide business in an age of globalization and compulsive integration—will plunge into the chaos and anarchy produced by the unabashed pursuit of the basest human instincts: greed, egoism, lust for power, envy, resentment.

A competing, though far less popular, modernist narrative paints quite a different picture. It insists on seeing the ethical vacuum at the heart of the modern experience in terms other than the demise of binding systems of values and universal visions of the good life, if contemporary evils are to be confronted effectively. This is the narrative championed by Musil, among others, the one in which Lyotard recognized the postmodern projection of modernism. In true Nietzschean spirit, this discourse accounts for the alleged lost foundations in terms of historical constructs that helped Western societies cope with a void that characterizes the human condition by concealing it. The modern condition, then, is about the unclouded perception of this void. More specifically, it is about the impossibility of presenting a lasting ground or unity of human existence, which is only perceivable as the intimation of an ineffable harmony as it announces itself in fleeting moments of happiness. Drawing on Kant's *Critique of Judgment*, Lyotard accounted for the impossibility of articulating this experience by pointing to a structural discrepancy between human faculties, namely, between our faculty to conceive and our ability to present, or, in Kant's framework, the intellect and the imagination. It is this constitutive gap between the faculties that makes the void a void and not the loss of an alleged, original ethical substance. Modern art, then, is about the effort "to make visible that there is something which can be conceived and which can neither be seen nor made visible"; it is about the impossible task of presenting the unpresentable. But, as Lyotard emphasizes, there are two possible reactions to this modern conundrum. The properly modernist response "allows the unpresentable to be put forward only as the missing contents." It remains trapped within a "nostalgia for presence" that melancholically twists its gaze backward and indulges, if only unwittingly, in a yearning for the bygone certainties and foundations. The more mature, postmodernist response, on the other hand, has lost that "nostalgia for the unattainable" and can thus place its emphasis on "the power of the faculty to conceive," on "the increase of being and the jubilation which result from the invention of new rules of the game."[4] Musil's narrative in *The Man without Qualities*, I believe, is deliberately nested between these two responses, "the attempt at clearing the slate and the intimation of a synthesis," as Musil summed up the aim of his project.[5]

In bringing up Lyotard's distinction between aesthetic modernism and postmodernism, I wish to focus on the peculiar nature of Musil's modernism, on the ways in which it differs from other, contemporary modernist paradigms, and on the reasons it appears ever more appealing to us today, at a time when our ears have grown increasingly deaf to the more familiar modernist message I have described above. What interests me, in particular, is Musil's investigation of the void that lies at the heart of the experience of modernity, as it is recounted in his essays, notebooks, and, most coherently and extensively, in his ambitious thought experiment *The Man without Qualities*. Musil's unfinished novel tells the story of an individual's quest for an "other" condition of being against the setting of the now exhilarating, now troubling kaleidoscope of modern life in Austria, one year before the Great War. This quest originates from the protagonist's personal experience of inner division as well as from the disjointedness of a decentered, modern world torn apart by an uncontrollable proliferation of life-spheres and expert cultures. In this elusive Other Condition the man without qualities believes himself to glimpse an unintelligible ethical foundation, which lies in the intimation of a fundamental unity and accord of human life. His attempts to raise this intimation to the level of ordinary experience and turn it into a principle of conduct are doomed to failure. Yet this failure was to carry a positive valence, according to Musil's plans for the novel. It was to portray the Other Condition as a void inherent in the human condition and to denounce the violence lurking in all endeavors aimed at surreptitiously filling this void with yet another absolute vision of the good life. In some sketches for the novel's conclusion, this violence is triggered by the hapless maneuvering of the Parallel Campaign and realized in the apocalypse of World War I. In this way, Musil's experiment was to point to the flip side of the nostalgia for fullness and presence that still dogged his time; it was to debunk its ill-concealed intolerance for difference, its desire to forcibly impose coherence and consensus, and its impulse to force the incommensurable perspectives of the modern world into the straitjacket of a single, purportedly unifying account. This attitude, as Lyotard claims, prepares "a return of terror."[6] It is a terror Musil was forced to analyze firsthand during the formidable ascent of fascist totalitarianism in the 1920s and 1930s.

The appeal of Musil's peculiar brand of modernism, then, lies in its invitation to acknowledge the ethical void as constitutive for the human condition and to cherish it as an opportunity for rethinking ethics in modernity. This study aims at tracing Musil's intellectual exploration of ethics by unfolding the Kantian framework that led Musil to interpret it as a void resulting from a structural discrepancy in the human mind. At issue is not, however, Kant's sublime incongruity between the power to conceive and the ability to present, as revisited by Lyotard, but rather a structural discrepancy between two incompatible states of mind, which are fleetingly bridged in the momentary bliss of aesthetic experience, as it arises through the unique coalescence of intellect and imagination in the judgment of the beautiful. Musil's original reappropriation of Kantian aesthetics, I believe, yields a modernist model for conceiving the relation of literature, ethics, and purposeful human action that speaks volumes to our time.

To this day, Robert Musil enjoys an ambivalent reputation as a widely respected but somewhat neglected author. His canonization in the early sixties failed to translate into the wide reception he craved and clumsily pursued in his lifetime. This relative neglect has been blamed on the complexity and large scope of the issues he chose to bring together, both in his essays and in his fiction. The intricacy and theoretical sophistication of his reflection, as has been said, is responsible for his reputation as a difficult author who is not readily accessible to a large audience. One must also add that Musil's works were not easily incorporated within the paradigms that controlled the reception of modernism up to the debates on postmodernism, which, in spite of important ideological differences, often appeared exceedingly preoccupied with delivering clear-cut assessments of authors and texts based on polarities such as high / low, right / left, engaged /apolitical, modernism /avant-garde.[7] When forced into interpretive paradigms dominated by either/or choices, Musil seems an indecisive thinker, indeed, the irresolute explorer of antinomies: the supporter of reason and an antimetaphysical, empirical approach to experience, and at the same time the proponent of mystical states; the champion of multiplicity and ambivalence, yet the advocate of partial solutions and of the importance of not suspending judgment; a professedly apolitical writer, yet a deeply engaged thinker. Even when compared with contemporaries whose reflection also displays a high degree of ambivalence and elusiveness, such as Benjamin, Adorno, or Bloch, Musil appears to be a thinker swimming against the tide, clinging to unfashionable lifesavers such as reason, scientific precision, partial solutions, or the seemingly ineffectual utopias of essayism and an inductive attitude at a time that saw the inexorable rise of totalitarianism in Europe.[8]

Musil's biography reflects the life of an intellectual whose clear sense of his merits and resolute commitment to his mission as a writer prevented him from entering the compromises and forming the alliances that would have secured him the influence and recognition he deserved.[9] Born in Klagenfurt in 1880, he was trained as an engineer, a mathematician, and an experimental psychologist. After his first novel, *The Confusions of Young Törless* (1906), was hailed as a literary sensation, Musil gave up a career in academia to dedicate himself completely to writing. At home in the culture of Vienna as well as dynamic Berlin, Musil soon won the respect and support of prominent writers and intellectuals, including Franz Blei, Alfred Döblin, and the influential literary critic Alfred Kerr. In spite of the high esteem in which he was held in contemporary literary circles, as documented by the prestigious literary prizes he was awarded in the 1920s, he never succeeded in garnering the favor of a broader audience, in part on account of his relatively slim and unsteady literary output. His largely unsuccessful attempts to secure a livelihood for himself and his family through his activity as an essayist and theater critic led to the financial difficulties that plagued him all his life. Toward the end of the 1920s, chronic financial straits and the frustration of having to compete for the attention of an audience seemingly hungry for coarser literary fare bred in him a growing bitterness, causing him to resent more successful writers like Thomas Mann and Hermann Broch. Nonetheless, by the late 1920s Musil had managed to consolidate his position in Berlin's literary circles. His reputation was further enhanced by the critical success of the first volume of *The Man without Qualities,* published in 1930. He failed to capitalize on this increased visibility, however, due to his inability to follow through, in a timely manner, with the second and final volume of the novel. The breakthrough of National Socialism in Germany in 1933 led to his gradual eclipse on the German scene. Increasingly plagued by writer's block and various ailments, Musil found himself working at an even slower pace on the sequel to the novel's first volume, which became the object of almost obsessive concern. Germany's annexation of Austria in 1938 forced him to leave Vienna with his family and seek refuge in Switzerland. At his sudden death in Geneva in 1942, he was still working on what appear to be relatively early chapters in the novel's second volume. The first postwar edition of *The Man without Qualities,* published by Adolf Frisé in 1952, lifted Musil's name from the oblivion into which it had plunged in the late 1930s and quickly secured him a reputation as one of the most accomplished and incisive novelists of the twentieth century. His inclusion in the pantheon of European modernism alongside writers like Joyce and Proust at last earned Musil the success that had eluded him during his lifetime.

Musil's modernist sensibility becomes fully comprehensible when considered in light of his distinctive stance on modernity, which set him apart from other prominent modernists and substantially informed his views on art and ethics. Musil saw himself as a representative of the generation of 1900, a generation of intellectuals and artists that had come of age amidst narratives of crisis and tales of redemption, who saw themselves confronted, as Hofmannsthal perceptively put it, with a present haunted by "ambiguity and uncertainty" and a "subdued chronic dizziness."[10] This malaise grew out of the difficulties in coping with profound, historical transformations in the physiognomy of Western societies. At issue are phenomena like industrialization, urbanization, and the mechanization of everyday life made possible by the extraordinary advances in science and technology in the second half of the nineteenth century. These phenomena produced the subversion of extant social structures, particularly as a result of the decline of old economic elites and the emergence of an urban working class, itself made more menacing by the rise of mass politics and mass culture under the aegis of highly polarized political ideologies. In the 1890s Nietzsche's critique of rationality detonated like a bombshell in the cultural arena, debunking the faith in an ontologically grounded, rational notion of truth that had sustained both scientific and philosophical inquiry well into the nineteenth century and opening the way for skepticism, relativism, and nihilism. But if the natural sciences had emerged comparatively unscathed from, and in fact even thrived on, their confinement within a skeptical and relativistic framework, the blow to the human sciences had been too great. It prompted a radical reorientation, in part along the lines of a philosophy of life that radicalized Nietzsche's critique of reason and often drew on an unspecified notion of experience, as well as on conceptually murky categories such as life, soul, spirit, feeling, and intuition. This perspective was often bolstered by self-indulgent irrationalism and unconditional resentment for the little-understood phenomena of industrialization, urbanization, specialization, and rationalization driving the development of modern societies. It bred a regressive cultural climate bent on seeking refuge in an emphatic notion of culture as the last depository of the innermost substance of human existence. The framework of cultural despair with which it frequently became associated found expression in the immensely popular narratives of corruption and decline spun by conservative thinkers such as Oswald Spengler, Walther Rathenau, and Ludwig Klages, as well as in the aggressive cultural chauvinism that culminated in the "ideas of 1914."[11]

In his early treatise on the novel, Georg Lukács delivered perhaps the most rigorous and sympathetic analysis of the modern condition from a perspective colored by the cultural despair of the early twentieth century. It is significant that Lukács also employs the image of a circle of life to weave together familiar themes of modernity, alienation, and ethical disorientation. In this way he seemingly foreshadows Clarisse's diagnosis of the human condition as a hollow ring a decade later. Lukács portrays the lost unity of human experience—whose echoes could still be perceived in the harmonious art of Greek antiquity—as consigned to the reassuring, enclosed horizon of a self-contained world that has not yet tasted the fruit of unbridled rationality. Life was for the Greeks a well-rounded circle endowed with a stable center of meaning from which all aspects of experience could be interpreted and organized. But the progressive and one-sided affirmation of a rational mode for confronting existence exploded the secure confines of the Greek world. It broke open its harmonious circle of life, letting the gray matter of Western civilization splatter across the stars in a whirlpool of cosmic dispersion.[12] In this way the moderns were made to bear the original sin of reason, a sin perpetrated by their ancestors when they yielded to the temptation to unleash the corrosive power of reason the Greek world had kept in check. It is important to note that Lukács's theory engages a much more sophisticated level of discussion than the rancorous attacks on reason mounted by less rigorous thinkers whose ideas Lukács nonetheless seemed to be echoing. His transposition of the development of rationality into a secularized version of the Christian tale of fall and salvation offers an idiosyncratic account of reason from the perspective of a beleaguered neo-Kantianism.[13]

In spite of superficial similarities, Musil's image of a circle of life summoned by Clarisse's ring evokes a very different vision of modernity and of the human condition—a vision hinging on a narrative not of loss and decline but rather of misrecognition and self-delusion. This difference is instructive, for it marks the distance separating Musil from the cultural pessimism that informs much German modernism. Through the tale of a deformation and successive rupture of the circle of life, Lukács's account is intended to capture the dynamism of history, envisaged as a process of dispersion and decline fueled by a disorderly diffusion of precious human substance, which the circle once contained. By contrast, Musil's image is fundamentally static and intimates a timeless condition rather than a historical development. The circle of life symbolized in Clarisse's ring is intact, yet its center is hollow. Nothing suggests that there ever was something at the place of the void. Precisely the nature of the void constitutes the main point of contention between Musil and Lukács. Musil did not believe that the ethical void was the result of an inauspicious development driven by a historical process of rationalization that culminated in a cultural crisis of unprecedented proportions. Rather, his investigations led him to see it in terms of a structural feature built into the human condition, a void which for centuries had been disguised, indeed surreptitiously filled with narratives postulating the existence of a primordial ethical substance, whether rooted in the Christian God or in some other metaphysical construct. For Musil, reason was not a culprit but the human faculty whose development had helped debunk these narratives by providing a medium for discerning and reflecting upon the void. Against the grain of the disparate narratives of decline and prophecies of doom that dominated the German cultural arena at the beginning of the twentieth century, Musil insisted on turning the prevalent perception of crisis into an opportunity for confronting the void at the heart of ethics.

If the perception of absence, of a missing ethical ground, either as the result of a loss or as a structural void, is at the very heart of modernist discourse, it hardly finds richer modulations than within Viennese modernism, from Freud's inquiry into an elusive unconscious to Kraus's desire to reinstate the forlorn language of old Austria, from Rilke's cajoling of ever absent angels to Kafka's negative evocation of elusive authority. Musil's debt to this tradition cannot be overstated, yet his distance from the Viennese is perhaps even more instructive for understanding the specificity of his modernist vision. Jacques LeRider has mapped the patchwork of identity crises in turn-of-the-century Vienna by calling attention to the link between the distinctive "loss of reality" that marks Viennese decadence and the demise of age-old strongholds of individual identity.[14] Hermann Bahr's oft-quoted proclamation of an irretrievable self remains perhaps the most trenchant expression of the collapse of traditional notions of subjectivity and selfhood in both science and philosophy under the onslaught of Nietzsche's critique of metaphysics and Mach's empiriocriticism.[15] The modern feeling of alienation became funneled into the perception of an inner dividedness, along lines of speculation that recast themes first articulated within German Romanticism on the eve of the nineteenth century. Accordingly, human life is portrayed as split between an ugly ordinary experience dominated by rationalization, modernization, specialization, soullessness, and mechanization on the one hand, and the intimation of an alternative realm that escapes language and thought and surfaces in fleeting moments of illumination on the other. While interest in this latter domain spawned whole new fields of inquiry in the human sciences, from the psychology of religion to the investigation of the unconscious, much Viennese modernism tended to focus its attention on the inadequacy of linguistic and conceptual structures for grasping and describing this alternative realm of experience. Following in Nietzsche's footsteps, Fritz Mauthner provided a formidable model for an investigation of language that was simultaneously a powerful critique of knowledge, as it proceeded from a fundamental identity between language and thought. At the same time, Mauthner's "mysticism without God" epitomized the peculiar mix of linguistic skepticism, suspicion of reason, and neomysticism that formed the hallmark of much Viennese culture at the turn of the twentieth century.[16] It found an emblematic document in Hofmannsthal's "Chandos Letter," which not only traced the simultaneous disintegration of language, thought, and shared moral coordinates, but also identified art as the new idiom that would grant expression to those moments of illumination into which ethical experience seems to have fled in the modern period.[17] In a similar attempt to delimit the realm of philosophical logic, Wittgenstein's *Tractatus Logico-Philosophicus* reasserted the affinity between aesthetics and ethics as two experiential realms, which are located outside the grasp of ordinary linguistic and conceptual structures.

With his first novel, Musil situated himself squarely within this tradition. *The Confusions of Young Törless,* from 1906, explores the disorientation of an adolescent first confronted with the perception of an inner split grounded in the intermittent, disquieting emergence of a prelinguistic, preconceptual mode of experience, which he glimpses in both the paradoxes of mathematical concepts and the sadistic abuse of a classmate at the hands of two boarding school bullies. But the resolution of Törless's inner trials is also symptomatic of the distance separating Musil from the "culture of nerves" of the *décadance,* for the boy's tribulations come to an end when he learns to accept this duality as a fact of life. As Alfred Kerr immediately recognized, Törless appeared to be a very different character from the emaciated and oversensitive youth populating the rarified tales of decadent literature. This is in part due to the fact that the novel's exploration of a split in human existence is not framed within the trendy linguistic skepticism and epistemological nihilism so characteristic of Viennese culture. What shapes Musil's inquiry is instead his background in the natural sciences and his subsequent training in the experimental human sciences during his Berlin studies under Carl Stumpf (1903–8), which culminated in his dissertation on Mach's *Analysis of Sensations.* It was during this time (and in the years leading to the outbreak of World War I) that Musil outlined the main contours of his aesthetic endeavor, which envisions literature as a medium that enlists the rigor, flexibility, and optimism of scientific thinking in the investigation of moral issues.

The scientific emphasis on factual observation and the primacy of experience enabled Musil to foreground the singular and contingent nature of ethical choices and expose the anachronism of the traditional view of morality, which is "in its method, static, with the fixed as its basic principle" and predicated upon the formulation of atemporal and universally transparent rules of conduct (*P* 63). A careful reader of Nietzsche, Musil well understood that the philosopher's merciless deconstruction of Western morality did not open the way to nihilism, but rather offered a fertile terrain for rethinking obsolete philosophical and moral categories. Musil likewise recognized in the antiessentialist and decentered notion of subjectivity that emerged from Ernst Mach's psychology a framework for a more realistic appraisal of individual identity. This led Musil to believe in the historical malleability of individual consciousness: "Good and evil, duty and violation of duty, are forms in which the individual establishes an emotional balance between himself and the world" (*P* 39). In his eyes, literature offered a flexible medium for highlighting the intricate tangle of material circumstances, social conditioning, personal history, feelings, emotions, and thoughts that frame moral choices, a medium that places the observer in the position to correctly appraise the singularity and contingency of the ethical, rather than treating it as an aberration. A perspective that affirms ethical singularity does not entail the utter dismissal of codified rules of conduct, however, but rather provides a corrective that highlights their contingency and limitations. The ultimate goal is to propose new, "appealing models of how one can be human, to *invent* the inner person," indeed, to find partial, contingent solutions to the pressing issues of the day (*P* 64). Within this frame, literature is reconfigured as a realm for the imaginative experimentation with creative alternatives to reality. It is sustained by an inductive attitude that treats the given, the reality of facts, as merely one actualized option of countless nonrealized possibilities.

Musil associated the writer's mode of operation with the movement of essayism, which he defined as the intellectual attitude bent on extending the methodological rigor of the natural sciences to the domain of radically singular events pertaining to art and ethics. His early insistence on a rigorous scrutiny of experience led him to distance himself from the irrationalism and anti-intellectualism that permeated contemporary discourse on art and, in his judgment, irreparably compromised the aesthetic experiments of Impressionism, Symbolism, and Expressionism alike. This faithfulness to the data of experience compelled him to reject as mystifications what he saw as the two primary ideological premises shared by these currents, namely, the polarization of a pure dimension of feeling on the one hand and a corrupt and oppressive rationality on the other, as well as its corollary, faith in art as an uncontaminated safe haven grounded in the pristine domain of the irrational. In Musil's eyes, the related cult of immediacy and postulation of a phantasmic intuitive knowledge presumably consigned to art not only wound up foreclosing the possibility of a long overdue inquiry into the fabric of aesthetic imagination and the mechanisms of aesthetic experience. It also fed into a rash suspicion of reason bent on blaming rationality for all the evils of civilization. In the vehement anti-intellectualism of his time Musil recognized the token for a misplaced longing to escape the troubled reality of a time of transition plagued by an endemic lack of "ordering concepts" (*P* 126). He believed that a balanced assessment of the role played by reason in the epochal erosion of Western metaphysical habits of thought was necessary to unravel the knot of contemporary cultural malaise. For him, the acceleration of processes of secularization and rationalization that had been under way at least since the Renaissance might well have precipitated the recognition of the groundlessness of moral systems at the beginning of the twentieth century, but they certainly had not caused their demise.

Much to Musil's dismay, however, the escapist tendencies of the 1910s were only magnified in the years following the First World War. The widespread desire to retrench and look to the past for comforting visions, which characterized the postwar years, prompted Musil to return to many of the issues he had addressed before the war. After serving as an officer in the Austrian army during the war, Musil moved back to Vienna, where he resumed his activity as an essayist and a theater critic. He set out to continue his inquiry into ethics in the longer essays from the 1920s and in *The Man without Qualities,* which he regarded as a decisive contribution to the crisis that was pushing his contemporaries into the embrace of all too "familiar fetishes of epoch, nation, race, Catholicism, the intuitive man" (*P* 127). Particularly, he insisted on distinguishing between the historical roots of the predicaments that haunted the newly constituted German and Austrian Republics on the one hand—their economic quagmire, their sense of violated national pride ensuing from the defeat suffered in the war, their riotous political climate too hastily blamed on democracy's presumed shortcomings—and on the other the perception of an ethical black hole that defined the modern condition. The moral and ideological vacuum so vociferously decried in the 1920s was not, Musil believed, the result of the liquidation of traditional moral certainties. Rather, it represented the unobstructed manifestation of a void that is constitutive for the human condition and whose unhampered perception had been made possible by the conditions of modernity.[18] Musil was adamant about underscoring the optimistic and emancipatory potential of a modern existence marked by ethical groundlessness, for "if it turns out that our innermost being does not dangle from the puppet strings of some hobgoblin of fate, but on the contrary that we are draped with a multitude of small, haphazardly linked weights, then we ourselves can tip the scales" (*P* 122).

The narrative I have spun so far paints a picture of Musil's intellectual engagement few would dispute today.[19] This consensus breaks down, however, when it comes to assessing the significance and validity of the theories Musil developed in the 1920s and 1930s based on his diagnosis of the modern condition. Drawing on sources as diverse as the secular studies on mysticism by Martin Buber, the phenomenological investigation of exalted emotional states by Max Scheler and Ludwig Klages, and the insights of gestalt psychology as well as the psychopathological inventory of Ernst Kretschmer, Musil recoded the fundamental split of human existence as the coalescence of two incommensurable states of mind in the individual: an ordinary condition presiding over everyday experience and another, ecstatic condition of feeling that emerges in fleeting moments of illumination. In keeping with his conviction that the aesthetic, and literature in particular, provides the most appropriate locus for an inquiry into this latter condition, Musil set out to explore it in *The Man without Qualities.* The novel's multilayered narrative offers an uncanny portrayal of the time before the Great War from the perspective of a postwar era that had failed to learn the lessons of the war and, as a result, was treading in the same dangerous paths that had caused the prewar order to collapse. The first volume, published in 1930, follows the vicissitudes of the protagonist Ulrich as he searches for an impossible, ethical center of gravity in modernity. His quest unfolds against the backdrop of the Parallel Campaign, a fictional political initiative mounted in Vienna in 1913. Under the pretext of planning the celebrations for Franz Joseph's seventy years of reign in 1918, the Campaign embodies a last, desperate attempt at providing much-needed ideological braces for the crumbling Austro-Hungarian monarchy, "a state just barely able to go along with itself" (*MwQ* I, 31). The second volume, of which only thirty-eight chapters were published during Musil's lifetime, in 1932 to 1933, and which otherwise dissipates in a myriad of drafts and variants, recounts Ulrich's investigation of that Other Condition of being in which the novel's protagonist believes to glimpse the source of ethical experience. Early drafts document Musil's intention to dramatize the failure of Ulrich's attempts to ground his life in this utterly moral condition, which he pursues in a mystical erotic relationship with his sister Agathe.

It is precisely the mystical vision that unfolds in the fragment of the second volume that has posed the greatest interpretive challenges. Its evaluation appears crucial for assessing Musil's aesthetic inquiry in the novel and the essays. Critics in the 1960s and 1970s often read the novel's development toward the siblings' asocial adventure as a token for Musil's desire to distance himself from the ugly political reality of the 1930s, a distancing that can be easily viewed as a retreat. For many, the eclipse of sociohistorical reality in the second volume represented a way for Musil to acknowledge that the rise of totalitarianism in the 1930s had rendered his early utopian visions—the related utopias of essayism and a scientific precision—ineffectual and dated.[20] Indeed, when the Nazi dictatorship put an end to Germany's democratic experiment in 1933, Musil's expressions of discouragement and self-doubt grew stronger and more frequent, as he and his Jewish wife Martha were forced to leave Berlin, where they had resided on and off since the 1910s, and establish their permanent residence in Vienna until 1938. At his death in Swiss exile in 1942, Musil had yet to flesh out the inductive attitude he had envisioned as the lesson his protagonist was to draw from his failures. This circumstance prompted some critics to even speak of a failure of Musil's overall project. What was not available to early commentators, however, were reliable and comprehensive editions of both the novel and the notebooks, which appeared in 1976 and 1978. The previously unpublished materials included in the newer editions show that the development in favor of the narcissistic "utopia of the Other Condition" had been planned at least since the mid-1920s, a circumstance that makes a reading of the Other Condition as Musil's resigned response to fascism difficult to sustain. Since the 1980s, readings informed by poststructuralist paradigms have seized on the mystical and ineffable qualities of this vision and related its failure to the novel's incompleteness and presumed incompletability. Within this frame, the novel has been read as anticipating a deconstructive understanding of language and literature.[21] If to this day Musil's novel is widely acknowledged as a document of uncontested literary value, the tentative, mystical character of its ethical visions has not ceased to puzzle readers, especially when put to the test of the political developments facing Europe in the 1930s.

This study offers a reading of the Other Condition as Musil's dramatization of an ethical void built into human existence. To this aim, I cast into sharper focus the mostly overlooked development of Musil's thinking on art and ethics over time, as he attempted to come to grips with the changing historical circumstances of the 1930s. This development takes the form of an increasing reliance on crucial concepts from Kant's *Critique of Judgment,* which Musil adapted to fit contemporary psychological paradigms. This focus on the gradual emergence of a Kantian framework makes it possible to grasp the fundamental continuity in Musil's reflection on literature and ethics. It not only dispels the impression of a dispersion or even regression under the pressure of the intractable problems of the Nazi era; it also provides an essential key to interpreting the novel's seemingly apolitical turn in the second volume, whose focus on the siblings' mystical adventure must be seen as a critical commentary on the yearning for absolute visions and definitive truths that propelled fascism to power. Musil's debt to Kant becomes especially evident in his longer, important essays from the 1930s. Reinscribing Kant's account of aesthetic judgment onto contemporary psychological and gestalt-theoretical paradigms, Musil identified a momentary, ecstatic state of the mind, which is triggered by a peculiar coalescence of the intellectual and emotional faculties and announces itself in the feeling of a disinterested pleasure. This special unison of faculties grants a glimpse into the otherwise ungraspable unity that grounds human life; it is therefore perceived as a thoroughly moral, alternative condition of being. Appropriating important arguments from the third *Critique,* Musil conceptualized art as a medium that allows for the ineffable unison of faculties to momentarily surface in ordinary life and thus serves as a temporary bridge between ordinary experience and the Other Condition. For Musil, this is the quintessential condition of the literary; it produces what Stanley

Corngold has termed a "nonconceptually cognitive," its peculiar feeling being suspended between cognition and feeling.[22] In Musil's account, the ecstatic experience triggered by aesthetic feeling favors a reshuffling in the individual's perception of reality and disrupts formulaic modes of experience, releasing the individual from the spell of established pictures of the world and opening up a space for the imaginative play with, and the emancipatory reaggregation of, given elements of experience.[23] Aesthetic pleasure is thus "dependent on intelligibility dawning,"[24] that is, it is predicated on the disclosure of a novel understanding of reality and is thus necessarily accompanied by a feeling of purposiveness. When further pressed to specify the ethical import of aesthetic experience vis-à-vis the ruinous political developments of the late 1930s, Musil went so far as to advance the hypothesis that the aesthetic balance of intellect and feeling is also the depository of an immanent, nongeneralizable principle of purposive human conduct, which is fundamentally aesthetic in nature, since it is guided by feeling and not by concepts. Musil claimed to recognize the deterioration of this principle in the stupidity that had led the Germans to yield to the temptation of fascism.

The Man without Qualities, then, dramatizes just this understanding of a structural discrepancy between two incommensurable states of mind, whose ultimately unbridgeable gap produces what humans perceive as an ethical black hole. Specifically, the novel stages its protagonist's failed attempts to close the gap between an ordinary and an "other" condition of mind, which, in the first volume, take the shape of an essayistic utopia aimed at raising the Other Condition to the cognitive level of ordinary experience. The second, unfinished part of the novel was supposed to recount the reverse attempt at plunging ordinary life into the Other Condition. The failure of the siblings' latter attempt, made more sinister by the outbreak of the war, was intended as a warning against the dangers of overdetermining the ethical by filling its cognitive void with yet another absolute vision of the good life. In Lyotard's terms, the novel undertakes the endeavor to understand the human yearning to present the unpresentable, that is, the Other Condition that grounds ethical experience. At the same time, it also invites the reader to acknowledge the impossibility and undesirability of this yearning and denounces the violence lurking behind the attempts to grant reality to the unpresentable. The fact that ethics turns out to be a void for language and thought does not entail a dysfunctional state, but it is perhaps the most profound insight into the human condition that modernity has gained. From this perspective, Clarisse's image of a hollow ring symbolizing the impossibility of human life contains a productive challenge to face the paradox of ethics, namely, the impulse, built into the human condition, to think of the most important principle that structurally eludes the experiential categories of ordinary life.

Given the lack of an ontological foundation for the novel's inquiry into ethics, the text is compelled to establish this grounding self-referentially, by raising the fundamental question of how it is possible to investigate ethics through the medium of art. That is, on a self-referential plane the text explores the conditions of possibility of its own inquiry, thematizing its relation to its object of investigation and specifying it by presenting the literary as situated at the intersection between ordinary experience and the Other Condition. Musil's novel raises the question of art's function in modernity from a perspective—that of the acknowledgment of the contingent coordinates of human experience—that sets it apart from many contemporary modernist endeavors. It identifies art as a privileged medium for acknowledging the singularity of ethical experience but also draws the limits of reflection on ethics in modernity, while self-reflexively formulating its own function and drawing its own limits. What emerges is an ethos that is paradoxically founded on the insight into the impossibility of articulating a permanent ethical foundation for the modern world.[25] It is a stance that accepts the coexistence and confrontation of various ideologies and language games not on the grounds of a presumed common foundation, but rather precisely because it recognizes the lack of such foundations.

It is important to note that the Kantian horizon that encloses Musil's reflection on literature and ethics is not a systematic network of principles. Rather, it is a reservoir of heuristic categories and productive images that frame the insights Musil derived in part from his scientific studies. In reconstructing this horizon, I not only aim to emphasize the originality of Musil's response within German modernism. I also wish to show that the notion of the writer and public intellectual, which Musil articulates partly in contrast to contemporary models, reflects a view of modernity that is especially timely today, for it helps scrutinize long-standing assumptions on the critical mandate of the intellectual and the artist.

Musil's reflection unfolds against the backdrop of rising modern intellectual consciousness at the turn of the century, as profound changes in the function of cultural elites, triggered by far-reaching social, economic, and political transformations in the fabric of Western societies, set the stage for the emergence of a new, relatively disenfranchised intellectual stratum.[26] The experience of alienation, marginalization, and social uprootedness spawned by confrontation with a rapidly changing economic and social landscape shaped the critical self-consciousness of intellectuals and writers in fundamental ways. It often gave rise to embittered accounts bent on interpreting the crisis of the intellectual's identity as the token of a more general crisis in modern societies. Peculiar for the German context is the recourse to an idealized notion of culture, viewed as the last endangered social realm that could still function as a bulwark against the threatening development of capitalist economy and mass politics.

Dagmar Barnouw has shown how the perception of a crisis in Weimar culture was inextricably bound to a sense of threatened intellectual identity, so much so that the articulation of the intellectual's critical mandate came to rely quite heavily upon a specific reading of the present as a time of crisis. In other words, the perception of a state of emergency, which distinguished Weimar culture, functioned as a source of legitimation and anchoring for the intellectual's critical discourse. By the same token, intellectual discourse itself was bound to reinforce the narratives of crisis that authorized it, even where it did not directly generate them. It would certainly be misguided to second-guess the motives or question the intellectual integrity of the German and Austrian intellectuals and writers who found themselves caught in this circle of critique and self-legitimation. Yet, as Barnouw has noted, the low degree of awareness demonstrated by many intellectuals when it came to reflecting upon their personal interest and self-implication in the narratives they were spinning often appears puzzling.

In examining the relationship between the perception of crisis and the articulation of the intellectual's and the artist's mission in Weimar culture, Barnouw exposes a troubling pattern of aloofness and self-delusion, which she traces to what she generally terms a "temptation of distance."[27] Distance assumes a twofold meaning in her careful account. In the first place, it denotes the perplexing hiatus separating the narratives produced by Weimar intellectuals and writers, on the one hand, and Germany's historical reality in the 1920s, on the other. In reviewing examples ranging from Franz Pfemfert's sanguine pacificism in *Die Aktion* to Thomas Mann's esoteric parable in *The Magic Mountain,* Barnouw notes how a great many of the thinkers under consideration proved to be dangerously prone to taking at face value their own fictional accounts of social reality, while failing to put them to the test of lived experience. In addition, distance—understood as the principled detachment from the powers that be, particularly from the presumably contaminating influence of extant political ideologies and institutions—functioned as a strategy for legitimizing one's account of reality as disinterested, uncontaminated, truthful, and thus inherently superior. In stylizing their social function as grounded in a privileged vantage point outside or above the social system and untainted by the dirty game of Weimar politics, paradigmatically embodied by Mannheim's free-floating intellectual, numerous thinkers failed to perceive and articulate their own implication and self-interest, for instance, in their self-attribution of a critical mission.[28]

Barnouw's nuanced account adds specificity to what has become an established assessment of the intellectual climate in Weimar culture,[29] a term she extends to some German-language writers in the first Austrian Republic. This assessment resonates with the thesis of an exodus impulse fostered by a mood of world repudiation and intolerance toward contemporary reality advanced by Norbert Bolz and Anson Rabinbach, among others.[30] It is significant that Barnouw singles out Musil as exemplary for an intellectual stance that does not yield to this temptation of distance on account of its commitment to confront the complexity of the present with an optimism guided by an open-minded, inductive attitude. Especially after World War I, Musil wondered aloud about his contemporaries' tendency to "turn away from the present" (*P* 176), that is, to withdraw from the challenges posed by contemporary reality and seek refuge in sterile fictions. In the aesthetic realm, Musil chastised what he termed a "senseless, deceptive, universal hunger for artistic redemption, for a Homeric simplicity in which we could, with all our differences, some day subside once again into unity" (*P* 34). He vehemently criticized what he saw as a related propensity to ground the intellectual's and artist's critical mandate in a presumed gift of intuition or some analogous, distinctive cognitive power, which would in turn grant him a position on the outside of degenerate social reality. In his discussion of modernism and postmodernism, Jochen Schulte-Sasse has outlined the implications of this stance, identifying in the dream of an aesthetic sphere untainted by the ills of the social body the driving impulse of both high-modernism and the avant-garde. Beyond their important differences, Schulte-Sasse argues, both discourses start from a view of art as a realm that is not—yet—completely permeated by the unrelenting transformations of technological progress and the mechanisms of monetary economy and instrumental reason at work in mature capitalist societies.[31] On account of its position outside the corrupt social body, art is thus said to provide an authoritative terrain from which critique can be launched. Drawing on conceptualizations of the aesthetic sphere by Herbert Marcuse and Odo Marquard, Schulte-Sasse argues that any critique that relies on the assumption of an aesthetic outside fails to reflect upon its implications in the social mechanisms it seeks to criticize. It thus runs the risk of becoming an instrument of consolation and compensation that unwittingly provides an outlet for the unresolved conflicts dogging the social body, thereby reinforcing the system in the very act of subjecting it to scrutiny.

Musil found in Thomas Mann an egregious example of an intellectual attitude that, under the pretense of unyielding critique, provided a site for at once articulating and defusing the contradictions haunting society. To be sure, Musil's distaste for Mann's self-serving stylization as the poetic moral consciousness of the German nation in the 1930s was not free of personal resentment for the incomparably more successful novelist. Yet Musil did not go too far when he noted that Mann, in his self-adjudicated critical role as Germany's public intellectual and a last, heroic spokesperson for humanism's threatened wisdom, did little more than refine the prejudices and convictions of his bourgeois audience, effectively reinforcing those prejudices in the very gesture of subjecting them to scrutiny.[32] Under the pretense of leading his bourgeois audience, Musil believed, Mann was actually being led by them. Prior to his death in 1922, the Jewish industrialist and politician Walther Rathenau also embodied an exemplary case of suspicious intellectual myopia, according to Musil.[33] Rathenau enjoyed enormous popularity in the first two decades of the century thanks to his prolific essayistic activity, which situated him at the intersection of cutting-edge debates in philosophy, psychology, and sociology. Musil acknowledged Rathenau's perceptiveness and intellectual breadth, yet he also recognized in his trendy dilettantism and occasional strategic intellectual laxity the representative vices of an epoch. It was not only that Rathenau's vision of a preindustrial, precapitalistic society frozen in an austere utopia jarred both with the present-day reality of mature capitalism and with Rathenau's own implication in it as a tycoon of the booming electrical industry. More important, Rathenau exemplified in Musil's eyes the yearning for absolute, all-encompassing perspectives that fed into a pernicious tendency to absolutize insights gained from one discipline or subsystem of society and magnify them into a body of coherent truths, endowed with the force of a new redemptive vision. Musil understood that in modern societies, characterized by what Max Weber described as the functional differentiation of life-spheres and the loss of unifying coordinates of orientation, the temptation was strong to make oneself and one's discourse the "center of a modest overview" (*P* 53), with the effect that "every little twig spreads out into a microcosm" (*P* 52). The skewed visions thus produced were ill equipped to deal with the modern plurality of competing cognitive discourses and specialized domains of experience. On account of the inevitable discrepancy between their reductive outlook on reality and the actual complexity of modern life, they fostered a mood of denunciation and condemnation of the present, which they charged with being unable to pursue lofty ideals and hopelessly marred by skepticism, nihilism, and the relentless proliferation of discordant ideologies.

Musil did not believe that the pluralistic structure of the modern world was inherently evil and should be overcome. Quite to the contrary, he saw in it an as yet unrecognized chance for progress and emancipation. He was convinced that art, and literature in particular, offered an especially well suited vehicle for critique and positive change. Aesthetic critique was not, however, to be anchored in the claim to a superior vantage point, presumably grounded in a position outside society that would enable the artist to retrieve an obfuscated truth or restore a lost, comprehensive horizon of meaning. Musil insisted that art remains at all times fully implicated in society as one of its functional subsystems. He believed that aesthetic critique is sustained by art's ability to trigger the estrangement and rearrangement of shared narratives of reality, which operates, at the level of production, through the combinatory power of aesthetic imagination and, on the side of reception, by means of a reshuffling of perceptions in aesthetic experience. Musil credited this combinatory ability with the power to challenge the status quo through the production of alternative visions, which are bound to enter into competition with our entrenched perception of reality. In this way, art can offer an imaginary foil to the real that challenges established views of the world while remaining firmly grounded in it. Accordingly, the critique to which literature subjects reality is inherently immanent and contingent, for it remains inextricably entwined with the social system it seeks to scrutinize. All it can produce are partial solutions that structurally beg for future reexamination and revision.

In his discussion of the intellectual attitudes that define modernism and postmodernism, Zygmunt Bauman lists three characteristics that capture the distinctively modernist quality of key theoreticians of modernity at the turn of the twentieth century. Bauman stresses at first the modernist insistence on acknowledging the "irreversible character of the changes modernity signified or brought in its wake," regardless of how positive or negative these changes may have appeared. Furthermore, modernity is presented as "an essentially unfinished" but also unfinishable project, its open-endedness being seen "as the paramount, perhaps defining, attribute." Finally, an important criterion for discriminating between more or less valuable modernist visions lies for Bauman in their relative temporal perspective and self-positioning. The visions that appear more dependable and informative today are those that recognize modernity as a "phenomenon with a rich pre-history but with nothing visible beyond it, nothing which could relativize or objectivize the phenomenon itself." Because there is "no outside vantage point" that could provide "a frame of reference for the perception of modernity itself," the more valuable visions are those that approach and represent it from the inside, as it were, from a sympathetic perspective that constantly reflects its own contingency, partiality, and self-implication.[34] These traits, which for Bauman frame the momentous reflection of Nietzsche, Freud, and Simmel, among others, provide a powerful description of Musil's modernist perspective. What further distinguishes Musil's modernist vision is its fundamental optimism, which the aforementioned modernists did not necessarily share. This optimism grounds in Musil's understanding of reason as a supple human faculty suited for illuminating the intricacies of modern experience. Musil's nondogmatic empiricism led him to recognize in the intellectual faculty not an adversary of aesthetic imagination, but rather one of its indispensable components. Hence his faith in the power of aesthetic imagination remained at all times dependent upon his trust in reason. Musil's reason appears, however, very different from the domesticated and fuzzy concept of humanism. It also has little in common with narratives prone to seeing in rationality the telos or inevitable blueprint of modernity. Reason represented for Musil neither modernity's normative framework, as in the Enlightenment model reclaimed by Jürgen Habermas, nor its inescapable fate, as in the bleak vision of a world dominated by instrumental rationality made famous by Theodor W. Adorno and Max Horkheimer. Rather Musil saw in rationality the single most significant shaping force of the modern period, indeed, the faculty humans are left with as a means of orientation once age-old religious and metaphysical certainties have collapsed, but by no means a destiny to be embraced or resisted. This belief in a nonnormative, nonfatalistic view of reason bestows upon Musil's account of modernity an open-endedness and an optimism that retained their force even in the face of rising totalitarianism. Its antiutopianism and antiapocalyptic quality contain a lesson that is still compelling today.

This study does not aim at the comprehensiveness of an intellectual biography. My purpose is rather to trace the development of Musil's thinking on ethics as it relates to literature and to the realm of purposive action. The themes and texts addressed here revolve around this central concern, which selectively guides my exploration of Musil's open-ended and productively unsystematic thinking. Chapters 1 to 3 outline the specific understanding of modernity that shaped Musil's investigation of art and ethics in the years around World War I. While chapter 1 revolves around Musil's first novel, *The Confusions of Young Törless,* chapters 2 and 3 draw primarily on Musil's essays and notebooks. My aim in these chapters is to illustrate how Musil's endeavor to optimistically confront the contingency and decenteredness of modern experience accounts for his peculiar position within modernism. Chapter 4 traces Musil's increasing reliance on Kant in his attempt to attune his reflection on art and ethics to the troubling historical events of the late 1920s and 1930s. Chapter 5 turns to *The Man without Qualities* as a thought experiment conceived as a self-referential testing ground for Musil's aesthetic project. The aesthetic and ethical endeavors outlined in the previous chapters provide a frame for assessing the protagonist's aesthetic utopia in the first volume. The final section interprets the quest for the Other Condition that develops in the fragmentary second part of the novel as a reversed mirror image of the utopian vision presented in the first volume. I argue that the symmetry between the utopian enterprises described in the two parts of the novel extended to their necessary failure. This failure was to carry a positive message, namely, the appeal to optimistically accept the modern reality of an ethical black hole while drawing on the more modest and sustainable utopia of an inductive attitude. In the postscript, I discuss the import of this last utopian vision for our day.

> As soon as we put something into words, we devalue it in a strange way. We think we have plunged into the depths of the abyss, and when we return to the surface the drop of water on our pale fingertips no longer resembles the sea from which it comes. We delude ourselves that we have discovered a wonderful treasure trove, and when we return to the light of day we find that we have brought back only false stones and shards of glass; and yet the treasure goes on glimmering in the dark, unaltered.
>
> —Maeterlinck, *The Treasure of the Humble*

1. *Törless* and the Delusions of Sensuality

This citation from Maeterlinck is found at the beginning of *The Confusions of Young Törless,* Musil's first novel, published in 1906. Through the metaphor of a treasure shining at the bottom of the ocean, which reveals itself as phony when brought to the surface, Maeterlinck articulates a central topos of Impressionist and Symbolist poetics, namely, the obscure presentment of a realm before language and thought that is presumed to provide the ultimate foundation for ordinary experience even as it eludes conceptualization. As Maeterlinck's image suggests, the fact that the objects retrieved from the sea appear worthless once examined by the light of day does not call into question the authenticity and preciousness of the treasure, which continues to glimmer undiminished in its deep-sea sanctuary. It is, rather, the very act of lifting those precious stones out of their submarine environment and of exposing them to daylight that undermines their authenticity and turns them into worthless glass fragments. The vision of a submerged treasure offers an apt dramatization for Maeterlinck's belief in the existence of a pristine, unconscious realm, a 'pure soul' that shuns verbalization through the prosaic language of everyday life and rather seeks expression in an 'active silence' or in the terse utterances of a mystical, poetic idiom.[1] Much like the treasure that loses its charms when brought to the surface, Maeterlinck intimates, this unconscious realm uniquely glitters in art but is irretrievably altered when translated into the categories of everyday life.

The Belgian lyricist and dramatist had become a sensation in the German-speaking world following the publication in 1898 of the German translation of his 1896 collection of essays, *The Treasure of the Humble,* from which the passage above is taken.[2] In choosing to introduce *Young Törless* by means of Maeterlinck's evocative image, Musil sought to relate his narrative of an adolescent's existential disorientation to a crucial sentiment at the beginning of the century, namely, the premonition that ordinary experience does not fully exhaust the possibilities of existence but rather unfolds alongside an alternative reality or state of being that discloses itself within normal experience in fleeting moments of illumination. Precisely this kind of mystical illumination forms the backdrop for Törless's experimentations and tribulations. Removed from the safe, nurturing environment of his family and placed in a boarding school, Törless is left to his own devices in the crucial transition from childhood to adolescence. The adults around him, teachers and educators, prove unable to offer any guidance, for they heedlessly cling to patently anachronistic notions of human experience. So Törless must face alone the now enthralling, now disquieting experiences that disrupt the placid routine of consciousness of childhood. The novel revolves around Törless's involvement with the blackmail and sadistic persecution of a classmate, the weak Basini. Basini's masochistic submission to his torturers as well as the allure of their transgressive sexual fantasies capture Törless's imagination, suggesting the existence of a realm beyond good and evil, in which the bliss of *Ich-Entgrenzung,* of a dissolution of the boundaries of the self and a merging with the objects of the outer world, finds a correlate in the release of sexual intercourse. Yet, as Törless soon discovers, the erotic relationship with Basini can grant a glimpse into the moments of bliss he is pursuing but cannot render them permanent. It is not a way to close the gap between ordinary consciousness and the exalted states of mind he fleetingly experiences. Significantly, Törless learns to come to terms with his divided consciousness when he is finally able to verbalize his troubling experiences. It is in the memorable conclusion of the novel, a trial-like scene in which Törless is called by the boarding school authorities to explain his involvement with Basini, that he realizes he has found a way of coping with the split between ordinary experience and his mystical illuminations. Even more important, Törless's uncommon eloquence and loquacity in this final scene seem to prove Maeterlinck wrong, at least in part. If it is true that ordinary language and thought may not do justice to the preconscious life of the soul, they still provide a valid means for coming to terms with its elusiveness.

The inquiry into an ineffable realm of experience obscurely associated with ethics, which forms the core of the narration in *Törless,* also constitutes the horizon for Musil's lifelong investigation of the relation between ethics and literature. Within German culture, the modernist paradigm that follows the path indicated by Maeterlinck interprets the intuition of an "other" mode of being as the token for the existence of an alternative realm beyond the constraints of reason and conceptual thinking, a realm to be tapped into through the nonrational medium of art.[3] Musil's first novel seems at first to fit this paradigm seamlessly, yet the resemblances are only superficial. Upon closer look, the novel marks Musil's distance from the literary decadence precisely as it modulates key themes of this tradition. It charts the course for Musil's distinctive inquiry into the modernist intuition of an ineffable ethical realm, setting the stage for the aesthetic exploration of an ethical void in his mature work.

Musil was twenty-six when *Törless* appeared in print. After interrupting his training as an army officer and, subsequently, as a mathematician and an engineer, he moved to Berlin to begin university studies in psychology and philosophy in 1903. He had written the novel in his spare time to fight feelings of purposelessness and disorientation that were gnawing at him even as he was busy making up for the humanistic training he had missed in secondary school.[4] The novel's manuscript was at first rejected by several publishers, until it came into the hands of the powerful Berlin critic Alfred Kerr, who instantly put his weight behind it, mediating between the young author and various publishing houses and helping make the novel one of the literary successes of the year. Kerr had immediately recognized that the primary virtue of Musil's narrative did not lie in its straightforward treatment of controversial issues such as homosexuality or the sexual education of adolescents, which nonetheless helped titillate the imagination of many a contemporary reader. Rather, it was the text's novel and refreshing account of a fundamental theme of Symbolist poetics that Kerr praised, namely, its ability to conjure up the reality of a young person struggling to make sense of his mystical, unfathomable presentments in a dispassionate, matter-of-fact, almost laconic style. It was the novel's complete lack of lyrical preciousness, of the sultry and verbose eroticism of some writers of the *décadence,* and, by contrast, its sure-handed, factual narration, which Kerr found innovative.[5]

Indeed, *Törless* represented for Musil an attempt at dealing with a central theme of decadent literature while avoiding the pitfalls of the literary *décadence.* In the popular works of D'Annunzio, Huysmans, Hofmannsthal, Andrian, and Schaukal, the presentment of an unspeakable realm of experience gave rise to a literary mode committed to the suggestive evocation of a void, now conceived positively as the nonconceptualizable core of existence, now experienced negatively as the threatening cipher of life's innermost vacuity. The young Musil had felt deeply attracted to this literature, as his early diary entries on Mallarmé and Baudelaire testify, yet by the early 1900s his fascination had all but worn out. He had found in Nietzsche's indictment of *décadence* stringent categories of critique, which enabled him to put his finger on the ostensive preciousness of decadent literature, its inconclusive flirtation with elusive sensations, its evocative and deliberately imprecise language.[6] In a diary entry from around 1900, Musil transcribed the by now famed passage from *The Case of Wagner* (1888) in which Nietzsche provides a most incisive characterization of *décadence* (*TB* I, 28–29). The style of the *décadence,* Nietzsche argues in the passage, bears witness to the modern circumstance

> that life no longer dwells in the whole. The word becomes sovereign and leaps out of the sentence, the sentence reaches out and obscures the meaning of the page, the page gains life at the expense of the whole—the whole is no longer a whole. But this is the simile of every style of *decadence:* every time, the anarchy of atoms, disgregation of the will, "freedom of the individual," to use moral terms—expanded into a political theory, "*equal* rights for all." Life, *equal* vitality, the vibration and exuberance of life pushed back into the smallest forms; the rest, *poor* in life. Everywhere paralysis, arduousness, torpidity *or* hostility and chaos: both more and more obvious the higher one ascends in forms of organization. The whole no longer lives at all: it is composite, calculated, artificial, and [sic] artifact.[7]

Perhaps no other passage offers a comparably concise and trenchant depiction of the literary decadence as a symptom of a larger modern condition, and it is hardly surprising that Musil would be so struck as to note it verbatim in his diaries. Nietzsche's famous indictment of decadence grows out of his diagnosis of the sick and declining civilization of the West, which he saw most eloquently exemplified in the success of Richard Wagner's music. Within this frame, decadent style comes to denote a cancerous growth of language and of the social body, a process by which the distinct constituents of an organism emancipate themselves from their natural environment and begin to thrive uncontrolled. While this process may at first translate into an exhilarating increase of being for the discrete element, such enhancement of the particular always occurs at the expense of the overall structure, for the individual parts can blow themselves up only by mercilessly gnawing at the whole. The result is a devastating inner disaggregation and hollowing out of the organism, which must result in its final collapse. But the collapse of the whole in turn deprives the individual cells of that life and blood that nourished them and gave them meaning; they perish as a result of having cannibalized the totality that contained them. And where there are still attempts at conjuring up the simulacrum of a totality, this manifestly appears feigned, contrived, inauthentic, artificial, as in the monstrous simulacra that are Wagner's operas.

The challenge that Nietzsche's depiction of disintegrating language posed to the philosopher and the writer was not lost on the generation that came of age after 1890. It fueled both the language skepticism and the linguistic experimentation that shaped the works of Rilke, Hofmannsthal, Kafka, and Andrian. Unlike his fellow writers, however, Musil appeared on the whole unconcerned with the subversion of the poetic enterprise that the erosion of language entailed. It is, rather, the ultimate bloodlessness and sheer boredom of D'Annunzio's smothering eroticism, for instance, or of Huysmans's stylistic exquisiteness that Musil rejected. The absolutization and fetishization of one aspect of experience at the expense of all others, as found in D'Annunzio's "aesthetic overvaluing of the detail, the distinct moment of beauty" (*D* 13), had to appear unconvincing in the long run, its aestheticist disengagement from lived experience pointless.[8] It may seem ironic that Nietzsche's disparaging definition of decadence would provide Musil with trenchant arguments for dismissing an early Nietzsche enthusiast like D'Annunzio. Yet it is undeniable that precisely the traits of aestheticism embodied by writers like the self-absorbed Italian poet and prophet were at once a symptom of and a means for expressing a pervasive experience of modernity. As clearly intimated in Nietzsche's diagnosis of decadence, the stylistic exuberance of the particular and the emancipation of the detail from the totality that contained it mirrored a broader desegregation of extant social and cultural structures. In the dictum that "life no longer dwells in the whole," the Nietzsche enthusiasts of the turn of the century saw a reflection of the formidable acceleration of modern life and proliferation of contexts of experience that had radically transformed human existence since the mid-nineteenth century. It distilled their response to the deep scars caused by apparently uncontrollable phenomena like industrialization, urbanization, intellectualization, and mechanization, by the excesses of a rampant capitalism and the threat of mass political movements.[9]

Max Weber sought to account for this troubling modern condition by pointing to century-old processes of specialization and differentiation, which in Western societies had brought about the affirmation of a rationalistic mode that had appropriated the modern scientific method in its pursuit of mastery over human nature and the natural world. Weber described how this instrumental form of rationality gradually managed to infiltrate and regulate all domains of experience, including the religious sphere, whose progressive secularization he detailed in his groundbreaking account of Protestantism. This rampant intellectualization had the effect of weakening Christianity's metaphysical claim to be the depository of life's ultimate, all-encompassing meaning. At the same time, Weber noted, the objective truth of science was not able to replace the value and meaning conjured up by religion and metaphysical speculation. As a result, the very development that had made reality utterly explainable and calculable also divested it of any coherent meaning and purpose. Thus, Weber saw intellectualization and secularization as the roots of the modern perception of a "disenchanted" world, a world that is once and for all stripped of an inherent meaning and consigned to fundamental indifference.[10] Modern reality becomes synonymous with an inordinate proliferation of partly interrelated, partly incoherent realms of experience—the economic, the legal, the religious, the political, the scientific—and is necessarily perceived as fragmented, disjointed, devoid of a center of meaning. Although Weber's account is not cast within the terms of corruption and decline that from Nietzsche migrated into the cultural pessimism of the turn of the century, it nonetheless strongly evokes Nietzsche's diagnosis of modernity in the above passage. Where the individual life-spheres have taken up a dynamic of their own and are undermining the unity of the social body, the result is either the hostility and strife ensuing from the clash of different validity claims, or the lethargy and paralysis produced by the impossibility of orienting oneself among them. Modern life, one could conclude with Nietzsche, appears as opaque, disjointed, overburdened, and inauthentic as Wagner's style.

The pervasive sense of crisis at the turn of the century was further exacerbated by the perceived threat to the foundations of knowledge posed by the fragmentation and specialization of cognitive discourses under way at least since the mid-nineteenth century. This development had led to the definitive emancipation of the natural sciences from philosophical discourse, thus undermining once and for all philosophy's traditional claim to serve as the *scientia universalis,* that is, as the deontological foundation for all other cognitive enterprises and the universal arbiter in their disputes.[11] Nietzsche himself had denounced the ossification of academic philosophy, chiding its proclivity to metaphysical daydreaming and its obstinate clinging to a systematic mode of speculation that had little to do with the exigencies of lived experience. If, on the one hand, he praised the natural sciences for establishing standards of cogency and truth that were grounded in factual observation and a sense of experimental adventurousness, he also decried the naïveté and smugness of the positivistic faith in science and scoffed at the heedless extension of positivism to the human sciences. As he argued in his meditation "On the Utility and Liability of History for Life," historicism, the purportedly value- and ideology-free examination of history modeled after the natural sciences, delivered a troubling view of human experience as an array of epochs and events that are devoid of an intrinsic telos and can only retrospectively be invested with meaning. The ensuing insight into the historicity—that is, the contingency and lack of necessity—of supposedly timeless epistemological and cognitive categories undermined the endeavor of both science and philosophy at their foundation without apparently offering any concrete alternative. While modern science actually profited from its confinement within a skeptical and relativistic framework, the historicist vision of existence dealt the human sciences a substantial blow, opening the door for epistemological skepticism and nihilism.[12]

Fritz Mauthner's momentous reflection on language and overall intellectual trajectory (1849–1923) can serve as an exemplary case to illustrate the skeptical fallout of the loss of faith in language and knowledge at the turn of the century. A Bohemian-born, German-speaking Jew who established himself as a successful journalist and satirist after moving to Berlin in 1876, Mauthner had received both Nietzsche's critique of reason and Ernst Mach's functional notion of the self. Taking as his reference points the philosophical traditions of medieval nominalism and English empiricism, he set out to explore the structure of language and thought in his voluminous *Beiträge zu einer Kritik der Sprache* (*Essays on a Critique of Language,* 1901–2), which combined philosophy of language, epistemology, and linguistics. Mauthner's work is primarily devoted to demonstrating how human language is a fundamentally metaphorical construct that lacks any direct correspondence to, and any grounding in, the objects of reality. While it is adequate as a means of communication, language (and thought in general, since Mauthner equated the two) does not produce knowledge, for it does not stand in any necessary relation to the real. It follows that what we hold to be knowledge is nothing other than a delusion made possible by our disregard of the essential metaphoricity of language. After the turn of the century, Mauthner began to point a way out of the nihilism entailed in his radical critique of knowledge by increasingly foregrounding the mystical undercurrent implicit in his theory of language. His last work, *Gottlose Mystik* (*Mysticism without God*), published in 1924, one year after his death, reproposes a theme that consistently runs through his reflection, namely, the diagnosis of a modern condition defined by the unreliability of language and knowledge:

> Meanwhile the pale sickly humans had learned thinking and language from the black serpent, the whole of their petty reason, and had cultivated all kinds of yearnings—since they were too wretched for the only great, productive yearning—, without real faith, fruitless yearnings. Also their puny yearning for the unattainable, the invisible, the unknown. And they prayed with words to the stammering word creations of their impotent yearnings, for they knew that the great, strong, omnipotent yearning was the only creator, the creator of heaven and earth, of gods and humans.[13]

The mythical tale in which this passage is inserted recasts the Judeo-Christian narrative of humanity's fall from Eden to recount the dissipation of a primordial yearning, which preceded thinking and reflection and was sustained by true faith. This—not closer defined—yearning was displaced when humans surrendered to the temptation of a black serpent that promised them thinking, reason, and knowledge. Since receiving these dubious gifts, humans sought to rekindle the fire of that primordial longing, but their attempts only produced a dispersion of that original desire in a myriad of fruitless longings. These are worthless creations made of language, which humans worship with prayers that are also nothing but language. In spite of occasional conceptual inconsistencies, Mauthner's account powerfully conveys the sense of humanity's helplessness in trying to break loose from the iron cage it has itself erected through language and rationality, and whose only hope resides in the feeble, ineffable memory of that primordial yearning that is the source of all life.

What interests me here is the exemplary path that leads from doubting the adequacy of language to altogether challenging the possibility of knowledge, to invoking the return to a mystical, intuitive grasp of experience, and, finally, to seeing reason, along with its offshoots conceptual thinking and ordinary language, as the chief obstacle in the path to this intuitive modality, or, as in Mauthner's pseudoreligious account, as the original sin of humankind. It is a narrative that radicalizes Nietzsche's critique of positivist science and instrumental reason. In its coarser variants it is prone to blame all evils of modernity on the corrupting influence of rationality and to preach the eruption of primordial, unconscious forces as a remedy. This theme pervades diverse cultural undercurrents of the time, from the cultural pessimism of *völkisch* nationalists like Julius Langbehn and Moeller van der Bruck, to the yearning for rejuvenation at the heart of the variegated Youth Movement, to the anti-intellectualism and vitalism that fueled the propagation of life-philosophical doctrines at the beginning of the century.[14]

Musil's investigation of an alternative realm of experience in *Young Törless* can also be read as inflecting this theme.[15] The novel explores the disorientation of the individual who must confront the split between a disjointed and meaningless ordinary experience—Nietzsche's cancerous growth of the detail that has made itself autonomous from the whole—and the intimation of moments of mystical illumination, whose bliss is however not translatable into the categories of ordinary life. The question is whether and to what extent Törless's tribulations in the end also engender a suspicion of reason that subscribes to the diagnosis of the modern condition described above. The narration opens with a glimpse into the dreary routine of boarding school life, which appears dominated by boredom and vacuity. Törless, the single child of a well-to-do bourgeois family, is shown as he squanders his time in the hope that some extraordinary occurrence will shake him loose from the intellectual and emotional lethargy that has befallen him since his passage to puberty. This hope feeds on the boy's occasional experience of peculiar moods or states of mind, in which ordinary events, things, and people appear to him as transfigured. These experiences are for Törless like an elastic horizon, which seems intelligible and full of sense when intuited at first, yet recoils into incomprehensibility any time he endeavors to encompass it in thoughts and words (*T* 25). The adolescent initially finds a way for pursuing these singular moments in the sexual encounters with the prostitute Bozena. What impels him to overcome his repugnance for the aging prostitute and engage in a singular "cult of self-sacrifice" (*T* 31) made of sexual discharge and moral debasement is the chance of breaking loose from the world of the convict: "It thrilled him to have to leave behind everything that normally enclosed him, his privileged position, the thoughts and feelings inculcated in him, everything that gave him nothing and oppressed him" (*T* 31). But Törless is really after the intimation of another world beneath the reassuring surface of bourgeois existence. When two of his classmates discover in their peer Basini the culprit of petty thefts that have plagued the boarding school for some time, their plan to coerce him into a sadistic program of atonement and purification becomes for Törless an occasion for observing closely the psychological mechanism that allows an individual to violate fundamental principles of conduct and trespass into an engrossing world "of adventure, full of darkness, mystery, blood, and unimagined surprises," a world that exists next to the familiar one, "in which everything took place in regular and rational ways" (*T* 44).

The whole experiment becomes even more mesmerizing when Törless learns that part of the punishment devised by his schoolmates for the helpless Basini involves degrading sexual acts. As he allows himself to become a spectator and a passive accomplice in Reiting's and Beineberg's tortures, he begins to realize that the two worlds between which he feels torn are two facets, or "faces," of the same reality; in fact, they are the very signature of reality's fundamental duplicity and ambivalence (*T* 57). Hence, Basini can at times appear like an ordinary thief, while at others he seems to hold the dark secret to an altogether different mode of being. And this in turn leads to the startling discovery that what Törless perceives as an unfathomable world behind ordinary experience is actually an obscure force deep inside him, which appears at once enthralling and potentially destructive: "Is it a universal law that there is something within us that is stronger, bigger, more beautiful, more passionate, darker than we are ourselves? Something over which we are so powerless that we can only aimlessly scatter a thousand seeds until suddenly one of them sprouts forth like a dark flame that finally towers over us?" (*T* 103) It is the experience of a split between his conscious self and its darker side that haunts the adolescent and prompts him to search for a passage connecting the two worlds, a connection that would enable him to at least raise the obscure presentment of the other reality to the categories of the ordinary one: "He felt the need to persist in his search for a bridge, a context, a comparison—between himself and that which stood silently before his mind" (*T* 72). Language and conceptual thought seem to offer no assistance in this regard. As Törless must discover time and again, they exclusively encompass the ordinary side of things, and the attempts at employing them for incursions into the other world only make this world recede into silence.

It is, quite unexpectedly, a paradox of mathematics that provides Törless with an image that sheds light on his experiences. In one of the novel's most celebrated scenes, the adolescent finds himself marveling at the use of imaginary numbers in some classes of computations. As he notes with astonishment, the beginning and the end of such computations display real numbers, yet the path that leads from one to the other rests on a numerical construct that lacks the positive reality of ordinary numbers. "Isn't that like a bridge," Törless asks, "consisting only of the first and last pillars, and yet you walk over it as securely as though it was all there?" (*T* 82) What makes the mathematical bridge truly notable is its unquestionable ability to connect the two banks of firm numerical land, and yet the two banks are "connected to one another by something that doesn't exist" (*T* 82). In other words, the calculation with imaginary, nonexistent numbers yields concrete, practicable results that are expressible in real numbers. Far from being the fruit of a whimsical speculation the mind entertains in idle moments, the imaginary bridge forms an indispensable requisite for reaching the opposite bank; it represents a necessary feature of the calculation. But what is this prodigious bridge made of between the two ends that mathematicians call real? What does it mean that the mind is able to cross this nonexistent bridge as though it were walking on a real one? What kind of "other" reality is the mind engaged with without being able to perceive it as real? These are the issues that Törless must grapple with as he confronts the duplicitous nature of experience and that he finds magnified in Basini's case. If mathematicians have come up with a formalized procedure for crossing the bridge—namely, the imaginary numbers—perhaps one could also find the missing link between the two realities whose split is inscribed deep within Törless. Yet, the boy's inquiries with the mathematics teacher yield little fruit, for the young teacher becomes uneasy when asked to look beyond the narrow confines of his mathematical routine and to discuss the transcendent assumptions on which his mathematical edifice rests. Even as he halfheartedly mentions Kant's immanent inquiry into the limits of reason and knowledge, his best advice for Törless is to simply accept the mysteries of mathematics as an article of faith.

By contrast, Reiting's and Beineberg's physical involvement with Basini seems to offer just one such bridge. As Törless has himself experienced with Bozena, the physical arousal of sexuality seems to contain the obscure promise of a seething, passionate world of fulfilled experience, finally released from the meaningless constraints of bourgeois society. Sensuality comes to embody for the adolescent an authentic, original source of force, a protection against the alienating intrusions of the outside world, perhaps the very foundation of his innermost self: "he felt for the first time that there was something in his sensuality . . . that no one could take from him, that no one could even copy, something that protected him against any form of alien cleverness like a very high, a very hidden wall" (*T* 97). When one night Basini, who is infatuated with Törless, slips into his bed, Törless's newly gained confidence in the liberating force of sex helps him overcome his last inhibitions toward homosexual intercourse. And yet the consummation of his sexual desire is also what begins to undermine Törless's homoerotic attraction to his classmate, for it teaches him to distinguish between the turmoil of his awakening sexuality and the intimation of a world beyond the ethical constraints of ordinary reality, which he had associated both with Basini's criminal deeds and with his torture at the hand of his power-hungry classmates. As Basini increasingly appears to Törless nothing more than a petty thief and the undignified victim of a lewd persecution, Törless's fascination with him turns into disillusion, disgust, and, finally, indifference. At the end of his emotional peregrinations, Törless finds himself trying to sort out the sense of shame and guilt that befalls him at the thought of his involvement with the Basini case. This, in turn, helps him draw an all-important lesson:

> He knew only that he had been following something still undefined along a path that led deep within him, and that it had left him exhausted. He had grown used to hoping for extraordinary, hidden discoveries, and in the process he had been led into the narrow, twisting chambers of sexuality. Not because he was perverse, but because his spiritual situation was temporarily aimless. And that very infidelity to something serious within him, something for which he had striven, filled him with a vague sense of guilt. . . . (*T* 129–30)

In pursuing the stirring of a nameless something deep inside him, in trying to identify that sixth sense that discloses an altogether different view of reality, Törless had come across and become entangled in the workings of sexuality. He had mistaken the release afforded by the senses for the emergence of that other face of reality he intuits, but cannot name. Quite remarkably, it is not the memory of his participation in Basini's debasement that feeds into his guilty conscience but rather the awareness that his sexual instinct actually misled him, in fact, that it distracted him from and caused him to betray that deeper self he was pursuing.[16] His learning path in the novel takes him to recognizing what sexuality is and what it is not, and this turns out to be a lasting lesson, as confirmed by the only insert that conspicuously interrupts the narrative flux to provide a glimpse into Törless's later life as a refined young man. If Törless's objective had been to find a door or a passage between the two sides of his self and thus heal the split haunting him, his failed experiment with sensuality enables him to learn to live with what has been termed a "dual vision."[17] It is in the novel's final scene, when Törless is called to explain his involvement in the Basini case to the unsuspecting and well-disposed boarding school superiors, that he finds fitting words to describe what he went through and what he learned:

> I know that I was indeed mistaken. I'm not afraid of anything any more. I know: things are things and will remain so for ever; and no doubt I will see them now one way, now another. Now with the eyes of reason, now with those other eyes . . . And I will no longer try to compare the two . . . (*T* 157)

It does not matter that the adults gathered in the headmaster's office become increasingly annoyed as they unsuccessfully attempt to make sense of Törless's explanations, because the reader has no problem grasping the meaning of the boy's words. Healing for Törless does not entail bridging the gap between the two modes of viewing reality but rather acknowledging this very gap as a fact of life. In his penetrating discussion of the novel, Alfred Kerr recoded this rift as a discrepancy between experience and verbalization, in fact, as a fundamental incommensurability of some experiences with language and thought. A certain feeling or state of mind, Kerr explains, makes the trusted images of ordinary reality vibrate with the obscure presentment of a different mode of experience, a mode that implicitly challenges the legitimacy of ordinary reality and appears all the more threatening as it eludes language and thought. In keeping with Musil's virtuoso use of visual metaphors in the novel, Kerr describes Törless's experiment as an attempt at flooding with light those inexpressible experiences that normally occupy a twilight zone of consciousness.[18] In pushing Kerr's image even further, one could portray Törless's fascination with Basini as a sort of hologram image that offers a picture of squalid abuse perpetrated against a vulnerable adolescent if seen from one angle but changes into an enthralling challenge to the moral categories of everyday life when observed from another. The eye cannot quite make out the image's contours to decide between the two; the impossibility for vision to correctly focus confounds perception and fills the individual with a nauseating dizziness. Yet the experiences of this twilight zone are no figments of the imagination, they are no less real than those that can be seamlessly put into words. If Törless had initially sought to erase them by raising them to the broad daylight of consciousness and language, he finally acknowledges that this is not possible. As he learns, the fundamental ambivalence and doublefacedness of experience is nested deep inside the individual's emotional life and cannot be undone.

Kerr must have recognized that Musil's first novel had all the right ingredients to make it a literary success, since it touched on themes that resonated deeply with fundamental concerns of its time. For instance, it confronted head on the question of human sexuality and its relation to morality, without shunning taboo issues such as the sexuality of children and adolescents, homosexuality, and sexual aberration, which formed the focus of diverse inquiries, from Krafft-Ebing's psychopathology of sexuality, to Freud's psychoanalysis and Weininger's influential philosophy of gender, to the merciless critique of the two-faced sexual morality of bourgeois society in the works of Wedekind and Schnitzler. Furthermore, Törless's precarious relation to language must have immediately recalled the plights of an illustrious predecessor, Hofmannsthal's Chandos, for whom the collapse of trusted linguistic and conceptual patterns becomes the symptom of a more fundamental disintegration of subjectivity. Indeed, Musil's narration seemed to provide a modulation for the skeptical reflection on language of many Viennese contemporaries by reframing it as the murky relation between thought and reason, on the one hand, and the realm of emotions and feeling, on the other. Finally, Törless's discovery that verbalization is nothing but a freezing in time of an inextricable knot of perceptions and feelings points to Musil's reception of the theories that revolutionized psychological inquiry in the latter decades of the nineteenth century, most notably the empiriocriticism of Ernst Mach. But while it is unquestionable that *Törless* inflects many crucial themes of the time, even more telling is the extent to which the novel ultimately fails to reinforce key sentiments expressed by Musil's contemporaries, while taking some issues in new, unexpected directions.

A case in point is Musil's engagement with Ernst Mach's revolutionary views on perception and subjectivity, which provide a frame, at least in part, for the depiction of Törless's beleaguered self and the perils of his "double vision." The impact of Mach's psychological theories on Viennese culture can hardly be overstated. Mach's empiriocriticism had become a lightning rod for the disquietudes and yearnings of many intellectuals and artists associated with Young Vienna following the reprint of his pivotal and thoroughly accessible *Analysis of Sensations* ten years after it had first appeared in 1886.[19] Beginning in the 1870s the Moravia-born scientist and philosopher of science embarked upon a radical critique of traditional epistemology that led him to challenge the status of central categories of scientific discourse—concepts such as time, space, matter, consciousness, the self. Embracing a radical epistemological atomism, Mach had come to view reality as being constituted solely within perception, in an automatic procedure that involves the arbitrary organization of the free-floating "elements" of sensations. From this premise followed that neither the perceiving self nor the outside world were self-contained, stable entities, independent from the event of perception. The self, Mach declared, is nothing other than a relatively stable cluster of sensations. While denying it any ontological or psychological grounding, Mach insisted that it retains an important place within epistemology and science as a pragmatic, economic construct. Mach's contemporaries did not fail to grasp the enormous ramifications of his dismissal not just of the Cartesian self but of any essential core of subjectivity. Hermann Bahr's optimistic endorsement of an insubstantial, functional notion of the self reflected the jubilation and the Nietzschean yearning for renewal with which some contemporaries sought to meet Mach's challenge.[20] Others, instead, saw their anxieties more aptly reflected in Otto Weininger's polemics against the Machian reduction of the human psyche to a mere "waiting room for sensations."[21]

Musil had first run across an edition of Mach's *Popular Scientific Lectures* in 1902, but it was not until his Berlin studies at the psychological institute headed by Carl Stumpf, between 1903 and 1908, that he had an opportunity to examine Mach's theories within a rigorous scientific framework. Musil's dissertation *On Mach's Theories* (*Beitrag zur Beurteilung der Lehren Machs*), which was submitted in 1908, two years after the publication of *Young Törless,* bears witness to his critical engagement with Mach's enterprise. His sympathetic analysis offered a favorable assessment of Mach's pragmatic view of the development of scientific discourse. It emphasized the advantages of Mach's notion of scientific models based on functional relations, which offered a sorely needed alternative to the traditional claim of science to provide explanations about the world based on principles, like that of causality, that essentialized the phenomena under observation. At the same time Musil did not hesitate to expose the troubling inconsistencies in

Mach's argumentation. Some of Mach's pronouncements, Musil noted, went well beyond the skeptical, empirical framework Mach had staked out for his enterprise and trespassed into the sheer speculative.[22] Musil's criticism demonstrates just how sympathetic he was toward Mach's enterprise. His critique was not aimed at Mach's radical deconstruction of outlived psychological and epistemological postulates, which Musil strongly endorsed, but rather at Mach's lack of consistency and methodological rigor in this pursuit. As a result of his endeavor to harness the intransigent monism and atomism of his assumptions, Musil believed, Mach had stepped into the very metaphysical traps he sought to warn others about.

Judith Ryan has vividly described the close relationship connecting the subversion of traditional notions of subjectivity in the wake of the new psychological theories between 1870 and 1900, on the one hand, and the extraordinary innovation and stylistic experimentation that shaped the literature of modernism, on the other. At issue is a quest for new modes of conceiving the relationship between the body and the mind, the emotional and the intellectual, reason and the soul, given the erosion of their trusted metaphysical substance. In drawing on the exemplary case of Hermann Bahr, one of the most astute cultural interpreters of his time, Ryan shows how the empiricist focus of the new psychologies was widely understood as establishing a primacy of immediate, sensual experience over the mediated data of consciousness.[23] Bahr's 1891 essay on "The New Psychology" contains the apology of a new literary style that perfects the lesson of naturalism by portraying the entwinement of sensations, feelings, and nervous stimuli in the individual before the intervention of consciousness.[24] Bahr's continued engagement with the new psychological theories, most notably his reception of Mach, culminated in his famous proclamation of an "Unsalvageable Self" in the homonymous section of his *Dialog vom Tragischen* (*Dialog on the Tragic,* 1904). Here the Machian insight into the fluidity of subjectivity is celebrated as a scientific validation of Nietzsche's appeal to jettison all limiting notions of a stable, self-identical subject. But Nietzschean is also Bahr's polemics, in the *Dialog,* against the stifling influence of reason and the intellect, which he pits against the regenerating power of instinct and the senses. As Bahr maintains, language and thought prove unable to express the intoxication of the individual who, after shedding the false constraints of selfhood and becoming one with the world around him, attains the heightened state of being typical of ecstatic experience.[25]

Törless's sultry erotic experiment with Basini seems to at first unfold according to the script laid down in Bahr's *Dialog*. The adolescent's discovery of sensuality as a source of strength that uniquely defines him initially resonates with the Machian undoing of the self celebrated by Bahr, which serves the purpose of shattering the false cocoon of bourgeois subjectivity and of returning to an immediacy of experience that is primarily grounded in the senses. However, the lesson Törless learns from his tribulations is quite different from that preached in the *Dialog*, for the adolescent comes to realize that the release of sexual desire in his involvement with Basini bears only a superficial resemblance to the dark world he intuits in moments of inexpressible epiphany. While it is true that this world is consigned to a particular emotional state, a condition that eludes thoughts and words, one should not conclude that any state that is not yet formed through consciousness can grant access to it, like, for instance, the arousal of the senses typical of sexuality.[26] As mentioned above, Bahr's appropriation of Mach stands in the service of a Nietzschean polemics against the intellectual mediation of consciousness, which stands accused of thwarting and reifying the data of experience, and on behalf of an immediate and authentic existence that can be made visible in the immediate tangle of sensations, emotions, and nervous stimuli of mental life. His notion of consciousness as a derivative and secondary force bound to impose an inauthentic form on the sensuous, spontaneous life of the individual is in keeping with Mach's uncompromising monism, which disavowed any fundamental distinction between the physical and the psychical, the senses and the mind. By contrast, in Musil's novel sensuality possesses a primordial, instinctive, unmediated quality that is bound to be mistaken for the "other," inexpressible emotional state, yet is *not* identical with it, as the boy discovers when he realizes that sexual release is not a way to reach into the "other" world. That Törless in the end learns to live with his dual vision can also be seen as a departure from Mach's monism. His realization that thought, language, and, by implication, knowledge are incommensurable with the alternative realm he intuits implicitly disavows Mach's conviction that all facets of experience are ultimately reducible to the observable and knowable elementary structure of sensations. Indeed, dualism is all but ruled out in Törless's final acceptance of split consciousness.[27]

In reviewing the extraordinary Nietzsche reception that shaped the avant-garde movements of the turn of the century, Steven Ashheim has underlined the privileged role attributed to eroticism and the senses as the last bastions of an immediate experience that is not yet corrupted by the corrosive influence of modern, sickly civilization. The corollary of this faith in unmediated experience is often a pervasive polemics against the stifling influence of reason, conceptual thought, and scientific knowledge, which are blamed for the perceived inauthenticity and distortions of modern life. The Nietzschean demand to restore authenticity to human life by reclaiming the unerring guide of instincts and the senses finds an echo in the pointed suspicion against language and thought that is peculiar for Viennese culture, a suspicion that Musil's novel at first sight also seems to endorse. Törless's preverbal glimpses into an alternative mode of being intimate the possibility of an intuitive existence that, in eluding the mediation through language and thought, is able to disclose an altogether different picture of the real—a mystical experience that closely recalls the mute epiphanies experienced by Hofmannsthal's Lord Chandos. These epiphanies cast into doubt the ability of language and thought to encompass what is most precious in human existence. For Chandos, this doubt extends to a radical skepticism with regard to the adequacy of language as a medium for representing and negotiating experience.

Upon closer look, however, *Young Törless* decisively foils the expectations of those readers who seek in it a testament to the language crisis of Vienna 1900. To be sure, the adolescent's painful realization that language is bound to fail him when he needs it most represents a recurrent theme in the narration. The newly discovered inability of language to convey the experience of the "other" world uncovers a more general disjuncture between language and reality. Once made aware of the gap separating language from experience, Törless is compelled to regard even the successfully verbalized experience as little more than a lie:

> It was a failure of words that tormented him then, a half-awareness that the words were merely random excuses for what he had felt.
>
> And today he remembered the picture, he remembered the words, and he clearly recalled lying about that feeling even though he did not know why. . . .
>
> He felt the need to persist in his search for a bridge, a context, a comparison—between himself and that which stood silently before his mind.
>
> But however often he had calmed himself with a thought, that incomprehensible objection remained: you're lying. (*T* 72)

Because language and thought do not come clear with what matters most, one could conclude, they deserve to be generally distrusted. If they fail in this most important task, in fact, what vouches for the reliability and authenticity of ordinary experience in general, which they help shape and mediate? Yet Törless never draws these conclusions, because he never goes so far as to blame his inability to articulate his other experiences on presumed shortcomings of language and thought. His sense of the accidental and untrustworthy quality of language grows out of his insight that ordinary language proves unable to function as a "bridge" between him and the ineffable experiences that confront him. The important lesson Törless learns at the end of his tribulations is not that language should always be mistrusted. Language, as Törless comes to realize, proves to be a fine tool for ordinary experience but is inadequate for capturing the experience of the "other" world. Rather than disavow language for what it cannot accomplish, at the end Törless pledges that he will never endeavor to compare the two realms again, that is, he will never again stare at the "other" realm with the eyes of the intellect and of conceptual thought.

Hannah Hickman has offered a compelling account of Törless's relation to language by closely comparing the adolescent's linguistic troubles with those of Lord Chandos. For Chandos, words and concepts are indispensable braces of subjectivity. Once closer scrutiny—symbolized in the image of a magnifying glass—uncovers the fundamental rift separating language from experience, the very structure of the self reveals itself as inauthentic and begins to unravel, just as a lie dissipates under the pressure of truth. Hence, what is at stake in Chandos's magnified gaze is the ultimate disintegration of the self. Hickman points to a similar image in Musil's novel, showing how, however, the magnifying lens is used by Musil not to denote the disintegration of subjectivity but rather to point to a distortion of sight: "For Musil on the other hand, magnification produces *distortion:* the insistence on using words in situations where their use is inappropriate leads, it is true, to greater definition, as in a magnified image; but *ipso facto* the resulting excessive precision results in falsification of the original emotional experience."[28] This is in keeping with the warning contained in the Maeterlinck passage at the beginning of the narration, which reminds the reader of the pointlessness of trying to raise the deep-sea treasure to the surface, of endeavoring to express that which is inexpressible. Nevertheless, the narration does not simply come full circle. Törless's troubling experiment does not merely confirm what was stated at the onset, and the lesson he learns does not simply contain an endorsement of Maeterlinck's poetics of silence. Jerry A. Varsava rightly notes that the boy's awareness about the limits of language is not a point of arrival but rather a point of departure in the narration. Even as the adolescent ends up recognizing that ordinary language is inadequate to encompass the stirrings of the other world, his own successful verbalization of the problem in the final, trial-like scene represents an enormous step forward. To be able to express that there are emotional realms that recoil from the gaze of language and thought, to be able to acknowledge and explain to others that one's split self is grounded in this incommensurability, constitutes a tremendous achievement, an achievement that cures Törless of his afflictions and helps him find his way to adulthood—though, to be sure, as the sensitive and skeptical aesthete that is portrayed in the only flash-forward of the novel.[29]

What is at stake in Törless's tribulations is how to properly articulate the relationship between the intellect and feeling, the mental and the emotional, the mind and the senses. If it were framed within the terms of an imbalance between the intellectual and the emotional faculties, Musil's treatment of this question could be seen as validating the pessimistic account of modernity offered by Mauthner and endorsed by many contemporaries. It appears doubtful, however, that Musil's articulation of this crucial theme was meant to reinforce that widespread diagnosis of the modern condition that advocated the renewal of humankind through a liberation from the oppressive grip of reason and the release of primordial, irrational forces. In other words, the issue is whether Musil believes that the adolescent's plights ought to be traced back to an imbalance between the intellectual and the emotional faculty.[30] In a letter from March 1905, Musil relates to a friend his insecurities about the merits of the novel, which he claims to have just completed. The letter reads as an apologetic attempt at preempting criticism of some ambitious aspects of his project—for instance, the characters' stylization and the lack of traditional psychological analysis. In spite of all its flaws, Musil suggests, the narration conveys a firm fact: "the world of feeling and that of the intellect are incommensurable." He cites the example of the emotional power of music, particularly its ability to summon an unfathomable emotional world: "what a misjudgment to try to clarify music through words and thoughts."[31] But all art forms share this quality, he continues, for art is the realm that encompasses feelings and emotions that can be neither satisfactorily articulated nor conceptualized. While this discussion seems to set up a familiar opposition around polarities such as mind and feeling, the intellectual and the emotional, ordinary life and art, the latter part of the letter makes clear that the incommensurability of the emotional and the intellectual worlds does not necessarily entail an antagonistic relationship between the two. Rather, incommensurability implies the challenge of expressing that which at first lies outside the scope of expression:

> I know that I now grasp the painting as the only person in this room and I do not quite know how and with what. I can convey my impression only by means of quite improper words. And yet the certainty with which I grasp it is indescribably strong. In other words, it is as though there were a person in me to whom the painting speaks . . . and [as though] my actual person, as which I possess myself (and we believe to possess ourselves only to the extent that we can comprehensibly grasp ourselves) only barely seized its shadow.[32]

This passage recalls Törless's disquieting awareness of an elusive 'other' to which his conscious self is unable to relate by means of language and thought. But this characterization adds an important element to the by now familiar theme of inner dividedness, in that it ties the emergence of the shadowy side of the individual to the moment of aesthetic experience. The artwork elicits a response from the shadowy self whose clarity and persuasiveness can be felt but not properly articulated by the conscious self. There is no mention of a hostility between the two, let alone an antagonism between feeling and the intellect, the emotional and the conceptual. Rather, the issue is how to find ways for expressing that which eludes verbalization, for pushing the limits of the sayable in order to become acquainted with the invisible person that lies beneath one's conscious self. And this is not just a description of Törless's learning path but also a characterization of Musil's own literary experiment in the novel.

The currency of the experience recounted in Musil's first novel—that is, the glimpse into an invisible reality that eludes the established automatisms of perception, conceptualization, and verbalization—can be assessed by reviewing the eclectic attempts at expanding the experience of the natural world beyond the traditional confines of perception at the turn of the century. These endeavors encompass phenomena as diverse as the popularity of spiritualist and occultist practices, the resurgence of faith in a mystical, intuitive knowledge of the world of turn-of-the-century theosophy and anthroposophy, or the quest for capturing the spiritual content of experience in the sensuous medium of art, which drove the experiments of avant-garde painters like Wassily Kandinsky and Franz Marc. While the sensational advances in the natural sciences, from Röntgen's discovery of X-rays to Marie

Curie's investigation of radioactivity, greatly augmented the scope of material experience, they also simultaneously called attention to the limitations inherent in the scientific method and to the need for pursuing alternative ways for disclosing the intangible reality presumably hidden behind the material world. These experiments were nurtured by hope that a holistic, intuitive grasp of reality would provide ways for overcoming the pervasive sense of crisis linked to the modern phenomena of modernization, specialization, and mechanization, so as to disclose new coordinates of orientation and ethical horizons. It is an intellectual constellation that takes its cues from the early Nietzsche to rediscover in art and aesthetic experience not just an alternative terrain of experimentation but also a medium for reinvesting human experience with the meaning lost in the wake of modernization.[33]

The renaissance of interest in Romanticism in the latter decades of the century falls within this framework. Romanticism was the first deliberate endeavor to explore within the medium of art those layers of reality which lie outside the grasp of conceptual cognition and are presumably consigned to the ethical depths of a submerged, unconscious self or the unfathomable magic of the natural world.[34] Shortly after completing *Young Törless* Musil noted in his diaries his intention to "apprentice himself" with the Romantics and the mystics, whom he had encountered through the mediation of Ricarda Huch's influential monograph on the German Romantics (*D* 87).[35] The rough poetological program Musil outlined as a reaction to Huch's work is all the more remarkable as it exhibits the profound differences that separated him not just from the literary decadence but also from the contemporary neo-Romantic renaissance. Musil's main concern in this regard is how to articulate the proper relation between the intellectual and the emotional faculties in the pursuit of the unfathomable ethical reality humans are given to glimpse in mystical moments of illumination. In a long diary entry written just a few days after the letter to Frau Tyrka, which contains the *Törless* commentary discussed above, Musil engages Huch's discussion of the early Romantics. At issue is the Romantics' belief that the submerged layers of consciousness are key to understanding "finer ethical relationships" (*TB* 138) and thus represent the source of authentic human behavior. The Romantic opposition between "visible person" and a submerged "soul"[36] certainly resonates with the experiences of Musil's young protagonist, who feels divided between a daytime self and its preconscious shadow. The issue becomes how to pursue the investigation of this shadowy side, an investigation that, as Musil assumes, is best conducted within the literary medium. The details he lays out for his plan to learn from Romanticism are quite revealing: "The only critical activity to perform here," he writes, "is to reduce their [the Romantics'] ideas to the pure 'senti=mental' core, i.e., to cut out anything that is only possible from a specific metaphysical point of view, for example in terms of Schelling's philosophy of nature" (*D* 87). The objective is to strip Romantic speculation of its metaphysical baggage until its "senti-mental" core is revealed. The meaning of "senti-mental" is specified through a contrast with the practice of aestheticism: "What would be the attitude of Jena [the Jena Romantic circle] to d'Annunzio, for example? They would feel that the mental was missing in his work. They might possibly find that his sensuality was plebeian" (*D* 87).

The juxtaposition of early Romanticism and D'Annunzio, the Nietzschean standard-bearer of aestheticism and the decadence, is significant because it suggests that Musil sees the Romantic polarity of consciousness and the unconscious, the visible person and the soul reinscribed in the modern dichotomy of mind and feeling, intellect and the senses, reason and emotion. Within this frame, the modern celebration of the sensual appears like another way for liberating the unconscious self. But this is the fruit of a misunderstanding, Musil warns, for the modern practice of extolling sensuality only superficially resembles the Romantic inquiry into the unconscious. As Musil maintains in his remark on D'Annunzio's plebeian sensuality, the modern exaltation of the senses represents "a culture of the physical in order to bring relief to the spiritual" (*D* 87). Within "the Modern movement," the false juxtaposition of intellect and the senses relegates sensuality to a mere escape valve without even beginning to understand its true import. It is a dualistic practice that sets up an artificial opposition between the mental and the physical, an opposition that, one might add, lends itself to skewed polarizations, to demonizing the one side in order to better romanticize the other. Hence, it tends to bracket out the mental as inferior, unworthy, or even damaging. On the whole, this represents a deep misunderstanding of the Romantic enterprise. This is why, Musil concludes, the early Romantics would miss a crucial 'mental' or intellectual content in D'Annunzio.[37]

It is in critiquing, a few days later, an essay by the Swedish reformer and feminist Ellen Key—published in 1905 in Samuel Fischer's influential avant-garde journal *Die Neue Rundschau*—that Musil has an opportunity to define more closely what he perceives to be the flaws in much contemporary reappropriation of Romanticism. The essay, "Die Entfaltung der

Seele durch Lebenskunst" ("The Unfolding of the Soul through the Art of Life"), elaborates on some aspects of Key's revolutionary pedagogy, which she outlined in her influential *The Century of the Child* (1900). The essay's emphasis on the role that art is called to play in the development of the individual makes it into a manifesto of the neo-Romantic revival at the turn of the century. Weaving together several neo-Romantic themes, Key delineates an emancipatory program centered around the harmonic growth of the individual's soul. Art represents an indispensable source of nourishment for the soul, which encompasses the preconscious or unconscious source of vital energy in any individual and forms the essential, underground current that sustains the life of the community. Citing examples of "Lebenskünstler" ("artists of life") ranging from antiquity to modernity, Key reproposes the central Romantic trope according to which life itself should be shaped following a process that emulates the artist's creation of the artwork. Central to this program is the cultivation of all aspects of human nature, in order to ensure the harmonious unfolding of the self. Several factors have come to jeopardize the harmonic growth of the individual in the present. Alongside the propagation of capitalistic greed and a stifling educational system, Key points to the excesses of intellectualization and of an aggressive form of rationality, which are responsible for thwarting the instinctual life of the soul.

Musil is deeply moved and at the same time troubled by Key's observations. As he puts it, she brings back "a line of thinking" that he had at some point embraced and from which he now feels alienated (*D* 92). Over several days, he takes her ideas apart in his notebooks, going through her essay point by point in search of the reasons for his irritation. Many of Key's ideas closely recall Huch's account of Romanticism, yet the Swedish reformer goes one step further in her discussion of Romantic themes, which she weaves together in a revolutionary life program for the incipient twentieth century. Her line of argumentation further departs from Huch's in that it construes and rhetorically exploits a pronounced opposition between soul and reason, the instinctual/emotional and the intellectual. If, on the one hand, Key expressly states her concern with avoiding the sentimental, inconclusive exaltation of feeling in which she identifies a pitfall of historical Romanticism, it is undeniable that her association of an underdeveloped "soul" with the suppressed instinctual life of the individual stands in the service of a polemics against reason that lends support to the prevalent diagnosis of the modern condition as corrupted by rationality, scientific thinking, intellectualization, and the like. At the end of his painstaking examination, it is as though a burden had fallen off Musil's shoulders, as he admits to being "sobered" up. "Her idea of making soul the subject of study brought me redemption. . . . Beyond these things, however, she fails. What soul is and how soul is to be nurtured are full of contradictions. She has simply gathered together, in a rather uncritical fashion, what has been written on the subject" (*D* 95). But if one major flaw of Key's piece lies in her eclectic and unreflected rehashing of other people's positions, Musil finds that "the most fruitful source of contradiction" resides in her criticism of reason (*D* 96). This is punctuated by a naive longing for the innocence of the child and the primitive as well as by the hackneyed pantheism "of those simple people whose heart is heavier than their head." "Key polemicizes against reason" (*D* 96), Musil concludes disapprovingly. While her aim of drawing attention to the submerged layers of consciousness is laudable, her ensuing critique of reason remains spurious and tendentious and does little to shed light on the problem at issue.

Musil's investigation of a prelinguistic, preconceptual mode of experience in his first novel only superficially inflects the neo-Romantic theme of a split individual consciousness. Musil's concern with drawing a line between contemporary neo-Romanticism and his own inquiry arises from his suspicion toward the dichotomizing categories habitually employed in framing the problem. Because conceptual thought and language prove unable to grasp the other self, faith is placed in the possibility of experience that is not mediated through them: intuition, emotion, the senses, eroticism. The split in the individual is then simplistically construed as an opposition of reason and the nonrational, the intellect and the senses, life and art, rational civilization and intuitive culture. This narrative portrays reason as an obstacle that prevents access to the nonrational source of experience, which can be tapped into only through an irrational art. This polemics against reason and on behalf of intuition pervades virtually all the aesthetic experiments that flourished in the first decades of the century, from aestheticism and Symbolism to Expressionism and Surrealism. With *Törless,* Musil clearly moves in a different direction. While the novel reaffirms the perceived incommensurability of the world of the intellect and the world of emotions, it also makes clear that this gap is not necessarily a matter of a skewed relationship between the two or of an unbalance that ought to be rectified. A last comparison with Chandos will be instructive in this regard. Chandos's experience is framed within a narrative that portrays the young aristocrat as having fallen out of an original condition of oneness with the cosmos, a condition he once enjoyed in his adult life. By contrast, Törless's dividedness announces itself as a prerequisite of adult consciousness. In raising the question whether all adults are plagued by an inner split, Törless makes it a precondition of the transition to maturity. In other words, in Törless the gap between an ordinary and an other, ineffable realm is portrayed not as an anomalous condition that should be reversed but rather as the state of mind of adulthood, a state of mind one deals with by accepting the incommensurability of the two realms. Or, to speak with Törless, by realizing that one cannot apply the gaze of reason to the other realm. Reason, conceptual thought, and language do not become an obstacle or an enemy to be fought, because divided consciousness is portrayed not as a fall from a past state of grace but rather as the precondition of the passage to adulthood.

The conclusion of Musil's first novel should not be read as an invitation to renounce the investigation of the unfathomable "other" realm, though. The issue becomes rather to what extent and within what medium it is possible to push the limits of expression in order to capture the ineffable substance of the ethical. Echoing the response of Symbolist and decadent poetics, Musil finds in literature an appropriate medium of investigation. However, his evolving notion of literature parts ways with the aesthetic discourse of decadence, which remains locked within an often unreflected irrationalism. Instead, Musil productively draws on his training in the natural sciences to redefine literature as an ambitious intellectual enterprise informed by an open-minded empiricism and scientific precision. This inquiry does not set up a programmatic opposition between the intellect and feeling. It instead seeks to uncover their interplay without preconceived ideas, endeavoring to productively exploit the distinctive "sentimental" quality of the literary.

2. The "Mathematical Man," or The Advantages of Scientific Precision

In a short essay from 1913 Robert Musil embarked on a singular, passionate discussion of mathematics aimed at elucidating an overlooked aspect of mathematical speculation.[1] Though the text partially reflects Musil's engagement with the discipline as part of his doctoral studies in Berlin, one would be ill advised to seek a technical discussion of the expanding horizon of mathematical research at the dawn of the twentieth century. Instead, Musil reframed mathematics as a model for bold intellectual inquiry, which promised to revolutionize the human sciences. While the discipline's utilitarian aspects, that is, its application in the development of science and technology, is generally recognized, an important side of modern mathematical thinking has yet to be acknowledged, Musil claims. He describes this aspect as the willingness of theoretical mathematicians to confront openly and constructively the contingent foundations of their discipline. Musil outlines the rise of the modern 'mathematical consciousness' as follows:

> All the life that whirls about us, runs, and stops is not only dependent on mathematics for its comprehensibility, but has effectively come into being through it and depends on it for its existence, defined in such and such a way. For the pioneers of mathematics formulated usable notions of certain principles that yielded conclusions, methods of calculation, and results, and these were applied by the physicists to obtain new results;

> and finally came the technicians, who often took only the results and added new calculations to them, and thus the machines arose. And suddenly, after everything had been brought into the most beautiful kind of existence, the mathematicians—the ones who brood entirely within themselves—came upon something wrong in the fundamentals of the whole thing that absolutely could not be put right. They actually looked all the way to the bottom and found that the whole building was standing in midair. But the machines worked! We must assume from this that our existence is a pale ghost; we live it, but actually only on the basis of an error without which it would not have arisen. Today there is no other possibility of having such fantastic, visionary feeling as mathematicians do. (*P* 41–42)

As in *Young Törless,* here too the audacity of mathematical constructs becomes the medium for startling discoveries. These are made possible by a "visionary feeling" that Musil attributes to mathematicians. This imaginative feeling has led them to assume, for instance, that mathematical principles might be ultimately groundless, in a move whose epistemological ramifications go well beyond the issue of the accountability and sustainability of a single discipline.[2] In fact, the mathematicians' presumption in the end entails that our whole civilization is founded upon an "error." More precisely, civilization owes its very existence to this error, for mathematical calculations are at the heart of the development of modern science and technology. This insight leads to concluding that our existence is no more than a "pale ghost." However, the circumstance that the mathematical edifice hovers in the air rather than grounding in firm epistemological foundations is not too alarming a realization, for the machines, perhaps the most important outcome of the scientific revolution, work nonetheless. The significance of the mathematician's imaginative feeling can hardly be overstated. It not only carries the insight that a groundless, that is, totally contingent system can still be completely operational. It also helps the mathematician view the contingency of modern civilization, that is, its lack of ultimate grounding, not as a threatening condition, as an abnormal state to be overcome, but rather as the very condition that made civilization possible. What is then the error to which Musil attributes the rise of civilization? In the context of his argument, the term error does not refer to a presumed falseness of the foundations of mathematics, which would imply the existence of, and related quest for, true, noncontingent ones. The image of an edifice hovering in the air rather suggests that the mistake resides in assuming the possibility of noncontingent grounding—certainly a productive mistake that propelled Western epistemology and science up to the late nineteenth century.

Musil's mathematician appears all the more exemplary in that he does not feel mortified by the intellectual scandals made possible by his subversive imagination; quite to the contrary, he proudly wears them on his sleeve. His advantage lies in his willingness to come to grips with the data of experience, albeit without dismissing insight into the mediated, constructed nature of this data. This anchoring in experience accounts for the mathematician's frankness and openness in confronting the insight into the contingent foundations of his discipline. As such, it distinguishes the imaginative enterprise of mathematics from the dreamy speculations of the philosopher (*P* 42). This attitude, which disavows all escapist dreams or regressive nostalgias, represents for Musil the optimal model for the intellectual and the writer of the future:

> It is foolish to maintain that this is all a matter of mere knowledge, for thinking has long been the goal. With its claims to profundity, boldness, and originality, thinking still limits itself provisionally to the exclusively rational and scientific. But this intellect gobbles up everything around it, and as soon as it lays hold of the feelings, it becomes spirit. Taking this step is the task of writers. (*P* 43)

Only historical convention can explain the present confinement of bold scientific spirit to the domains of the natural sciences and a primarily instrumental rationality. It falls to the writer, Musil suggests, to adopt it as a model for an innovative inquiry into those realms that do not pertain to science. If scrutiny into the basic coordinates of scientific thought made possible revolutionary achievements such as quantum mechanics and the theory of relativity at the beginning of the twentieth century, the same revolutionary results could be attained in the human sciences, Musil believed. In virtue of its boldness and frankness, modern mathematical reflection had uncovered unexplored intellectual territory, showing that science, and civilization in general, are not necessarily harmed by insight into the contingency of their foundations. Musil's writer is ready to extend this inquiry to the realms of art and ethics, in fact, to undertake an investigation of ethics that starts not from the fiction of atemporal moral laws but from the elusive emotional quality of ethical experience.

Musil's dream of infusing literature with the spirit of science must be seen against the backdrop of the cultural ferment triggered by the crisis of the human sciences in late nineteenth-century Europe, a crisis that shaped German intellectual discourse well into the interwar period. Wolf Lepenies has recounted the main stages of this crisis by tracing the realignment of disciplinary discourses that accompanied the rise of sociology in the second half of the nineteenth century. His account focuses on sociology's attempt to occupy the discursive and cognitive space separating literature from science. This was a space traditionally delimiting a literary practice bent on the empathetic presentation of singular human experience, on the one hand, from the neutral and systematic categorization of the natural world in scientific discourse, on the other. In essence, Lepenies narrates the story of that intellectual mood known as cultural pessimism by reconstructing the ways in which the epistemological divide separating the natural sciences from the humanities became ideologically reinscribed, around the turn of the century, onto the rivalry between the Enlightenment tradition of faith in science, reason, and progress and a neo-Romantic exaltation of the intuitive life of 'man,' portrayed as endangered by the excesses of the cold spirit of science and instrumental reason. The ensuing polarization of art, culture, feeling, and intuition, on the one hand, and rationality, systematic thinking, and the natural sciences, on the other, produced an understanding of reason and feeling, science and literature as functionally incompatible.[3]

Musil's project is inscribed in the same frame of disciplinary and ideological displacements outlined in Lepenies' account of sociology's challenges. What makes his endeavor remarkable, however, is that it fails to endorse the reductive dichotomy of art and science, feeling and reason, that informs much of the discourse on art in the first decades of the century. Instead it effectively explodes it. Musil rejected as reductive the prevalent view of science as a narrowly utilitarian practice aimed at the mastery of nature and locked into an irreducible antagonism with the intuitive domain of art. Instead he believed that the open-endedness and attention to experience of scientific reflection could provide a model for an adventurous intellectual journey into new aesthetic and ethical terrain—those radically singular moments of epiphany explored in *Törless.* At the same time, the productive cross-fertilization of literature and the scientific spirit he envisioned does not have anything in common with the naive claim to scientific objectivity of naturalism. Infusing literature with the exact spirit of science would necessarily produce different criteria of cogency and precision than those of the natural sciences, Musil believed. These should be criteria suited for grasping the distinctive "senti-mental" quality of the literary. At stake is a specific balance of feeling and the intellect that enables the writer to explore the realm of situated, ethical experience with the accuracy and rigor of science. Musil's fascination with ineffable mystical states places him in good company with prominent modernists such as Walter Benjamin, Ernst Bloch, Hermann Broch, Hugo von Hofmannsthal, Marcel Proust, and James Joyce. What sets him off, however, is his declared trust in reason, which grew out of his belief in the central role that the intellect plays in aesthetic experience. Musil's growing persuasion about the intellect's contribution to artistic process forms the focus of this and the following chapter.

The immediate prewar years were a time of intense essayistic activity for Musil, as he strove to make a name for himself by contributing to leading literary periodicals in Germany and Austria.[4] In 1909 he gave up the prospect of a secure academic career when he declined a position as academic assistant at the side of Alexius Meinong, who held a chair in philosophy at the university of Graz.[5] Upon leaving Berlin in 1910 he relocated to Vienna, where he accepted a post as a librarian at the Technological University. He hoped that this occupation would allow him to dedicate his best energies to writing, but he proved unable to endure the constraints of the job. He was soon granted an indefinite leave from the post after coming close to a nervous breakdown. While in Vienna Musil actively cultivated the personal relationships and literary contacts established in Berlin, among them the one with his best friend and intellectual rival Johannes Allesch, a trained experimental psychologist who would become a leading figure in the psychology of art, and with Franz Blei.[6] In spite of the disappointing reception of his second work of fiction, the two novellas published under the title *Vereinigungen* (*Unions*) in 1911, Musil proved successful in securing, in 1914, a prestigious editorial assignment in Samuel Fischer's *Neue Rundschau.* He was however unable to reap the fruits of this increased visibility, for his career at the *Rundschau* was cut short by the outbreak of World War I. Musil was first stationed in South Tirol as an officer in the Austrian army and subsequently assigned a post as the editor of an army newspaper, which he held until the end of the war.[7]

Musil's appointment to the *Rundschau* appears even more remarkable in light of the fact that the journal, generally regarded as the leading avant-garde periodical published in German, had printed a scourging review of both *Törless* and *Unions* in 1911. The author of the review, Jacob Schaffner, made no attempts to tone down his sarcasm as he discussed the flaws of the newly published novellas:

> Of these stories the publisher (Georg Müller) remarks that nothing happens in them, something one cannot dispute. In a twentieth century that thunders with historical events it takes courage to demand that poetry also present occurrences. . . . There is no poetical form, rather everything is couched in haze and fog. The soul of this poetry lies in premonitions.[8]

Schaffner's criticism in this passage targets the narrative paucity of the two stories, which focus primarily on the elusive states of mind of the main characters. The first novella, "The Perfecting of a Love," recounts the story of a happily married middle-class woman who, prompted by the inexplicable compulsion to probe the depth of her love for her husband, commits adultery with an occasional acquaintance, a man she finds repulsive. The second narrative, "The Temptation of Quiet Veronica," revolves around the bewilderment of a young woman who feels torn between two men, a priest and a brute, and whose erotic fantasies include an encounter with a dog.

Schaffner's unsympathetic response to Musil's second work of fiction was by no means an exception. The novellas left most critics disconcerted and were cooly greeted even by Alfred Kerr, Musil's most influential proponent. Critics saw themselves justified in likening the novellas' radical narrative perspective, aimed at recording impalpable states of mind and borderline experiences, to a trendy introspective practice bent on evoking fuzzy presentments and indefinite moods in a nebulous style. Given the focus on transgressive sexual experiences in *Unions,* some critics rushed to note the connection to the unhealthy disclosure of human depravity in *Törless,* stamping Musil as an author reveling in the sick and the perverse.[9] By the same token, they located the appeal of the two stories in the ambivalent evocation of lewd situations, ostensibly meant to titillate a reader's basest instincts. But what must have been even more dismaying than the accusations of moral turpitude is that several reviewers explicitly or implicitly placed the novellas within the very tradition of psychologizing decadent prose from which Musil had sought to distance himself, at times closely echoing Musil's own critique of the decadent "culture of the nerves." Yet a look at Musil's diary entries that relate to the drafting of the short stories shows just how distant Musil was from the horizon of *fin de siècle* decadence and at the same time helps reconstruct the development of his distinctive poetological program.

In an entry from August 1910, Musil tries to clarify for himself the issues at the heart of the trials endured by the young protagonist in "The Temptation of Quiet Veronica": "What is actually her problem? . . . What does she want? . . . A longing originates in her for a class of hardly fathomable, yet in some way defined experiences. Like in God. Strong and yet impersonal experiences" (*TB* 223). Veronica's enigmatic, dreamlike behavior, Musil suggests, is driven by the longing for a hardly representable class of experiences that stand in close proximity to the experience of the divine. As in *Törless,* these ecstatic moments are situated at the intersection of the erotic and the ethical. Musil glimpses in some works of naturalism an attempt at capturing just this type of experience. In authors like Hamsun and Zola he finds the intimation of a peculiar "emotion," of a modality of feeling that is directed at a "nameless object that is represented for the first time" (*D* 120). The shortcoming of their works lies, however, in a "lack of awareness of their actual goal" (*D* 120), that is, in their inability to consciously reflect on the attempt at exploring this untapped affective territory. This inability makes of naturalism "a promise that has never been kept" (*D* 120).

Naturalism further provides an occasion for raising the question of the appropriate means for presenting these experiences within the medium of literature. Upon rereading, in December 1910, an essay by Alfred Kerr that had appeared a few months earlier in the *Neue Rundschau,* Musil reminds himself of the importance of grounding narration in the depiction of events, rather than moods: "One should not paint mood but allow the desired measure of lyricism to grow from the shaping of facts" (*D* 128). After all, the narrative virtuosity Kerr had praised in *Törless* lay precisely in the subtle lyricism emanating from the dispassionate, matter-of-fact tone of the narration. Musil seems to ask himself here how Kerr's injunction to narrate facts and not moods would apply to the far more atmospheric narration of his novellas, in which events are elusively refracted through the prism of the protagonists' consciousness. This bold narrative perspective represents in many ways a radicalization of the objective pursued in his first novel, namely, to grasp and present "things that so far have been inexpressible" (*D* 128). The objective to delve into the mind of the protagonists to give voice to the inexpressible is once again contrasted to the prosaic practice of some naturalists. The problem with Ibsen's works, for instance, is that they deal with "things that one could discuss with every sensible person" (*D* 128). Why draw in literature, Musil seems to be asking, if the problems at stake can be addressed within a communicative medium that is, so to speak, more ordinary than the literary?

Upon completing, a few days later, a draft of the Veronica story, Musil seeks to once again define the substance of his literary practice by setting it off from that of naturalism. In reflecting upon the puzzling behavior of the main characters in his novellas, he notes that what he was really after were "the true (ethical, not just psychological) determining factors of activity. For Hauptmann's and Ibsen's people are not determined; what impels them does not impel me" (*D* 129). The problem with Ibsen and Hauptmann, thus, is that they fail to convey the deeper motives that would account for their characters' behavior. In spite of a superficial psychological verisimilitude that supposedly grounds their actions, the reader fails to identify empathetically with them, that is, to grasp the ethical, not just psychological, "triggers" of their behavior. At stake is the endeavor to decompose the atomic structure of emotional states and reach into the very fabric of ethical experience.

Musil's confrontation with naturalism is aimed at defining the principal challenge at the heart of the literary enterprise, namely, the difficulty of presenting the emergence of mystical moments in ordinary experience without becoming mired in the evocation of precious moods or fanciful states of mind typical of the *décadence.* At the same time, the task of literature itself becomes more clearly defined. Literature appears as the medium that is uniquely suited for presenting hardly communicable states of mind located at the periphery of ordinary experience. These borderline experiences grant access to some hidden ethical triggers of behavior, those triggers that traditional psychological inquiry fails to uncover.

Naturalism's unredeemed promise lay according to Musil in its insufficient understanding of those shadowy experiences it unintentionally summoned. By the beginning of the century new literary experiments had flourished at the intersection of fiction, feuilleton, and philosophical inquiry, continuing the legacy of the literary decadence by investigating, from often eclectic disciplinary perspectives, those mystical moments of illumination that naturalism had disregarded. An analogous quest for reaching through to a nonconceptualizable, mystical mode of experience drove some of the most innovative avant-garde experiments within German culture, most notably that of the Blue Rider group in Munich, which, under Wassily Kandinsky's leadership, conceptualized art as the modern medium that uniquely grants access to a supernatural, spiritual world presumably obstructed by the material one.[10] Some book reviews from 1913 document Musil's engagement with this aesthetic horizon, colored by vague neo-Romantic and cultural-pessimistic moods. In responding to works by

Margarete Susmann, Hetta Mayr, Hermann Bahr, and Walther Rathenau, Musil finds himself compelled to deplore the halo of bad metaphysics that engulfs their inquiries into borderline, mystical experiences. A paradigmatic example is Hermann Bahr's *Inventur* (*Stocktaking*), a collection of essays that appeared in 1912 and which Musil reviewed a year later.[11] What catches Musil's eye is Bahr's endeavor to define aesthetic cognition in terms of an elusive type of truth, an insight Bahr borrows from Goethe, the larger-than-life cultural icon of the time. Without posing the question about the difference between aesthetic cognition and other practices of knowledge, Musil notes, Bahr proceeds to generalize this insight and to cast into doubt the possibility of all knowledge, which results in a largely predictable rearticulation of epistemological skepticism. The way out of nihilism is then found in a notion of religion, in Bahr's own words, possessed by those "who through feeling become aware of a higher certainty of life than the intellect can convey, and who are immediately certain of the right way even without proof" (*GW* 9, 1452). The inner certainty of this secularized religious feeling lends itself to support the ideal of an intuitive, "combative goodness," which, as Musil notes, forms the core of a fuzzy vitalist program devoid of any intellectual cogency. Yet the consistency of Bahr's writing is not to be found at the level of logical argumentation; it lies rather in the general tenor of his arguments: "This book places a light emphasis on all things alogical and quietly depreciates everything that has to do with the intellect" (*GW* 9, 1453). Precisely this discreet fascination with the irrational and low-level hostility toward reason, Musil believes, are indicative of a general attitude among contemporary intellectuals and artists, which grows out of their inability to come to terms with the 'intellectual passion' that drives the exact sciences in the present.

The problem with works like Bahr's is that they fail to develop an open-minded, innovative approach to the investigation of borderline experiences and instead explain them away through recourse to a thinly disguised metaphysics. For this reason they have little to offer beyond a surrogate of forlorn religious narratives cast within a lax conceptual framework. But even more damaging is the polemics against reason that implicitly or explicitly drives much of the argumentation. This suspicion of rationality is rooted in a basic misunderstanding, which equates the emergence of mystical experiences with the workings of a pristine, irrational domain presumably subjugated by reason. One of the most extensive elaborations on this intellectual position is found in the cultural-pessimistic pamphlets of Walther Rathenau, the prominent essayist and tycoon of the electric industry who rose to the position of foreign minister in the first years of the Weimar Republic and was murdered in a right-wing terrorist attack in 1922. The fact that Rathenau counted among the most popular authors of Samuel Fischer's publishing house did not prevent the *Rundschau* from printing, in 1914, Musil's polemical review of Rathenau's influential *Zur Mechanik des Geistes oder Vom Reich der Seele* (*On the Mechanics of the Spirit or Concerning the Realm of the Soul*), which had appeared the year before.[12]

Rathenau's pamphlet unfolds as a pseudophilosophical inquiry into the allegedly threatened spiritual life of the modern individual. In a messianic and evocative style, Rathenau weaves together familiar themes of cultural pessimism, particularly a critique of the soullessness produced by modernity's intellectualization and mechanization and an appeal for preserving the allegedly threatened domains of intuition, soul, and transcendence. Musil acknowledges the importance of Rathenau's inquiry into the modern "spirit" and "soul," concepts grounded in the experience of an intermittent mystical condition bordering on the ethical and about which too little is known. Yet a fundamental flaw vitiates Rathenau's enterprise, namely, its apparent aim to turn the mystical condition it seeks to illuminate into the basis for a philosophical system (*P* 56). As Musil observes, while Rathenau claims for his investigation a standpoint relatively uncontaminated by the dissecting mechanism of reason, he also fails to see that this very claim is uttered within the same discursive rationality that the claim is supposed to disavow. The inevitable result of such an unreflected approach is a pseudosystematics based on concepts strenuously distilled from highly elusive experiences and harnessed by camouflaged rationalizing narratives. The unacknowledged generalizing gesture of these narratives inevitably fails to do justice to the singular experiences it purports to grasp. Musil finds it hardly surprising that Rathenau's investigation ends up providing little more than a predictable "*program* of a human type" (*P* 54) based on an idealized moral script—richness of soul, love, intuition, generosity, faithfulness—that flies in the face of the complexity and ambivalence of lived experience. It winds up bolstering a critique of modern civilization that shuns factual observation and instead recycles vacuous clichés of the time:

> despite all the modernity, the world is here being carved up once again into heaven and hell, whereas it is *between* both, made up of some kind of mixture; and it is precisely from such a mixture (which still needs much more study) of good and evil, sick and healthy, egoistic and self-sacrificing, that the questions of the earth blossom forth. (*P* 55)

Rathenau's arguments come to epitomize for Musil a widespread intellectual proclivity to confront reality by reducing its complexity to a host of neatly outlined dichotomies, such as mind/feeling, rational/nonrational, socialism/capitalism, community/society, culture/civilization. Musil takes issue not so much with the dichotomies themselves as with the practice of branding one pole as unconditionally and unequivocally bad, or, alternatively, of advancing the prophecy about a utopian end of differences, a paradisaic overcoming of oppositions. In Musil's eyes, both strategies unduly simplify the complex relations of different spheres of experience, yielding a Manichean view of the world more suited to setting up scapegoats than to facing productively an intricate reality.

Besides being one of the most visible German literati in the 1910s, Rathenau was a powerful industrialist with access to influential political circles. Musil's polemical review was undoubtedly a daring move for a comparatively little known author.[13] Yet his criticism did not constitute a self-serving *ad hominem* attack aiming at easy publicity. Musil's essays from the early 1910s develop a wide-ranging critique of the intellectual mood he found exemplified in Rathenau. Within this framework the industrialist appears as an emblematic representative of the countless "literati who have become hostile to analysis and flatter themselves with synthesis" (*GW* 8, 1008), that is, of a widespread tendency to eschew laborious intellectual analysis in favor of glamorous syntheses. Musil traced this attitude back to a "yearning for the simplification of literature and of life, for a Homeric or religious mood, for unity and wholeness" (*GW* 8, 1009)—in other words, to a naive longing for simple, backward-looking solutions to the intractable problems of the present. To Musil, the anti-intellectual, antiscientific, antimodern bias of the cultural pessimism Rathenau embodied grew out of a critique of reason that took its cues, at least in part, from the dilemmas of mature capitalism. At issue was an intellectual stance bent on blaming the plights of modern societies on the "rationality of middle-class society" (*P* 22), an instrumental type of reason that takes economic success as its undeclared criterion of truth. Rathenau's work then exemplifies the dangers of this intellectual attitude particularly in its proclivity to use the intimation of insufficiently understood mystical experiences as a foundation for a bogus transcendence founded in an idealized, nonrational realm. It is a discourse that longs for liberation from an allegedly oppressive rationality, while taking the side of a nebulous intuitive knowledge, presented as the panacea for all the problems of a weak and sickly society. For Musil, an analysis closer to experience would show how feeling and intuition, far from providing the basis for a distinct knowledge, represent an indispensable component of all cognition, including the so-called scientific, rational knowledge—the exclusive emphasis on the intellect in cognitive processes being a mere historical convention:

> But there is no emotional *knowledge* or other, second kind of knowledge that could exist in opposition to science. . . . There is only *one* knowledge, but to esteem in the gathering of knowledge only the achievements of reason is merely a historical convention. (*P* 23)

Scientific precision, Musil believed, could provide an antidote to precisely this type of metaphysical transfiguration of the poet and the artistic process in virtue of its emphasis on factual observation and commitment to continuously reassessing its self-imposed epistemological bounds. Musil saw the restriction of scientific thinking to the domain of mainstream science as the outcome of a historical process that did not respond to any factual necessity. In his eyes, a century-long development had inexcusably confined 'exact' thinking to a circumscribed domain of phenomena, which, in virtue of their iterability, measurability, and predictability, allow for generalization and systematization and thus lend themselves to technological applications and economic returns. This historical development fed into the misconception that rigorous thinking could not be extended to the other main realm of human existence, namely, the domain of singular phenomena. Musil's objective was to turn this situation on its head: "Scientific reason, with its strict conscience, its lack of prejudice, and its determination to question every result again the moment it might lead to the least intellectual advantage, does in an area of secondary interest what we ought to be doing with the basic questions of life" (*P* 34).

In his attempt at thinking outside the box when addressing the issue of a relation between mind and feeling, the rational and the nonrational, Musil saw himself compelled to switch the focus away from the presumed advantages or threats posed by specific human faculties like reason or intuition, in fact, to move away from a subject-centered conceptual framework altogether. He assumed that human existence unfolds within two distinct domains of experience defined by the nature of their respective phenomena, which he awkwardly termed ratioid and nonratioid (*ratioïdes* and *nicht-ratioïdes Gebiet*) in an effort to avoid more familiar and misleading binaries. The ratioid, the domain proper to science and knowledge, encompasses those phenomena that are iterable, measurable, and verifiable. These phenomena allow for systematization, for elaborating laws and principles that lend themselves to articulating a "far-reaching spiritual order" (*P* 48) that makes mastery over nature possible. If the focus on regularities and verifiable phenomena in the ratioid makes it possible to create the illusion of stable coordinates and firm reference points in a domain of "rule[s] with exceptions" (*P* 63), this illusion becomes impossible in the realm of the nonratioid, which comprehends the "other half" of human existence, namely, judgments and values, ideas and ideals, ethics and aesthetic experience:

> In this region facts do not submit, laws are sieves, events do not repeat themselves but are infinitely variable and individual. There is no better way to characterize this region than to point out that it is the area of the individual's reactivity to the world and other individuals, the realm of values and valuations, of ethical and aesthetic relationships, the realm of the idea. (*P* 63)

The singular facts of the nonratioid—those facts related to ethical and aesthetic judgments, for instance—do not allow for abstraction and systematization but draw their meaning exclusively from the situation in which they are embedded. Accordingly, the non-ratioid is defined by a fundamental "dominance of the exceptions over the rule" (*P* 63). Significantly, Musil refuses to define either domain in terms of a specific faculty, as in: the intellect dominates the ratioid, feeling rules over the nonratioid. Instead he emphasizes the nature of the phenomena that make up the two domains, and that demands specific modes of observation. Some phenomena are easily grasped by means of the criteria of rational cognition, namely, establishing regularities, drawing general conclusions, ordering and anticipating experience through abstraction and systematization. For others these criteria of observation do not yield as much. These latter phenomena form the nonratioid realm.

Musil's characterization of ethics as encompassing a realm of singular experience constituted his declaration of war on the taxonomy of laws and guidelines that framed contemporary thinking on morality. It was quite ironic, Musil thought, that an age bent on professing its uncompromising aversion to reason and science would endorse a moral system controlled by the very generalizing and categorizing strategies proper to the realm of the ratioid. Musil's first published essay focused on these very issues in addressing the question of art's relation to morality. The text, published in the Berlin cultural periodical *Pan* in March 1911, represented his response to a high-profile case of censorship involving the periodical itself.[14] The core of this case was the admissibility of the "obscene and sick in art," as the title of the essay reads—certainly a vital issue for an author whose first novel had been critiqued for reveling in the portrayal of human depravity. Musil voiced his protest against the objective he perceived to be at the heart of the censor's decision, namely, to tame and control aesthetic practice by reducing it to a didactic exercise centered around the depiction of edifying moral cases. In this first essay Musil draws on arguments that revived the age-old polemics on the morality of art dating back to Lessing's rejection of neoclassical aesthetics in the eighteenth century, warning against conflating the immorality of a represented event with the immorality of the aesthetic object that represents it and wondering aloud about the feasibility of the demand to present healthy moral situations without ever touching on unhealthy ones. Two unpublished essay fragments from the same period push this reflection even further as they focus on the inconsistencies of current thinking on morality.[15] They both explore the incongruity of moral thinking that regards itself as a "science of experience" (*Erfahrungswissenschaft*), yet operates with criteria and principles that are at best idealized fictions. These are the by-product of a compulsion to reduce human behavior to quantifiable and categorizable variables in order to make it fit into a manageable taxonomy of laws and guidelines. The resulting behavioral and moral laws, authorized in part by a misconceived understanding of scientific rigor, are then made to support an age-old understanding of morality as predicated on the correlation of duty and happiness (*GW* 8, 1306). The irony of this approach, Musil intimates, is its purported empiricism. Because if the moral sciences were to truly practice the empirical precision they preach, this would make their scaffolding of precepts and rules collapse:

> Once placed on the terrain of facts . . . the moral science should recognize that laws are not so easy to grasp—what is a law in one domain becomes lawlessness in the other . . . and what is law in a given domain is even here shot through with contradictions. One may think of the simple prohibition against killing with its exceptions for legal jurisdiction, for the duelist, the warrior—with its restrictions for the inferior, the intoxicated, the sick, which nonetheless cloud the sphere of the norm. (*GW* 8, 1305)

As a rule, ethical experience has been expected to conform to a system of abstract guidelines and universal laws harnessed by a rigid logic of good/bad, just/unjust, desirable/undesirable. Yet the absolute claim that moral laws place upon human behavior must inevitably clash with the complexity and ambivalence of concrete experience. Even the least controversial of moral precepts—such as the injunction "Thou shall not kill"—requires a befuddling array of exemptions or exceptions to make it work in ordinary life, for instance, to allow for those practices that are authorized in the interest of the state, such as war killings or capital punishment. According to Musil, the problem lies with the legalistic framework of Western mores, which remains grounded in a pseudo-objective notion of law that can only address the deed but not account for the doer. This framework proves inadequate in confronting, for instance, the all-important issue of individual accountability. In the case of the prohibition against murder, it is ill-equipped in attributing personal responsibility for the killings perpetrated because of insanity, or in a fit of rage, or under intoxication.

Musil's first formulation of more fruitful thinking about morality is found in a brief essay that appeared in *Der Lose Vogel* in 1913, "Moral Fruitfulness." The text opens with a playful discussion of two conceptual cornerstones of the empirical moral sciences, namely, the opposed notions of altruism and selfishness. These turn out to be little more than simplifying fictions deployed by the moral philosopher in the interest of a pragmatic ordering of existence. Because, as Musil argues, our concrete experience of altruism and egoism or, for that matter, of good and evil appears to be incommensurably more intricate than any of these abstractions:

> evil is not the opposite of good, or its absence; evil and good are parallel phenomena. They are not fundamental or ultimate moral antitheses, . . . but rather practical and impure summations. Diametrical opposition between good and evil corresponds to an earlier stage of thought that expected everything from the dichotomy; in any case this opposition is not very scientific. (*P* 38)

As this passage suggests, good and evil are not clear-cut opposites but rather entwined occurrences. The abstract categories normally used to denote them are little more than imperfect summaries, since they fail to convey the tangled connections that make them complementary rather than irreconcilable opposites. Musil is here not speaking on behalf of an amoral vitalism of Nietzschean derivation, though. The point is not to altogether deny the possibility of distinguishing between good and evil but rather to emphasize the need for overcoming a dichotomizing habit of thought bent on deploying abstractions, which may appear beguiling in their straightforwardness but are of no use in accounting for the complexity of lived experience. The difficulty lies in the fact that the central experience of morality has at its core a barely communicable state of mind; according to Musil:

> morality actually begins only in the solitude that separates each person from every other. That which is incommunicable, the encapsulation in the self, is what makes people need good and evil. Good and evil, duty and violation of duty, are forms in which the individual establishes an emotional balance between himself and the world. What is most important is not only to establish a typology of these forms, but even more to comprehend the pressure that creates them or the distress on which they rest, and these are infinitely various. The act is only a stammering language for expressing whether we are dealing with a hero, a saint, or a criminal. Even a sex-murderer is, in some cranny of his soul, full of inner hurt and hidden appeals. . . . (*P* 39)

The ethical triggers of human conduct have little to do with the moral principles that are abstracted from behavior, for they originate in an almost solipsistic state of the mind. Good and bad, the observance or violation of ethical norms are ways for humans to respond to this condition by establishing an affective balance between themselves and the world. Even the aberrant acts of a compulsive sexual murderer can be traced back to an intricate tangle of motives, affective responses, and environmental influences that must be carefully considered in their utterly singular configuration. Musil's sympathetic evocation, at the end of the essay, of the plights of the sexual murderer who finds in repugnant acts the only available mode of establishing a relation with the world will no doubt leave many of today's readers as disconcerted as it most likely left Musil's own contemporaries. One will wonder why to make his point about ethics Musil chose one of the most repulsive criminal profiles. Musil's example recalls the hypothesis, explored in *Törless,* according to which sensuality occupies an emotional territory in some way close to that of ethics. Hence the deviant behavior of the sexual murderer can potentially disclose insights into those levers of ethical behavior that go unrecognized in ordinary experience. Extreme cases of criminal behavior—Musil goes to significant length to avoid the term "immoral"—might provide an ideal testing ground for his presumption that ethics has little to do with trusted metaphysical constructs such as free will and is rather consigned to blind moments of illumination. In other words, the focus of this essay lies in the attempt at bracketing out conventional notions of morality in order to pursue an intuition of what ethical experience might actually be.[16]

Musil's iconoclastic discussion of morality in this early essay must be seen as an attempt at implementing the program outlined in the "Mathematical Man" and aimed at extending the rigorous thinking of science to those realms that lie outside it, most notably ethics. Exact thinking enables the observer to recognize that science and knowledge are embedded in the domain of a relative certainty, whereas questions of value, of meaning, of interpretation of experience fall into the domain of the unique and incommensurable and thus do not allow for certainty and unequivocal results. It follows that applying the rigor and precision of scientific thinking to the realm of ethics entails precisely the opposite of seeking to establish regularities and rules for moral conduct. It involves acknowledging the singular and utterly contingent character of ethical events, as well as attempting to account for them without effacing their singularity. Musil fruitfully deployed the notion of function developed within modern mathematics and physics as the cornerstone of innovative ethical thinking, which overcomes the rigidity of absolute moral categories:

> Good appears not as a constant, but as a variable function. Only intellectual dullness has kept us from finding a logical expression for this function, which satisfies our need for the unequivocal without suppressing the many-sidedness of the data. Morality is as unlikely to collapse because of this as mathematics is to die from the same number being the square of two different numbers. (*P* 114)[17]

In his dissertation Musil had analyzed Ernst Mach's appropriation of the concept of function for the domain of psychology, which made it possible to describe mental processes as a network of potentially infinite correlations between disparate elements and forces. In Mach's and Musil's use, function helps identify regularities and correspondences in such relations as pure data of observation, that is, without drawing on the fiction of causal explanations and laws that abide by the notion of necessity. When applied to the realm of morality, the concept of function appropriately foregrounds the situatedness, complexity, and potential ambiguity of ethical experience. To be sure, this perspective jettisons the dream of morality as a system of general principles. It does not preempt or absolve from ethical judgment, though, but rather calls for a reexamination of ethics that treats ambivalence, multiplicity, and contingency as unavoidable conditions of moral choices.[18]

Precisely the desire to recognize the uniqueness of ethical experience prompted Musil, a trained psychologist, to distance himself from psychology, certainly one of the crown disciplines enlisted by the empirical moral sciences: "The object of psychol[ogy] is the general case. [The object of] literature the personal case" (*P* 46). The problem with psychology, even with its new experimental branches, is that even where it pursues a rigorously descriptive empiricism it remains governed by the compulsion to generalization and systematization of established scientific discourses.[19] For this reason, "Psychology belongs to the ratioid area, and the multiplicity of its facts is by no means infinite. . . . What is incalculably multiple are only the soul's ways of working, and with these psychology has nothing to do" (*P* 64). If psychology aims at presenting general cases under which to subsume individual instances within the frame of causal relations, the goal of literature is to outline singular constellations of meaning, to present individual motives that can be empathetically conveyed by establishing an emotional bond with the reader. Literature thus appears as the domain uniquely suited for the investigation of those singular occurrences that make up ethical experience. But if the literary appears as a borderline domain of premonitions, ambiguities, and singularities that cannot be grasped by the systematizing and rationalizing procedure proper to psychology, the role that the intellect plays in this inquiry remains nonetheless crucial. One of Musil's most incisive statements of the role played by the intellect within the literary is found in an essay from 1913, "On Robert Musil's Books," which contains a trenchant response to the attacks leveled against *Törless* and *Unions.* The essay takes the form of a whimsical conversation on the merits of modern fiction that involves a "literary geologist" (a pompous amalgam of critic and academic); a writer of presumably sound mores and healthy emotions; and Musil himself. The setting for this conversation is the cavernous space of Musil's own brain, depicted as a surreal lunar landscape. While the writer launches into a critique of Musil's works that satirically revisits some of the charges leveled by reviewers like Schaffner, the Musil character attempts to set the record straight by offering a more innovative concept of narration than the shopworn one endorsed by his interlocutors. As he notes, in times immemorial the purpose of fiction might well have been to recount powerful experiences in order to neutralize their magic. At least since the rise of the novel, however, a new development has set in, which requires

> the depiction of reality finally becoming a subservient tool of the person who is conceptually strong, who uses it to slink up on recognition of feelings and upheavals of thought. These are not to be grasped in the abstract and in concepts, but only—perhaps—in the flickering of the individual case. They cannot be encompassed in the completely rational middle-class business-minded person, but through less consolidated units that transcend him. (*P* 27)

In the present, it is the "conceptual" person who avails herself of the potential harbored by fiction to explore emotional insights and intellectual commotions that cannot be grasped by means of the generalizing structure of conceptual thinking. Art can pull this off, the character impersonating Musil contends, in virtue of its status as "something halfway between the conceptual and the concrete" (*P* 27), that is, as a hybrid between the conceptual/general/abstract and the concrete/singular. This in-between status of art is in turn reflected in the ability of the poet to articulate feeling through the intellect: "What the writer creates by way of great feelings is an interpenetration of feeling and understanding" (*P* 29). Determined to debunk the commonplace understanding of art as a realm of pure feeling, the Musil character adamantly maintains that feeling alone is impersonal and undifferentiated. This leads him to underscore the essential intellectual component of art: "The decisive elements [of a work of art . . .] are—despite a comfortable prejudice on the part of the writer—ideas" (*P* 29). The whimsical setting of the conversation, Musil's own pulsating and rumbling brain, further corroborates this insight, in that it allegorically presents the imagined conversation as a fiction that could be spun only within the 'intellectual' space of Musil's brain.[20]

In emphasizing the aesthetic as the realm of the singular, Musil places himself within a tradition that in German culture extends from the *Sturm und Drang* to the now self-complacently decadent, now sternly ascetic modernism of the early twentieth century via the Romantic experiment. This tradition follows Kant's momentous characterization of the aesthetic as an experience not subsumable under concepts, that is, not entirely conceivable in terms of rational cognition. However, Musil does not share one of the most significant corollaries of this tradition, namely, the belief that art is also the realm of an alternative knowledge based on the preeminence of feeling and intuition. At issue is the neo-Romantic understanding of the poet's distinctive gift as consigned to a presumed 'intuitive knowledge' that grounds an 'exceptional' personality. As Musil notes in an essay from 1918, which takes on the task of describing the writer's cognitive modality, "in truth the writer is an outsider only insofar as he is the person who pays attention to exceptions. He is neither 'madman' nor 'visionary,' neither 'the child' nor any other deformation of reason. Nor does he apply any different kind or capacity of perception than the rational person" (*P* 64). Far from relying on faculties that are essentially different from those of the 'rational' individual, the writer operates in a domain that is partly governed by a logic different from that which characterizes repeatable and verifiable phenomena. Accordingly, his mission is dictated by the singular nature of the experiences under investigation and not by an alleged poetic gift or inclination. Rather than claiming for himself some phantomatic, intuitive knowledge, the writer is called to cultivate a type of thinking whose "sentimental" quality points to a peculiar interplay between intellect and feeling.

This mode of thinking is specified by Musil's distinctive articulation of essayism, which constitutes for him the medium for achieving "the strictest form attainable in an area where one can*not* work precisely" (*P* 48). In a much-quoted essay fragment from 1914, Musil presents the essay as both a mode of writing and an intellectual attitude that inhabits a space between science and art, ratioid and nicht-ratioid realms. Like science, it proceeds by establishing connections among facts and objects; however, the facts with which it operates are not generally observable and the connections it establishes are utterly singular.[21] The hallmark of an essay, as Musil succinctly puts it in a review of essay collections from 1913, is

> that its inner substance is as hardly translatable into conceptual thinking as a poem into prose language. . . . Its thoughts are intricately bound to a terrain made of feeling, will, personal experiences and such connections among complexes of ideas, which receive and refract light only in the mental atmosphere of a unique inner situation. They do not lay claim to universality . . . they are snapshots of situations that can only be grasped through snapshots. They respond to a suppler, though no less strict logic. (*GW* 9, 1450)

The essay appears here as the medium that extends the precision of science to the realm of singular human experience, enabling the reader to grasp the tangle of personal responses, ideas, and feelings that pertain to unrepeatable situations. Although the image of the world it presents cannot lay claim to general validity, it is nonetheless informed by a strict logic. However, this logic attends to a category of experiences that can be captured only by singular snapshots. Musil found in the maverick literary critic and friend Franz Blei the model for an essayist who could most successfully perform that "articulation of feeling through the intellect" that for him was at the very heart of essayism and of the literary enterprise in general (*GW* 8, 1024). It is significant that the most notable gift Musil praised in his friend was precisely what other contemporaries viewed as Blei's greatest flaw, namely, his protean "changeability of views" and intellectual restlessness. Far from pointing to superficiality and intellectual capriciousness, as Blei's critics charged, these qualities exemplarily embodied for Musil the perspectival movement and fundamental open-endedness of essayistic thinking, fulfilling the criterion of an examination of experience pursued from the standpoint of its irreducible singularity and exuberant inexhaustibility. As a singular, fluid, yet rigorous modality of thinking, essayism draws on the healthy relativism of science to free meaning from reification, thus releasing the established images of the world from their semantic fixity and moral ossification. It therefore provides the intellectual terrain on which ethics and art touch: "For me, ethics and aesthetics are associated with the word *essay*" (*P* 48).[22]

Within this essayistic horizon, the task of literature configures itself as an investigation of experience that does not yield to the compulsion of the unequivocal but offers an interpretation that respects the infinite, particular constellations of the disparate factors and motives underlying human actions. At stake is however more than just a retrospective hermeneutics of life, more than the demand to make sense of what happened. The aesthetic program engendered by essayism consists of an experimental permutation of the elements of experience that draws on an unprejudiced combinatory logic: "dissolving souls into their elements and unlimited permutation of these elements; here everything is related to everything else and can be built up from these elements" (*P* 13). Thus the writer's task entails discovering "ever new solutions, connections, constellations, variables, to set up prototypes of an order of events, appealing models of how one can be human, to *invent* the inner person" (*P* 64). The final objective is to devise viable and desirable alternatives to the way things are while proceeding from a frank examination of the given, by means of an open-minded, experimental procedure that releases a "freer ethical thinking" (*P* 13). Much like the scientist, the writer applies himself to the rigorous investigation of facts, in a cognitive quest that involves both intellect and feeling, mind and intuition.

But whereas the scientist is able to attain what appears to be firm knowledge due to the peculiar character of the facts in his or her domain of inquiry, all the writer ever achieves are partial, contingent solutions that pertain only to the situation for which they are devised.

Appropriating the exact thinking of science enabled Musil to embark on an immanent investigation of ethics as the realm of utterly singular experience and ineffable illuminations that have little to do with laws and precepts of conduct. Literature configures itself as the medium for grasping human experience in its irreducible singularity, Musil believed, in virtue of its peculiar senti-mental quality or, to use another Musilian formulation, of its being nested between intellect and feeling. I have emphasized Musil's conviction about the role the intellect plays in the aesthetic process to mark the distance separating him from those contemporaries who saw in art a realm of pure emotion untainted by rationality. In the 1920s Musil found himself compelled to add specificity to his vision in an effort to respond to the cultural crisis of the years following World War I. His aesthetic articulation of feeling through the intellect constitutes perhaps the least investigated aspect of Musil's thinking in the postwar period. It resulted in a conceptualization of aesthetic experience that modulates key images of Kant's *Critique of Judgment.*

The age: everything that has appeared in the War and after the War was already there.

—Musil, *Tagebücher*

3. World War I and the Troubles of a "Time Devoid of Ordering Concepts"

This terse judgment that Musil jotted down in 1920 neatly captures his assessment of World War I and the postwar period. What makes it intriguing is that it runs utterly counter to a widespread mood in postwar Germany. Musil's claim that all that occurred during and after the war had its roots in the prewar period would have startled many contemporaries, who would have rather agreed with observers like Stefan Zweig in seeing the war as an event of cataclysmic proportions that had ushered in a modern world of unbridled appetites and senseless violence that bore no meaningful connection to the old European order it had displaced.[1] Precisely Musil's refusal to see in the war a radical break between two utterly different ages constitutes the main point of contention between him and contemporaries like Zweig. Modris Eksteins's reconstruction of the cultural horizon that framed the outbreak of the Great War can help put Musil's assessment into perspective. Eksteins conjures up the powerful sense of weariness with nineteenth-century Western culture and humanity that prompted so many Germans and Europeans to enthusiastically embrace the war as a chance for radical renewal. This very spirit of rejuvenation, he argues, provided a frame for the distinctive horrors of World War I.[2] Eksteins's main point is that the haunting newness of the war, with its abdication of fundamental rules of humanity and horrors that defied imagination, had been made possible by a cultural and ideological climate that predated it, a climate that was much more pervasive than the coterie of intellectuals and artists who explicitly engaged in the cult of violence or directly advocated the conflict. Musil's judgment reflects a similar emphasis on the continuity between the cultural climate of the prewar years and the situation created by the upheavals of the war. In Musil's eyes, the war had accelerated and made conspicuous the irreversible transition from a nineteenth-century view of reality as governed by an intelligible order of meaning to insight into the opaqueness and uncontrollability of a modern world devoid of universal points of reference. While the war had not created a new world, it had certainly helped make plainly visible the direction of change in which the prewar order had been moving, for instance by exposing the bankruptcy of outlived notions of personhood, self, morality, and community. At the same time, it had also exhibited the need for filling the void left by these notions with new models of individual and collective experience. At stake was for Musil a concerted intellectual and spiritual effort aimed at creating a new "spiritual organization" (*D* 275) that could offer examples of social coexistence more suited to the reality of decentered societies.

Musil also pointed out another unrecognized element of continuity with the past, the persistence of many prewar habits of thought that had led to the collapse of the old order. He saw that instead of imaginatively responding to the challenges of the postwar years, his contemporaries were hastily seizing old narratives and metaphysical crutches that had been discredited by the war; these were often cloaked under visions of radical renewal and redemption. Anson Rabinbach has examined the apocalyptic discourses that negotiated the historical rupture of World War I in German culture, reconstructing a widespread mood prone to confronting the catastrophe of the Great War by drawing on an attitude of both world repudiation and messianic expectation.[3] Musil keenly distanced himself from such apocalyptic visions. In their yearning for revolution, for disrupting the oppressive flow of inauthentic history, for utterly erasing an ordinary experience guilty of being grounded in false being, he glimpsed the token for a pernicious brand of idealism that had persisted into the postwar period. This 'bad' idealism fed on a regressive attitude bent on projecting the existence of a messianic 'outside' of experience from which alone redemption could come. The very idea of the war as a radical rupture was for Musil a delusion that blinded many contemporaries to the fact that they were treading in the old paths of destruction. Musil pointed to all-too-familiar phenomena such as the regressive nostalgia of cultural despair, the humanist compulsion to tackle intricate ethical questions by drawing on absolute moral principles, and the naive cult of irrationality and irresponsible neglect of experience that in his eyes marred the aesthetic experiments grouped under the label of Expressionism. His intellectual and aesthetic endeavor in the 1920s is framed by desire to contribute to the spiritual reorganization of the present he held to be indispensable, a task he pursued in a series of essays and in his fictional works, especially *The Man without Qualities.* This task required setting the record straight with regard to the prevalent valuation of the war, of the new world it had presumably created, and of the crisis that haunted it.

Upon being drafted in the war, Musil was stationed in South Tirol and subsequently assigned the editorship of a military newspaper. At the end of the war he became close to the activist circles around Kurt Hiller and Robert Müller. He was, however, soon put off by the naïveté of their political views—most notably, their self-fashioning as a political vanguard called on to sacrifice in order to lead an unenlightened *Volk.*[4] During the transition to the new republican government that followed the breakdown of Austria-Hungary, he found temporary employment in the Foreign Office and in the Ministry of War in Vienna. As his negotiations to regain his editorial position at the *Neue Rundschau* floundered and the modest patrimony he had inherited from his parents disappeared in the inflation of the postwar years, Musil scrambled to make a living from his activity as an essayist and a theater critic in Vienna. The respect he had garnered in literary circles won him, in 1923, the post as vice-chairman of the Austrian society for the Protection of German Writers, which was chaired by the prominent Hugo von Hofmannsthal. Thanks in part to Alfred Döblin's engagement, in 1923 he was awarded the Kleist prize for his drama *The Visionaries* (*Die Schwärmer,* 1921),[5] which represented his most ambitious project next to the monumental narrative of *The Man without Qualities.* Due to the technical difficulties of staging Musil's probing 'conversation drama,' the play was not performed until 1929, when it premiered in Berlin in a radically abridged, unauthorized version. Embittered by the flop, by chronic financial difficulties, and by nervous ailments, Musil continued work on the novel, which since the mid-1920s had become virtually the sole focus of his fictional writing. The gamble on the novel proved right. The first volume of *The Man without Qualities,* which appeared in 1930, received high critical praise.

Musil never forgot that he, too, had become caught in the collective euphoria unleashed by the war in the summer of 1914. In an essay published in September of that year he had disavowed his early apolitical stance and hailed the conflict as an epochal opportunity to defend the Germans' besieged cultural heritage and restore a specifically German community (*Lebensgemeinschaft*).[6] Even if this text engages a far higher level of argumentation than the truculent proclamations with which many distinguished German intellectuals welcomed the war, it is not hard to imagine the embarrassment it retrospectively brought Musil, whose enthusiasm had quickly cooled off upon experiencing the war firsthand. Yet precisely the disconcerting circumstance that he, too, had been sucked into some enthralling experience obscurely evoked by the war made him all the more interested in exploring which hidden human levers the war had pressed and what it had revealed about human nature. In his eyes, a correct diagnosis of the years leading to the war was crucial for uncovering the roots of the crisis that haunted the postwar period. He looked back at the two decades preceding World War I as an epoch of great intellectual turmoil and frenzied developments in the sciences, which were nourished by faith in the advent of a radically new era. His postwar essays paint an ironic yet sympathetic picture of the intellectual ferments of those years, emphasizing the confusion but also the fertility of the disorderly exchange among conflicting worldviews:

> I take my examples once again from the literary sphere: there was irrationalism along with rationalism. The idea of the experimental novel, and S. Fischer's authors, expecting redemption through feelings, through a human short circuit. Nietzsche and socialism. The materialist view of history and the early stages of idealism. Humanism and anti-Semitism (or racial theory). Thus, internationalism and nationalism as well. European art and regional art. The poetry of the metropolis and the Catholic church. Monism, Free Christianity–church. (*P* 152)

The ideological confusion of the prewar years was for Musil inscribed in the litany of ideological opposites that battled each other in the cultural arena—rationalism and irrationalism, Nietzschean elitism and socialism, materialism and idealism, humanism and racism, internationalism and nationalism. These highly polarized visions all shared in hindsight a common denominator: a bold spirit of experimentation and a positive sense of the future, indeed, a "will to be different and to do things differently from the way people had done them in the past" (*P* 170). With the outbreak of the Great War the widespread calls for jettisoning the old order seemed to find a radical, traumatic fulfillment. While Musil thought it impossible to overstate the extent of suffering and devastation the war had brought upon the old continent, he was also persuaded that the conflict had at least proven the last ideological vestiges of the late nineteenth century bankrupt. But in the newly founded Weimar and Austrian Republics little had survived of the prewar spirit of experimentation. Here the sense of disorientation produced by the collapse of traditional identities and the transition to new political and social orders was exacerbated by the harsh economic crisis of the immediate postwar period. The distance from the confused euphoria of the prewar years could not have been more striking. The violent eradication of established structures and reference points, Musil recognized, had left a void that was perceived to be intolerable. The modern reality of specialized-life spheres was experienced as an insufferable "Babylonian madhouse" (*P* 128) torn by disparate beliefs and ideologies. In the face of an existence "devoid of ordering concepts" (*P* 126) Musil saw his contemporaries drown in an all-too-traditional "need to seek a foothold" (*P* 127), in that very same quest for fixed points of reference that had been discredited by the war. Where the prewar yearning for renewal had given way to a widespread perception of doom and decline, he noted, "the remedy is nearly always sought regressively in turning away from the present" (*P* 176). While Musil acknowledged that at stake were truly troubling phenomena of modernity, he could not help but denounce his contemporaries' proclivity to shun an open-minded examination of the problems and their causes, which he saw instead replaced by the emotional use of trendy catchwords—the heedless mechanization and intellectualization of the modern world, the domination of instrumental reason and reckless capitalism, the loss of religion and traditional values. The correlate of this withdrawal from the present, Musil noted with dismay, was a condemnation of modernity's alleged evils on account of sweeping generalizations and simplifications. Rather than recognize in the present the clean slate so many had advocated before the war, his contemporaries were now dismissing it as the degeneration of a previous, purportedly more desirable state, "the disintegration of an earlier condition that is supposed to have been more solid" and whose loss purportedly amounted to "the loss of dogmas and guidelines, the dissolution of bonds; in a word, a decline" (*P* 163).

Musil's interest for understanding this cultural mood is reflected in his confrontation with some of the foundational texts of cultural pessimism, from Houston Stewart Chamberlain's *Foundations of the Nineteenth Century* to Thomas Mann's *Reflections of a Non-Political Man,* which he extensively excerpted in his diaries. These excerpts testify to his sustained scrutiny of key themes that inflected the cultural-pessimistic message of decline, from the opposition of civilization and culture, to the incompatibility of true art and modern politics, to the pernicious effects of rationalization, intellectualism, and materialism.[7] His most extensive response to the cultural-pessimistic constellation is found in an essay on Oswald Spengler's *The Decline of the West,* which appeared in Efraim Frisch's *Der Neue Merkur* in 1921.[8] Spengler's monumental historical-philosophical treatise, published in two volumes in 1918 and 1922, combined a Nietzschean model of cultural cycles with a historiographic approach based on a willful, if suggestive, theory of historical forms. Its appeal for the postwar generation lay in its claim to provide an account of the presumably inevitable degeneration of Western culture into civilization—a phase that in Spengler's historical morphology immediately preceded the death of a culture, and that contemporaries found inscribed in the cataclysm of the war. Though Musil acknowledged Spengler's bold enterprise as an attempt at providing a model for that intellectual and cultural renewal he himself advocated, his essay aims at targeting those flaws in Spengler's approach that he saw as symptomatic of a widespread intellectual mentality: "When one attacks Spengler, one is attacking the age from which he springs and which he flatters, for his faults are its faults" (*P* 139). A case in point was the methodological capriciousness of Spengler's historical morphology, whose touted analogical framework appeared to be founded on little more than idiosyncratic comparisons. Musil sought to elucidate the arbitrariness of Spengler's analogies by offering a whimsical example of possible similarities linking the world of butterflies to that of Chinese civilization:

> There are lemon-yellow butterflies, and there are lemon-yellow Chinese. In a certain sense, then, one can say that the butterfly is the winged, middle-European, dwarf Chinese. Butterflies and Chinese are both familiar as images of sexual desire. Here the thought is formulated for the first time of the previously unrecognized commonality between the great ages of lepidopteral fauna and Chinese culture. That butterflies have wings and the Chinese do not is only a superficial phenomenon. (*P* 136)

The droll juxtaposition of the butterfly and the Chinese, hinging as it does on a superficial, randomly selected resemblance (the color yellow), helped illustrate how Spengler's morphological approach revealed more about the cultural prejudices of the observer (the Chinese as a symbol of lust) than about the object under investigation. The sarcasm of Musil's fabricated example was not so much aimed at Spengler himself as it was meant to expose the intellectual laxity and gullibility of an age that hailed his erratic theory of forms as the dawn of a new historiographical method. Above all, it sought to uncover the roots of a pervasive mentality that despised empirical observation and was happy to tolerate all breaches against cogency and precision. This antiempirical, anti-intellectual bias, Musil believed, ultimately authorized the countless factual inaccuracies in Spengler's text, as well as his characteristic strategy of seizing upon trendy terms from the natural sciences, which appeared programmatically hollowed out of their original meaning and made to fit Spengler's own prefigured theses:

> Spengler is speaking approximately; he works with analogies, and these are always right in some sense or other. If an author is bent on referring to concepts by the wrong names or even confusing them with each other, one can eventually get used to it. But some key symbol, some kind of ultimately unequivocal connection between thought and word, must be sustained. Even this is lacking. (*P* 135)

At issue was for Musil an unacceptable imprecision of thinking and argumentation, a tendency to neglect or erase important distinctions for the sake of a suggestive argument, an unjustifiable reliance on the force of bold but not closely inspected metaphors, the employment of generalizations and grand claims that did not stand the proof of analytical thinking. But Spengler was also emblematic in his endeavor to seek methodological validation in some elusive form of intuitive knowledge, conveniently pitted against an allegedly vulgar and pernicious type of intellectual cognition. Musil saw in this trite stereotyping of reason and intuition a prewar cultural crutch that was enthusiastically being revived in the postwar period:

> But that finally the entire substance of intuition amounts to the fact that one cannot say or treat what is most important; that one is skeptical to the extreme in matters of reason . . . but on the other hand unspeakably credulous toward everything that happens to pop into one's mind; that one doubts mathematics but believes in art-historical fabrications of truth like culture and style; that, despite intuition, one does the same thing the empiricist does in comparing and combining facts,

only worse, shooting with smoke instead of bullets: this is the clinical picture of the mind, the aesthetic mind, of our age, softened by immoderate, advanced addiction to intuition. (*P* 145–46)

In sketching the clinical picture of the intuitive aesthete—presumably the preferred audience for Spengler's work—Musil pointed to the intellectual dishonesty of a cultural ideology that claimed to avoid the pitfalls of a sterile empiricism and barren intellectualism, yet dabbled in the same domains as the empiricist and the rationalist while exempting itself from their methodological standards.

It is telling that the final section of the essay on Spengler singles out the artistic credo of Expressionism as the aesthetic corollary to the cultural mood that fueled works like *The Decline of the West.* Spengler, the intuitive aesthete, and the Expressionist were for Musil revealing symptoms of an age that did not suffer from excessive influence of the "understanding, as has been said again and again, but one that does not have its understanding in the right place" (*P* 149). It was indeed the Expressionist's dim intellect that made him appear as the prototype of an artist prone to squandering fundamental insights of art and condemned him to mouthing empty phrases, indeed, words that lacked the weight and check of empirical reality (*P* 149). Musil's antipathy for Expressionism is well documented in the numerous critical remarks that pepper his essays and diaries throughout the 1920s and that are mainly aimed at denouncing the flawed ideology he glimpsed in this aesthetic current rather than at attacking individual artists. He viewed this ideology as an aberration that tainted the artistic aspirations of the time and ruined the practice of contemporary drama. The reasons for his contempt are most comprehensively illustrated in an essay from 1922, whose immediate pretext was to offer a critical review of the past theatrical season in Vienna.[9] In trying to account for the scanty quality of the plays staged in Vienna the previous year, Musil pointed out what he saw as the fundamental error of Expressionist aesthetics, namely, its unstated assumption "that the writer should not think but rather feel, that he should immediately speak to a common sense of feeling by circumventing more analytical mental activity" (*GW* 8, 1097). At issue was a notion of the artistic process predicated on uninspected notions of immediacy, feeling, and intuition, which turned the artist into an irrational champion of pure emotion presumably able to tap into some secret well of life. In response to the Expressionist's claim of having thereby achieved a clean break with past conceptions of art, Musil noted how precisely this hypostatization of art as the source of some irrational knowledge was already part and parcel of Impressionism (*GW* 8, 1097).[10]

What caused the Expressionists to unwittingly persist in the errors of their predecessors, Musil believed, was nothing other than their repudiation of intellectual analysis and the related inability to practice lucid self-examination. As a result, where the Expressionists believed in bringing about the new by distilling the synthetic meaning of life from immediate experience, they actually did not go beyond translating trite tenets about human existence into an exalted and pathetic language—the good old values of humanism rehashed in a diluted version of socialism. The familiar symptom was a yearning for totality and synthesis: "The further essence of Expressionism is that of a synthetic method in contrast to an analytical one. The Expressionist renounces analysis. . . . Therefore he leans toward dogmatism. He therefore tries to find a new 'world-feeling' in the way in which a chemist tries to find synthetic rubber. What limits him is that no purely synthetic technique exists" (*D* 254–55). Pursuing the quest for restoring wholeness to a splintered modern existence, Expressionism attained a synthetic view of life by exempting itself from a comprehensive analysis of experience and hypostatizing untested insights into revelations.[11] What the Expressionists wound up presenting as the presumably spontaneous expression of the artist's soul were little more than shopworn phrases, which fell short of concealing the intellectual vacuity of their works. Musil unmercifully likened this practice to a barking of ideas, "for indeed the invocation—with two exclamation marks instead of a question mark—of great ideas of humanity like suffering, love, eternity, goodness, greed, woman, blood, chaos, etc., is no more valuable than the lyrical expression of a dog that barks at the moon" (*GW* 8, 1097). Even the few plays he singled out in his review as worthy of attention were fraught with problems. In discussing Franz Werfel's *Bocksgesang* (*The Song of the Buck*) and *Der Spiegelmensch* (*The Mirror Man*), for instance, Musil deplored that the plays' intriguing framing devices were barely filled with any worthy content. While he conceded that their precious network of allusions to the masters of literature—Fontane, Goethe, Byron, Ibsen, Maeterlinck—attested to a skillful display of literary mastery, he also noted that such mastery could not make up for the randomness of their plot and overall intellectual emptiness (*GW* 8, 1099).

The pitfalls of Expressionist theater further pointed to a larger problem that had haunted drama at least since the latter part of the nineteenth century. Musil set out to discuss this historical development in two other major essays that also start from a commentary on the bygone theatrical season to offer broader reflections on the state of contemporary theater.[12] For Musil, modern drama had arisen as a privileged vehicle for the propagation of the bourgeois notion of education (*Bildung*), which he saw paradigmatically inscribed in Schiller's idea of theater as a 'moral institution' and the vessel of an aesthetic education devoted to conveying purportedly universal virtues of humanity. This was a powerful ideological instrument that had sustained the drive to cultural hegemony and political affirmation of the bourgeoisie since the Enlightenment. The transition to a stage of mature capitalism, Musil believed, had coincided with the exhaustion of the bourgeoisie's initial ideological impulse, resulting in the reification and bureaucratization of the concept of *Bildung*. The erosion of the edifying imperative in drama had led, on the one hand, to redefining drama as a predictable form of entertainment based on reshuffling few characters and themes and, on the other, to the cult of an abstract notion of effect (*Wirkung*) and emotional impact pursued for its own sake (*GW* 8, 1120–21). In the contemporary demand that "a dramatic work . . . should not have any higher aim than its effect" (*GW* 8, 1120) Musil recognized a trend to favor the manipulation of the audience's affects over the production of substantial and innovative intellectual content. Related phenomena were a disproportionate emphasis on theatricality and the indefensible worship of star actors and their performances, which had displaced the appreciation of the plays' literary/intellectual qualities. For Musil, dramatic performance in the present exhausted itself in the evocation of feigned moods and artificial feelings, which had little to do with the emotional world of real people and instead corresponded to a trite repertoire of affects. It was their conventional character that the audience was able to recognize and identify with, not a reflection of lived experience:

> The element of the actor thus comprises elements that do not exist. Indeed, these elementary outbreaks do not seize the mind. They rather seize upon ideas of the mind that preexist in the viewer and only with the help of these seized ideas the viewer themselves. . . . What is performed are chain views and effect traditions; not passions, but rather actors who act out passions, not persons but mirrored persons and in general some sluggishly revolving state of tradition. (*GW* 8, 1107)

The presumably archetypical emotional outbursts modeled by modern actors did not grip the spectators via some direct affective impact but rather resonated with conventional concepts of what emotions should look like. These had been implanted in the audience via the mediation of an aesthetic tradition, which had become engulfed in the self-referential evocation of reified signifiers. Musil decried this aesthetic practice for its inability to capture the intricacies of contemporary reality and for the related propensity to offer a contrived and misleading image of human experience. Much like the Expressionists' inclination to cloak tired commonplaces under the mantle of prerational revelations, this theatrical tendency exempted itself from a serious scrutiny of modern reality, thereby dodging what Musil held to be art's fundamental duty, namely, to offer new models for being human based on a careful observation of present experience. In its unreflected cult of emotions and intuition it was also prone to squandering the distinctive, intellectual potential of art, that potential that for Musil was consigned to a specific mix of intellect and feeling (*GW* 8, 1098). It was this source, Musil believed, that could and should be tapped into in the quest for a new spiritual organization of the postwar era.

Musil singled out Spengler's mercurial philosophy of history and the vacuous pathos of the Expressionists as emblematic of the revival of damaging intellectual attitudes that had dogged the prewar years: anti-intellectualism, antiempiricism, and the cult of fuzzy notions such as feeling and intuition. He found it ironical that the mistakes of the prewar period were being repeated precisely in those areas that prided themselves on being most innovative. He saw in them a regressive longing for anchoring individual and collective experience in permanent models of interpretation that purported to transcend immediate, contingent reality. A similar "need for the unequivocal, repeatable, and fixed" saturated reflection in the realm of ethics and morality, which Musil saw as dominated by a frenzy for the unequivocal, the inability to deal with the ambiguities of a time of transition, and a compulsion to force the unique event into general categories of interpretation and judgment that did not take into account its constitutive singularity (*P* 182). Humanism exemplified the anachronisms of moral thinking driven by a tendency to systematization and standardization. In Musil's eyes, the humanist demand to articulate an unambivalent and universal notion of desirable humanity expended itself in assembling an erratic selection of lifeless examples that did not bear any relation to the richness and uniqueness of particular experience. Musil never tired of mocking the humanist reverence for sublime figures like Goethe and Lessing, whose great lives, depicted as "self-contained, unique totalities" were made to carry unequivocal exemplary character and "educational value" (*P* 132). He sardonically asked what would happen if one extended to the natural sciences the humanist practice of inventorying personalities, epochs, and cultures to establish models of morality. If one were to follow this procedure in a discipline like physics, he noted, the highest accomplishments would not rise above the biographies of Kepler and Newton (*P* 132–33).

Musil glimpsed an analogous eagerness to circumscribe and stabilize fixed notions of humanness in the idealized visions of community put forth by ideologies as heterogeneous as nationalism and socialism. In spite of conspicuous ideological differences, both doctrines shared a troubling reliance on antiquated notions of the self-contained individual defined by an immutable essence, which they turned into the cornerstone for variously modulated constructs of the national community. In so doing, they were compelled to ignore, for instance, the lesson taught by the war about the fundamental manipulability and moral 'formlessness' of human beings, who had proven to be "every bit as capable of cannibalism as of *The Critique of Pure Reason*" (*P* 121). Nationalism, in its reliance on the pseudoscientific concept of blood and race, and socialism, with its naive belief in the fundamental goodness of human nature, its abstract ethos of an "altruism of fraternity," and the ensuing notion of the state as an "institution for human perfectibility" (*P* 109), drew on remedies taken from a transfigured past rather than engage in a candid confrontation with the present. In evoking "a false 'we' . . . that does not correspond to reality" (*P* 111) they catered to a diffuse need for permanent foundations and thereby reflected a kind of thinking that was by definition drawn to exceed the limits of experience and trespass into the realm of metaphysical speculation. For Musil, it was a stance that proved utterly inadequate to face the challenge of the postwar period.

Persuaded that it was imperative to name the ideological impulses linking phenomena as diverse as cultural pessimism, Expressionism, and political ideologies like nationalism and socialism, Musil traced their pervasive need for absolute certainties back to a widespread cultural mentality grounded in a harmful type of idealism. At issue was a stance that pretended to account for experience by measuring it against a set of ideas and ideals located in a realm beyond ordinary life. This was a system of fixed reference points beyond reality to which reality was expected to conform. This pernicious idealism was marked by fixation on preformed notions about the way things ought to be and by a lack of concern with examining the underlying assumptions that anchored and legitimized such notions. As Musil described it,

> we stabilize our ideals like Platonic-Pythagorean ideas, immovable and unalterable, and when reality does not conform to them we are in a position to regard this very fact, that reality is only their 'impure' realization, as characteristic of their ideality. (*P* 113)

Experience must lose out when it is judged by standards that are grounded in a realm alien to it. Inevitably, this kind of idealism is prone to disavowing present reality as the inadequate, blemished realization of otherwise unattainable ideals. Musil thought that the antimodern mood of condemnation, the resentment, and the rancorous escapism of the postwar years grew out of the type of idealism that thrived on the discrepancy between an idealized notion of 'the good life' and a reality that failed to live up to it. William Connolly has traced this attitude back to a quintessentially modern anxiety, an anxiety that was most incisively described by Friedrich Nietzsche. For Connolly, modernity is defined by a dilemma that reaches far back into the history of the West, as far as the dawn of Christianity. On the one hand, the modern period is marked by the eclipse of century-old metaphysical certainties and absolute points of reference—God, reason, the sovereign, the community. On the other hand, it harbors the belief that life becomes meaningless without those certainties, in fact, that losing the possibility to ground our experience of the world in a metaphysical outside entails opening the gates to nihilism. To get out of this bind, the moderns have staged attempts to artificially keep alive some substitute of that outside, as a totality of meaning anchored in a dimension that lies beyond the alienating experience of this world. It is an operation that breeds violence, Connolly argues, because its underlying quest for an ordered and harmonious world entails oppressing and enslaving multifarious life.[13] Connolly identifies another troubling reaction to this dilemma, which he terms a passive nihilism: "The passive nihilist admits the inability to ground his highest values in a transcendent standard, but this admission leads him to devalue this world, to despise the world because it has deserted his ideals." This attitude also spawns violence, this time as the rage of the self-righteous individual who is all too willing to participate in the destruction of a world marked by unredeemable corruption.[14]

Musil recognized that the present "craving for a 'metaphysical bang'" (*P* 129) engendered both attitudes described by Connolly. He was aware of the potential for violence harbored by such metaphysical nostalgia, for he clearly saw the harmful consequences of a tendency to formulate ideas that had no bearing on actual reality and that were constantly frustrated by a world that failed to conform to them. To this regressive attitude Musil opposed a more fruitful kind of idealism, a stance committed to close examination of ordinary life, in order to devise hypotheses and models about the way things could be done differently:

> I call idealism the forming of reality according to ideas (and I would call following successful ideas until the next stage of realization is achieved only idealism in the second degree). Therefore, when life does not live up to a system of ideals, I am not able to see much idealism in them. One should finally realize that it is not that life fails to conform to ideals out of disobedience, as in school, but rather that the mistake must lie with the ideals. (*P* 113)

The ideals Musil championed were not based on allegedly atemporal criteria of value but were to be judged in terms of their ability to transform reality according to contingent standards. They presupposed the willingness to face the present and place the utmost emphasis on factual, rigorous, yet open-minded examination of experience, following the healthy spirit of scientific experimentation.

It is this antiapocalyptic view of the modern condition, informed by an 'empirical idealism,' that guided Musil's specific account of the present. Without denying the current diagnosis of "inexpressible multiplicity" (*P* 175), of a modern world plagued by the inordinate clash of conflicting worldviews and lacking firm reference points, Musil rejected the prevailing evaluation that stigmatized the present as an age of decline. He was instead determined to take a fresh look at the historical circumstances that had produced such a chaotic world, starting with the upheaval of World War I. He saw the war as the culmination of an acute ideological crisis that had dogged late-nineteenth-century societies, indeed, as the self-induced implosion of a social and political order that had outlived its time: "This explosive stimulus, with which the human being liberated himself . . . was the renunciation of middle-class life, the will for disorder rather than the old order" (*P* 112). For this reason, none of the prewar values and ideologies, if restored, could contribute to solving any of the current problems. The present crisis could not be helped by idealizing the past and advocating a return to traditional remedies, such as "faith, prescientific thinking, simplicity, humanity, altruism, national solidarity, subordination of the citizen to the state: the abandonment of capitalist individualism and its frame of mind" (*P* 176), for it was that very past that had carried the seeds of its own destruction.

The perspective that presented the war as the collapse of a no longer viable social order also enabled the observer to view the present as a time of transition rather than an age of decline. Echoing Max Weber's thesis of a Western modernity shaped by processes of rationalization and differentiation, Musil believed that European societies were caught in an irreversible process of internal 'decomposition' and differentiation that was responsible for the proliferation of specialized domains of experience and cognitive discourses (*P* 130). This meant for the individual an enormous increase in the complexity of everyday life. Having to deal with ever more specialized realms of life, each governed by partially incommensurable principles, the average person was bound to become overburdened with questions he could not master. When seen in this light, the current malaise vis-à-vis modern civilization was nothing other than a cipher for

> the burdening of individuals with questions whose very words they hardly understand (witness political democracy, or the newspapers). That the individual reacts in a completely pathological fashion is only natural: nowadays we expect the average businessman to make intellectual decisions whose conscientious deliberation would boggle the mind of a Leibniz! (*P* 130)

It was the increased complexity of life brought by modern advances like mass democracy and its ancillary phenomena such as the mass media that made modern reality appear opaque and out of control. The very identity of the individual had become the contested terrain on which disparate institutions and social formations staged their struggles: "State, nation, Church, profession, class, gender, etc. The individual cannot fully belong to any of these groups because they are in conflict with each other. Here, too, the issue is one of struggles between different kinds of apparatus" (*D* 335). It was only understandable, Musil thought, that the average person would feel overwhelmed and react in a pathological manner—that is, by rejecting the present and wishing a return to some idealized, idyllic past and a more manageable rhythm of life. Much as Musil acknowledged the distress of the individual caught among the competing claims of disparate institutions and ideologies, he did not believe that the differentiated structure of modernity could be undone. He thought it was imperative to acknowledge the present as a yet unrecognized new condition rather than as the purported degeneration of a more desirable state of affairs. The current divisions and fragmentations would then finally appear as the distinctive property of the new order: "Diversity as a quality of the future" (*P* 176). Musil was convinced that affirming the multifariousness and decenteredness of modern societies was key to recognizing and exploiting modernity's constructive potential. An open-minded examination of the present would then show how the modern condition had made possible the fulfillment of some of humanity's long-sought dreams:

> in the cellar of this madhouse we hear the hammering of a Hephaestian urge to create; humanity's archetypal dreams are being realized, like flight, our seven-league boots; seeing through solid bodies, and an incredible wealth of fantasies such as in centuries past were the blissful magic of dreams. (*P* 128)

Similarly, it was important to confront and reinterpret that "sense of contingency" (*P* 118) with regard to individual and collective experience, which was among the war's most troubling legacies. The war's sheer senselessness had made visible on a world-historical scale the lack of immanent necessity in human history, providing a traumatic fulfillment for the Nietzschean appeal to discard the trusted category of a teleological unfolding so crucial to the Western metaphysical tradition: "it is almost as if the events themselves were not necessary at all, but only accommodated necessity after the fact" (*P* 118). Musil conceded that relinquishing the notion of necessity had disquieting implications. If history has no meaning beyond the extrinsic accounts given retrospectively, then there are no transcendent guidelines that would allow humans to predict and shape the future. Yet he also emphasized the optimism entailed in jettisoning traditional notions of history as 'destiny' or 'lawful process' in favor of accounts that portrayed individual and collective existence as a sequel of 'situations' that do not obey any law of necessity: "People are not capable of changing laws; but they certainly can change situations in this sense, no matter how many immanent laws may have contributed to them" (*P* 170).[15] As he believed, this view of history as a sequel of situations could empower humans to shed the yoke of normative accounts of experience. Seizing and coping with this freedom meant living up to the true legacy of the Enlightenment, a legacy that needed to be reclaimed for the present: "for if it turns out that our innermost being does not dangle from the puppet strings of some hobgoblin of fate, but on the contrary that we are draped with a multitude of small, haphazardly linked weights, then we ourselves can tip the scales" (*P* 122).

A perspective that treated awareness about the contingency of experience as liberating rather than thwarting was also more suited for dealing with the new, bewildering insights into human nature granted by the war. Musil found that the war had finally cleaned the slate of the humanist notion of a European community, whose essential humanity was inscribed in presumably innate values that transcended national borders. The excesses of the war had taught contemporaries a very different lesson, a lesson that needed to be confronted without nostalgic moralism or self-interested finger-pointing:

> I would put it roughly as follows: people are an enormously indolent mass in every moral question. . . . I observe the monstrous degeneracies that the war caused to shoot up like mushrooms. The ruthless egotism of profiteering, of the peasants, of legitimate traders, the pompous presumption of the master caste with its Army General Staff, the hangman's composure with which the custodians of the new German order proceeded against anything that was alien to their spirit, the rejoicing with which the peoples of the Entente celebrated their Trojan victory (Wilson as the Horse). . . . And I come to the conclusion that I put forward before the war began—one of only a small number of Germans to do so—that in moral terms a human being is a misshapen thing, a colloidal substance that snuggles up to other forms rather than shapes [sic] them itself. (*D* 267–68)

The experience of the war had confirmed Musil's prewar view of ethics because it had exposed the illusionary quality of a view of morality predicated on the fiction of immutable categories and values, including the notion of a self-identical subject endowed with free will. The ease with which the war had turned respectable citizens into ruthless criminals had exhibited for Musil the fundamental "formlessness" of human nature, suggesting that humans lack any stable essence or essential attributes and are instead shaped in a constant exchange between individual and environment. This "theorem of human shapelessness" (*P* 167) did not necessarily lead to a nihilistic view of subjectivity and selfhood, Musil believed. It rather called for shifting one's perspective from the delusion of an immutable essence to the concrete analysis of the individual's interaction with his environment (*P* 178).

Accepting the theorem of shapeless humanity would in turn help cast a different light on the role of the various ideologies, whose disorderly proliferation was among the most troubling phenomena plaguing the present. Musil had little sympathy for those who deplored the corrupting influence of conflicting ideologies and instead emphasized how ideologies provided much-needed spiritual and intellectual direction, indeed, a horizon of meaning for an existence founded on contingent coordinates: "Ideology is the soul of life, even of everyday life. It not only reveals the character of this life, but forms it as well. . . . Ideology is: intellectual ordering of the feelings; an objective connection among them that makes the subjective connection easier" (*P* 173–74). Ideologies were for Musil contingent, spiritual molds into which life poured itself to acquire form. They shaped living forms as much as they were shaped by them and provided modern individuals with a sorely needed intellectual grid for ordering an otherwise amorphous emotional world. The growth of disparate ideologies in the present also represented a means to cope with the surge in complexity of modern life; in fact, it was a by-product of the need for mastering ever more specialized domains of experience. It was especially important to recognize the current proliferation of ideologies as an irrevocable development, because the process of differentiation that had triggered the inordinate expansion of disparate creeds and value systems could not be reversed: "Never again will a homogenous ideology, a 'culture,' arise in our Western society on its own. Even if it did once exist in the distant past (although we probably imagine it as too perfect), water flows downhill, not up" (*P* 130). Whether the nostalgically evoked civilizations of bygone ages were the expression of true cultural harmony or a delusion produced by an embellishing gaze onto the past, the current appeals for 'cultural unity' or for the advent of the ideology that could prevail upon all others in virtue of its intrinsic superiority missed the point for Musil. Instead, efforts were needed to create "social conditions that safeguard the stability and depth of ideological endeavors in general" (*P* 130). Musil demanded ways to foster the confrontation and interplay of ideological forces rather than abandon it to chance.

There is a characteristic abstractness in Musil's proposals, which at times makes them appear vague and impractical. One might ask, for instance, what concrete measures Musil envisioned in the task of fostering that productive exchange among ideologies he so ardently advocated. At the same time his suggestions seem vague, his position on specific issues or ideological stances appears unyieldingly critical, a criticism that did not spare even the standpoints with which he sympathized, like socialism.

In reading his essays and diaries, one often has the impression that the acumen of his observations prevented him from committing wholeheartedly to a cause, relegating him to the position of the interested but ultimately disengaged observer. On these grounds, Musil has been seen as an incarnation of the mandarin intellectual—the paradigmatic embodiment of the contradictions of high-modernism's elitism and lack of political engagement.[16] Before drawing such conclusions, however, one must consider the degree to which this position was consciously reflected by Musil. Musil was aware that he lacked the healthy dose of cynicism and self-interested pragmatism needed by the professional politician. He likewise lacked the activist's ability to take a side and intransigently defend it while denying or condoning its weaknesses and blindspots.[17] He was however also convinced that there was a qualitative difference between the realm of politics and that of intellectual reflection. While both fulfilled important tasks in the present, their different objectives also made their strategies and goals in many ways incompatible. Political activism was about unequivocally advocating the presumably truthful ideology that would once and for all mend the wounds of the present. By contrast, the thinker who had chosen to outline a broad intellectual framework suited for the spiritual reorganization of the present had to proceed differently. He was compelled to practice the virtue of essayistic reflection, Musil believed, of that open-minded and uncommitted exploration of an issue from various sides.

Some of Musil's remarks on socialism can serve as an illustration for the type of reflection he advocated and practiced. He was very critical of socialism as an ideology, not because he sympathized with its opponents on the right but because he thought that some of its tenets were psychologically unviable and doomed it to failure. For instance, he believed that the two main precepts at the heart of socialism, namely, the affirmation of the equality of all individuals and the imperative to love one's neighbor as oneself, had little anchoring in human psychology and could not possibly provide a foundation for collective life (*D* 257). He found it furthermore ironic that precisely these two precepts represented socialism's point of contact with Christianity, one of its main ideological opponents. In another diary entry, he compared the claims of the "Christian Socialist," who preached unconditional obedience to the community as a way to detach oneself from the enjoinment of the flesh and come closer to God, with those of the "red Socialist," according to whom the spiritual imperative of the Christian was a means for perpetuating the material exploitation of the masses. In spite of their differences, Musil saw that the two antagonists shared the same fundamental postulate, namely, "that the well being of society . . . represents the highest ethical good" (*TB* I, 575). It was placing the well-being of the community over that of the individual that made them both socialists. Precisely this tenet, however, deserved closer scrutiny. Musil thought that the individualism at the heart of capitalism was psychologically more sustainable than the starry-eyed communitarianism of socialism because it was grounded in a more realistic assessment of human nature. A diary entry from the period 1920 to 1926 takes up this point as it scrutinizes the ideological difficulties of socialism in its competition with capitalism. What made capitalism almost irresistible, Musil maintained, was its simple postulate that each "expenditure of money or effort" requires "something in immediate exchange," for this postulate draws on a fundamental inclination of human nature. As a consequence, "The question [of socialism][18] is not how to educate new people who, because they see things from a broader perspective, voluntarily take on unpleasant tasks; rather it consists in finding the compensating quid pro quo and taking account of human nature" (*D* 306). Socialism was well advised to consider human nature and rethink human relations in terms of an interested exchange if it was to prevail in its struggle against capitalism.[19]

These select passages documenting Musil's stance on socialism show how essayistic reflection enabled him to put his finger on the psychological weaknesses of this ideology from a nondogmatic perspective, which fruitfully acknowledged the criticism, but also the shared premises, of socialism's ideological opponents. It was this fluid and courageously mutable type of reflection that made it possible to navigate the archipelago of queer alliances and acrid disputes among disparate ideologies. For Musil, the intellectual mindset of essayism enabled the observer to avoid getting too bogged down in any one ideological quibble and instead made it possible to glimpse the strengths and shortcomings shared by antagonistic ideological positions. The goal was to attain a larger intellectual perspective than that of any one ideology and to put one's finger on the intellectual errors of the age, as Musil had done with his denunciation of the bad idealism of his time. The ultimate aim was to gain insight into the broader mechanisms of ideological exchange in order to articulate some desirable direction of change. As Musil himself defined the task at hand: "a life without systematizing but, nonetheless, with order. Self-creative order. Generative order. An organization that is not determined from a to z, but one proceeding from n to n + 1" (*D* 318). The order envisioned by Musil was not about formulating normative prescriptions but rather about steering the interplay of ideologies in a way that would leave it constantly open to negotiation. What enabled the intellectual to fulfill this task was not his inhabiting a superior vantage point located above or outside the exchange of modernity's ideologies and language games—the privileged perspective of Mannheim's "free-floating intellectual." It was rather the intellectual's commitment to empirical observation and a flexible use of reason, virtues potentially available to anyone, that assisted him in the task of articulating some kind of synthetic overview while affirming the impossibility of ever inhabiting an absolute, all-encompassing perspective.

Musil's vision of modernity was shaped by conviction that it was imperative to acknowledge the splintered reality of the postwar years and to articulate some contingent spiritual synthesis that would draw out the positive potential of the modern period. The difficulties entailed in this task are acknowledged in his 1921 play *The Visionaries,* which enacts Musil's idea of literature as a laboratory for exploring new ways for 'being human.' The text offers itself as a profile of its main characters, four long-time friends who have endeavored to embrace insight into the contingency of existence and the ethical open-endedness it entails. Yet their adult lives have become reified in an empty day-to-day routine, which is only intermittently haunted by memory of the ecstatic visions of their youth. Thomas, a university professor, has come to distrust and stifle his emotional side, withdrawing into a disengaged intellectualism. He finds his alter ego in Anselm, who, upon giving up the university career that was also his goal, has become locked in a quest for an ecstatic emotional condition he seeks to summon up through pathetic speeches and unaccountable, erratic behavior. Anselm is the lover of Regine, who in a series of extramarital relations has also been confusedly pursuing some ecstatic emotion she once experienced with her first, deceased husband. By contrast her sister Maria, Thomas's wife, has made of her quiet and trusting nature a virtue of goodness that is as unfulfilling as it is vapid. A series of events brings the friends together, offering them a chance for reckoning with their lives. They endeavor to understand how it was possible for the intuited passion of their youth to become a path to self-delusion, which led to spiritual sterility and, in the case of Regine and Anselm, to indefensible conduct. Especially Regine and Anselm must confront the question of what life is engendered by an ethos whose truthfulness lies in its mutability and contingency. How is one to assess such an ethos, which all characters in one way or the other pursued in their youthful visions, if one lacks firm criteria for honest and desirable behavior? No solutions are offered at the end, except that a reshuffling of the two couples takes place–the level-headed Maria chooses to follow the emotion-driven Anselm, leaving behind the cerebral Thomas and the instinctive Regine as a couple of sorts. While the text has been interpreted as suggesting the need for a better integration of feeling and the intellect in each character,[20] it remains unclear how the newly established relationships among the four friends will help each attain a more balanced relation of the two sides.

Musil's play contains the diagnosis of an existential condition he first described in *Törless.* It offers a dense dramatization of this condition, which makes few concessions to the need for dramatic development or for contextualizing specific issues and themes. In its intellectual density and complexity, the text represents Musil's response to the empty pathos and intellectual vacuity he associated with contemporary drama. Musil was fully aware that his ambitious thought-experiment demanded an extraordinary commitment from both its actors and its audience.[21] At the time of the play's publication he was already working on another fictional project, which was to allow for a large-scale inquiry into the issues explored in *The Visionaries,* namely, the novel *The Man without Qualities.* Musil regarded the novel as an opportunity for specifying and historicizing the ethical vision he had articulated before the war. He intended to show that the mystical experience of dispossessment linked to religion and art did not point to the existence of an ethical outside of experience, but, rather, to a different relation between feeling and the intellect, which was compatible with immanent and finite existence. This inquiry was to ground a model of ethics that relinquished the longing for absolute principles in favor of contingent coordinates more suited for coping with a modernity defined by decenteredness and devoid of a metaphysical outside. Musil appropriated key images from Kant's *Critique of Judgment* to account for the aesthetic configuration of intellect and feeling. His initial vision of art as spanning two distinct territories, knowledge and ethics, ratioid and nonratioid, evolved in a notion of aesthetic experience as connecting two distinct modes of experience, an ordinary and an unfathomable 'other' condition, each grounded in incommensurable states of the mind. The ethical ramifications of this vision were self-referentially put to the test in *The Man without Qualities.* When considered from this perspective, Musil's debt to Kant provides a key puzzle piece in the endeavor not only to understand the novel's aesthetic project but also to grasp the peculiar quality of Musil's modernist vision, which, as I will argue in the next chapters, revolves around a plea for embracing the modern void of ethics.

Non-ratioid, cultural problem.

—Musil, *Tagebücher*

Even aesthetic pleasure is according to Kant—whose aesthetics I could not appropriate, but whose formulations I can certainly call superb without further . . . subscribing to them :: still today appear penetrating and superb—aesthetic pleasure is judgment and feeling.

—Musil, *Der literarische Nachlaß*

4. Kant and the Ethos of Aesthetic Judgment

How is ethics to be conceptualized if one rules out the existence of a reference system located in some metaphysical realm beyond earthly experience? And how can one account for the ethical promise consigned to the mystical moments of illumination that characterize aesthetic experience? These are the thorny questions Musil found himself confronting in his reflection on art and ethics since the 1920s. He believed that what he had termed the nicht-ratioid, the domain encompassing ethics and art, was increasingly becoming a cultural problem in postwar Germany and Austria, for it provided a source of legitimation for redemptive doctrines cutting across disparate political ideologies, which were bent on disavowing the decentered reality of modern societies and on preaching the advent of new Archimedean points of reference. Musil's attempt at addressing these questions took the form of a reflection that appropriated key tropes from Kant's aesthetics. He was, however, not interested in reviving Kant's transcendentalism, as the passage quoted above makes clear. His return to Kant had likewise little to do with the contemporary renaissance of Kantianism in ethics and epistemology.[1] Rather, Musil discovered in Kant's *Critique of Judgment* a reservoir of tropes and images that enabled him to specify his developing notion of aesthetic experience as encompassing a modality of feeling alternative to that of ordinary experience and close to ethics. He primarily drew on his background in the empirical sciences and experimental psychology to define this alternative emotional modality. Nonetheless, the critical junctions of his thinking, that is, the reflection that connects and assesses his empirical findings on art, productively deploys central images and formulations stemming from Kant's aesthetics. Specifically, Musil followed Kant in describing the distinctive emotional quality of aesthetic experience in terms of a special interplay between the intellect and the faculty of sensibility—imagination in Kant's transcendental framework, feeling in Musil's empirical paradigm.[2] Much like Kant, Musil regarded this special interaction of human faculties as the site of an immanent principle of orientation. Through aesthetic judgment, he believed, art grants access to an ethical principle of conduct, which does not translate into specific precepts but rather allows individuals to act purposefully precisely in the absence of codifiable principles of behavior. The reappropriation of Kantian images thus helped Musil address what he saw as the key problem of contemporary ethical reflection, namely, the need for articulating a model of ethics that dispensed with the fiction of absolute metaphysical certainties while fulfilling the human need for a shared principle of orientation.

The Kantian framework was also instrumental in helping Musil underscore the intellectual component of aesthetic experience at a time prone to seeing in art the site of an unspecified "other" of reason.[3] Though framed by profoundly different historical circumstances, both Kant's and Musil's enterprises can be viewed as attempts at rescuing reason from the attacks of its detractors. These were, in the latter decades of the eighteenth century, the philosophical alliance of the skeptics and the empiricists, on the one hand, and resurgent religious gnosticism, on the other. For Musil, it was the irrationalism and cultural pessimism that found expression in the writings of Rathenau and Spengler, as well as the naive cult of intuition and anti-intellectualism that animated contemporary aesthetic experiments like that of Expressionism. The recourse to Kant's imagery allowed Musil to counter the current understanding of art as a realm of pure feeling at odds with the stifling force of the intellect. While conceding that art partakes of a peculiar emotional modality, Musil drew on Kant to underscore that the intellect was not an antagonist of feeling but rather its indispensable ally in aesthetic experience. The type of cognition afforded by the aesthetic was thus not to be seen as an alternative to the knowledge provided by rational discourses like science but rather as a complement to it. Musil saw the threats harbored by the anti-intellectualism and regressive idealism of his time become ominously concrete with the rise of National Socialism after the mid-1920s. Significantly, his references to Kant became more numerous and explicit as Germany's and Austria's political situation deteriorated in the course of the 1930s. His last published essay, from 1937, draws an unequivocal connection between the degeneration of aesthetic judgment in the German people and the distraught political situation of his day.

Musil's primary knowledge of Kant stemmed from his philosophical studies in epistemology. It is unclear whether and to what extent he was familiar with the tradition of philosophical aesthetics, although his diaries show that he consulted compendia of the history of aesthetics on his own. It appears that Musil did not initially realize that he was seizing on some well-known tropes of Kantian aesthetics. There are, however, indications that over time he became increasingly aware of the affinities between Kant's aesthetics and his notion of art.[4] The point, however, is not to look for convergences between Kant's critical method and Musil's eclectic empiricism. The aim here is rather to evaluate the import of the images and tropes Musil borrowed, at times knowingly, at times perhaps unwittingly, from Kant.[5] These images revolve around two main tropes: the idea of art as a bridge spanning two incommensurable realms of experience, which Musil redefined as two incommensurable states of mind in the individual, and the issue of the exemplarity of the artwork. They provide a nucleus around which Musil's eclectic thinking on literature and art over time congealed.

What prompted Musil to further specify his model of literature and of aesthetic experience in the course of the 1920s was in part a desire to move beyond the categories that dominated discourse on literature during the nineteenth century. In particular, he endeavored to discard the humanist notion of timeless artworks that are the solitary concoctions of a larger-than-life artist/genius and to advance a more timely concept of literature as a situated, time-bound practice that is shaped in the symbiotic exchange between readers and books. An essay fragment from the early 1920s takes up some familiar themes from Musil's criticism of contemporary literary practice to ponder the trivialized state of literature in the age of mature capitalism.[6] The text denounces the weak intellectual substance of literature in the present, seen as the product of a gushy idealism and fuzzy sentimentalism that squander the unique emotional potential of literature in the evocation of affects "that one later does not understand because they have nothing to do with the way one otherwise is" (*GW* 8, 1350). What makes this essay interesting, however, is not Musil's critique of the literary manipulation of feigned emotions, which plays on and broadens his analysis of contemporary drama presented in the previous chapter. The text is rather intriguing for Musil's acknowledgment that this kind of literature is also a manifestation of the times, for literature is not a realm detached from concrete life but rather a human activity whose function and social impact appear different in every age and culture (*GW* 8, 1349). This prompted Musil to advance his own alternative model of literature as a "moral laboratory" in which new analyses and partial overviews are tested on singular moral cases (*GW* 8, 1351). The literary process of offering possible solutions for unique moral constellations, Musil argued, crystallizes over time in a kind of "teaching about humans" that enables literary objects to serve as examples, which can speak to readers beyond the contingencies of different cultures and times ("One will never be able to impart this teaching without the examples," *GW* 8, 1352).

Musil further specified his model of literature as the time-bound interaction of readers with books in an essay from 1926.[7] Here he introduced the notion of an open-ended criticism as the intellectual and spiritual cement that turns the disorderly aggregate of readers and books into a coherent literary network. Criticism underscores the quality of literature as a "collective working concept" (*GW* 8, 1167). It consists in the work of processing the experience of reading, which Musil held to be the quintessential literary experience (*GW* 8, 1169).[8] Much like morality, criticism lacks absolute criteria of judgment, but it nonetheless possesses a system that is at once mutable and firm. It can dispense with universal criteria of value because it is an activity that is not grounded in some space outside or above literary practice but is rather one of its integral components:

> Criticism in this sense does not stand above literature, but is rather entwined with it. It integrates the ideological results into a tradition . . . and does not permit the repetition of the same without a new meaning. It is an interpretation of literature that turns into an interpretation of life. . . . That is why it represents both a less and a more, it remains in many ways indebted to the life that surrounds it, much like every ideological order, while bestowing on it some general quality. This criticism has little to do with a know-it-all attitude; it may make mistakes, for it never arises from one individual alone, but rather from entwined impulses, from the efforts of many, from an endless process of revisions, indeed, it is spurred from the critiqued books themselves, because every significant work has the ability to overturn everything that people had up to then believed. (*GW* 8, 1169–70)

Musil is here speaking to the sense of disorientation uttered by a community of literati prone to mourning the loss of absolute standards of taste in a culture marked by the rise of new media and the fragmentation of the cultural market. His notion of criticism seeks to acknowledge this modern reality. Criticism is for Musil not about judging literature against infallible standards of taste but rather represents a hermeneutic activity involving the interpretation of situated literary objects, which in turn yields an appraisal of contemporary human experience. This concept of criticism shifts the emphasis from the presumed intrinsic value of literary texts to the endless process of interpretive revisions they engender. Literature's ethical function, then, lies precisely in this time-bound, inherently partial process of interpretation and evaluation. Literature appears as a system in constant flux, a complex medium of meaning-production through which humans are given to test thorny moral issues and experiment with new solutions. Its partiality and time-boundedness well reflect the singularity and situatedness of moral questions.[9]

Both essays discussed above start from the premise that art is intimately related to ethics but fail to specify this connection in any detail. The reader is compelled to ask what, exactly, makes art into a "moral laboratory," what allows Musil to maintain that the examples consigned to literature have a moral valence at all, that is, where the exemplarity of literary texts is grounded. In his 1918 essay on the writer's activity, "Sketch of What the Writer Knows" (*P* 61–65), Musil had postulated the existence of two distinct domains of experience. On the one hand was the ratioid, defined by iterable and verifiable events like those under the purview of the natural sciences, and, on the other, the nonratioid, that encompasses the utterly singular occurrences of ethics. The writer's task lies in extending the methodological precision of the sciences to the singular realm of ethics. It was crucial to Musil to maintain that the writer avails himself of the same cognitive faculties as the scientist. What distinguishes him from the scientist is not a presumed poetic gift but rather a specific domain of operation, namely, that of singular facts (*P* 62–64). Assuming the existence of two distinct domains of experience served the purpose of avoiding the trap of positing a different kind of poetic cognition, that nebulous intuitive knowledge that exempted literature from intellectual accountability and relegated it to the ghetto of pure feeling. But the semantic instability of Musil's distinction between ratioid and nicht-ratioid in this early essay reveals just how far he was from having a satisfactory grasp of these issues. In fact, one passage in the text seems to undermine the essential difference between the two realms, suggesting that their disparity arises as a by-product of the given method of observation, grounded in rational coordinates, and is thus not an intrinsic property of the facts observed (*P* 62–63).

The instability of the polarity of ratioid/nonratioid in this essay, which denotes now an essential property of the facts under scrutiny, now a modality of observation, reflects Musil's uneasiness with hypostatizing two distinct realms of experience, art and ethics on the one hand, science and knowledge on the other. This distinction could be seen as replicating the inflated dichotomy between life and art or rational and nonrational that lent itself to bolstering the regressive critiques of the present that Musil was eager to refute. If at stake is not an essential quality of the facts under scrutiny, however, but a mode of observation that bears no necessary relation to what is observed, the whole distinction between the scientist and the writer really becomes one of observation—more specifically, of the criteria employed in observation. Musil's reflection in the 1920s unfolds as an attempt at shedding light on this issue and attaining a more nuanced understanding of art's relation to ethics.[10] A diary entry from around 1921 to 1923 registers an important recasting of the distinction ratioid/nonratioid, which is extended to denote a specific state of mind, namely, the state of mind of the individual in the ethical experience:

> What is an ethical experience?
> Two groups of experiences: those that can be fixed and transferred;
> those that cannot be fixed and transferred.
> These also called "ratioid" and "non-ratioid." (*D* 313)

In virtue of its utter singularity, ethical experience eludes fixation and, consequently, is comparatively difficult to communicate and share. It thus pertains to the nicht-ratioid. This passage is noteworthy because it shows how the nicht-ratioid has evolved from a class of objects and events endowed with intrinsic properties to an experiential mode alternative to the ordinary one. It illustrates Musil's shift to an understanding of art as consigned to a different affective modality, which brings it close to ethics. This turn is completed in a seminal essay from the mid 1920s, "Toward a New Aesthetic: Observations on a Dramaturgy of Film" (*P* 193–208). Here the idea of the writer's ability to span two domains of experience is reinterpreted as the momentary touching of incommensurable states of mind in the individual. The subtext for this development is a central trope from Kant's *Critique of Judgment,* the image of art as a bridge connecting two incommensurable realms.

The essay, which was published in *Der neue Merkur* in 1925, was inspired by the analysis of the new cinematic medium submitted by the

Hungarian essayist and film critic Béla Balázs in a book from 1924, *The Visible Person or the Culture of Film.*[11] It employs Balázs's observations on the artistic quality of the new medium as a springboard to address general issues relating to art and literature, particularly the question of the psychological processes involved in aesthetic experience. Film's artistic quality, Musil argues at first, is consigned to its ability to portray events that are reduced to moving shadows yet evoke the illusion of life. This ability to abstract from life while powerfully conjuring it up is for Musil a hallmark of all art forms, for aesthetic experience is grounded in a fundamental uncoupling from ordinary experience. This process of abstraction disrupts the individual's consciousness of reality, causing the rearrangement of its familiar elements into a new, initially unreal whole, which succeeds in displacing the previous picture of reality (*P* 195–96). In other words, art's impact lies in "exploding the normal totality of experience" (*P* 200), which in turn allows for the emergence of alternative visions and accounts of experience. However, it never really abandons the plane of ordinary existence, since it does not summon a novel world, a previously unthinkable reality, but rather operates by reshuffling the data of experience, favoring their reaggregation in a "summary leading to a new context" (*P* 195). In so doing, art stands in a fundamental antithesis to life, but not in the sense that it discloses an altogether different realm, a more authentic reality than ordinary experience. Art's antithetical relation to life rather resides in its ability to release the individual from the spell of established pictures of the world and to enable him to imagine alternatives in a realm of abstraction that is at once connected to and at one remove from ordinary reality.[12]

Art's function in modernity, Musil argues in summary, lies in this ability to renew our shared images of the world through the disruption of formulaic experience. But what triggers and sustains this uncoupling from experience? What grounds art's status at one remove from life? What do the artist or the artwork's recipient step back to, when they step back from ordinary life? At first look it may seem that Musil commits the same fallacy he eagerly critiqued in contemporary aesthetic reflection, namely, that of presenting art as a gate to a different, more truthful reality, an alternative world that might redeem the sins of the present. Musil's vision could not be more different, however. To be sure, in his model aesthetic experience allows for the emergence of something that is not part of ordinary life, and it is precisely the emergence of this 'something' that disrupts life's formulaic character. However, this realm does not form an alternative to ordinary life but instead represents its foil, its constitutive other, so to speak.

Accordingly, it can be perceived only negatively, as a void. Musil speaks in this regard of two fundamental states of mind that can be observed in the development of different peoples and civilizations. Human existence unfolds primarily within what he calls "the normal condition of our relationship to the world, to people, and to ourselves" (*P* 198), an experiential modality that is dominated by that instrumental use of reason that has made humans' mastery over nature possible. By contrast, the other modality is not easily characterized. Drawing on Lucien Lévy-Bruhl's important study of the culture of so-called 'primitive' peoples,[13] Musil assumes the emergence of an extraconceptual, empathetic mode of relating to the world, which was presumably prevalent in prehistoric ages and has become restricted to the realms of religion and art in mature civilizations (*P* 196). Across ages and cultures this experiential mode has been designated with different terms from the idioms of religion, ethics, and mysticism—love, contemplation, enrapture, quest for God. Despite the variety of descriptions, Musil maintains, it has not significantly evolved. Musil's recourse to metaphorical language emphasizes the difficulties of describing this alternative modality of experience:

> one finds again and again the presence of another world, like a solid ocean bottom from which the restless waves of the ordinary world have drawn back; and in the image of this world there is neither measure nor precision, neither purpose nor cause: good and evil simply fall away, without any pretense of superiority, and in place of all these relations enters a secret rising and ebbing of our being with that of things and other people. (*P* 199)

As this passage suggests, the 'other' condition entails a transfiguration of ordinary reality made possible by the erasure of the divide separating self and the world. While the emergence of this state leaves unmistakable traces in everyday life, shaping moral and ideal conceptions, Musil insists that it should not be construed as a dimension of being that harbors the concealed truth about human existence, a truth one could hope to transpose into the language of ordinary experience. This condition is nothing other than the "shadowy double of our world" (*P* 199), the foil to ordinary experience itself, and as such it is necessarily experienced as a void, a domain in which everything ceases: "the dark realm of the 'other condition,' in which everything provisionally ceases. This is the true and apparently unavoidable antithesis" (*P* 201).

The focus of this last statement is on the term "antithesis," which is meant to call attention to the paradoxical nature of any inquiry into the Other Condition. The problem is that once one has attained the 'other' state of mind, one will also have left behind those ordinary structures of perception and thinking that could help one grasp the condition thus uncovered. Conversely, any attempt to relate our experiences within the Other Condition in a causal and purposive manner does not further our knowledge of it but rather destroys it, "for, strictly speaking, no purely neutral state has any connection with other states; but if a neutral state should establish such a connection, it assimilates itself to consciousness or allies itself with the remainder of the self; it loses, in a word, precisely the quality that matters" (*P* 207). Because the two states are fundamentally incommensurable, applying the cognitive categories of ordinary experience to the Other Condition will inevitably erase its otherness. Yet if one leaves behind all the categories that structure consciousness, what remains is an unstructured condition that can be experienced only as an undifferentiated void.

Musil sees this antithesis as clearly inscribed in the expressly negative quality that distinguishes aesthetic experience. The paradoxical formulations of modern aesthetics—"purpose*less* movement" as the "essence of dance," "*non*-representational seeing" as the intuition of contemporary painting, and, more generally, Kant's momentous formulation of a "purpose*less* beauty and art" (*P* 201)—all bring to the fore the contradiction entailed in expressing within ordinary experience that which is incommensurable with it. In other words, art appears as a paradoxical experience, which favors the momentary touching between two mutually unintelligible conditions. As Musil argues in his concluding remarks, humans in the modern period permanently inhabit the dimension of ordinary experience and can apprehend the other realm only as a hypothetical limit:

> This condition is never of long duration except in pathological form; it is a hypothetical borderline case, which one approaches only to fall back repeatedly into the normal condition, and precisely this distinguishes art from mysticism, that art never entirely loses its connection with the ordinary attitude. It seems, then, like a dependent condition, like a bridge arching away from solid ground as if it possessed a corresponding pier in the realm of the imaginary. (*P* 208)

The permanent experience of the Other Condition is actually not impossible but amounts to a psychological disorder or to the estrangement from ordinary reality characteristic of mysticism.[14] Art distinguishes itself from mysticism in that it never completely severs the link to ordinary experience. As stated earlier in the essay, the possibility of a return to ordinary experience, that "point of contact with the normal condition" (*P* 205), is in art at least as important as its ineffable moment of rapture and estrangement. One can conclude that this partial grounding in ordinary experience constitutes the advantage of art over mysticism. While this link deprives art of any autonomy, in the sense of an operational realm of its own, it simultaneously enables it to serve as a bridge that rises from the solid foundation of everyday life as though it possessed its other end in the imaginary realm of the Other Condition.

This image powerfully reproposes Törless's quest for a bridge, a possible connection between the ordinary and the alternate state of mind, whose cleft represents the source of the adolescent's obscure anxieties. The film essay suggests that one such bridge is given in aesthetic experience. Precisely the image of art as a bridge spanning two incommensurable realms makes Musil's debt to Kant explicit. Though under very different epistemological premises, Kant had also found himself facing the problem of a gaping abyss between, on the one hand, the domain of nature and ordinary experience and, on the other, the realm of ethics and of an unknowable divinity—a gulf signifying the impossibility of grounding moral conduct in a transcendent, noncontingent realm.[15] To amend this situation, Kant conceptualized aesthetic experience, particularly the judgment of the beautiful, as the link between the otherwise incommensurable realms of nature and freedom, theoretical and practical reason—an enterprise to which the third installment of his critical philosophy, the *Critique of Judgment,* is dedicated. Specifically, Kant argued that the judgment of the beautiful in nature, while remaining excluded from the domain of knowledge, still enables humans to perceive the sign of a divine teleology beyond the contingent reality of the sensible world. In other words, aesthetic judgment makes the supersensible conspicuous in the sensible, not as a moral teaching one could translate into a system of conduct but as the sense of nature's overall purpose and meaning.[16] Kant was adamant in presenting this bridging not as the actual merging of physically distinct worlds but instead as the joining of faculties within the subject in recognizing the possibility of nature's overall purpose. Under Musil's different epistemological premises, Kant's idea of a bridge between the sensible world and the domain of morality is reconfigured as the momentary contact of two incompatible states of mind in the individual, namely, that of ordinary experience and that of its inaccessible foil, an ethical Other Condition. Musil's idea of art as a "dependent state" further recalls Kant's general characterization of the faculty of judgment. In the introduction to the third *Critique* Kant attributes judgment with a specific type of operation, while denying it a 'realm of legislation' or a domain of action of its own, so as to distinguish it from the faculties of understanding (*Verstand*) and reason (*Vernunft*). Notably, in Kant's framework it is precisely the absence of a distinctive legislative realm that enables judgment to serve as a link between the theoretical faculty of understanding and the practical faculty of reason, an argument that is echoed by Musil's vision of aesthetic experience as a dependent condition connecting the ordinary and the "other" conditions of existence.[17]

This reading of the 1925 essay suggests that Musil viewed the Other Condition as a secularized equivalent to the realm of freedom and morality, which Kant theorized as inaccessible to human cognition. Yet it appears not at all clear in this essay that the Other Condition possesses an ethical valence at all. Although a diary entry from the early 1920s defines it as the "basic state of ethics" (*D* 320), a discussion of its ethical import remains conspicuously absent from the essay on film. This is not surprising, if one considers the extreme terms in which Musil states his case in this essay. For once the Other Condition is declared to lie outside the conceptual and discursive categories of ordinary experience, very little can be said about it, not to mention speculating about its ethical significance. Musil was aware of this dilemma and oscillated between the intransigent position of the film essay and hope that further investigation might one day help shed more light on this condition, albeit from a cognitive position that was bound to remain fundamentally alien to it. In particular, an essay fragment from 1923 embarks on a more detailed inquiry into the ethical side of the Other Condition. Notably, it also further reappropriates and adapts Kant's understanding of aesthetic experience.

The text at stake is the fragment "The German as Symptom" (*P* 150–92), which is part of an essayistic triad aimed at offering a broad diagnosis of the crisis of the postwar years. The essay presents the pervasive sense of disorientation in postwar Germany and Austria as symptomatic of a broader crisis of Western civilization fueled, at least in part, by inability to properly acknowledge that elusive realm of human experience Musil called the Other Condition. The text offers Musil's most comprehensive exploration of the "other" realm, and one can surmise that the difficulty of this endeavor was responsible for its remaining a fragment. What appears to be the last of several drafts breaks off, quite tellingly, in the middle of a section dedicated to the "profane religiosity" of the Other Condition (*P* 191). Precisely the tentative character of Musil's exploration makes it a good place to trace the development of his thinking on this issue as well as its Kantian resonances. My discussion will focus on the last two sections, which contain a detailed discussion of the Other Condition.

If the emphasis of the film essay lay on the incommensurability of the two realms/states of mind and on the role art plays as a momentary bridge between them, this fragment undertakes to define more precisely the alternative modality of feeling that marks the Other Condition. Specifically, it pursues Musil's insight that the 'other' state of the mind consists of a full empathetic identification with the world, which represents the remnant of an archaic modality of relating to reality displaced by the intellectual mode prevalent in modernity.[18] Musil focuses on the state of contemplation that, along with a state of dionysian rapture, represents one possible realization of the Other Condition. If in ordinary experience the relationship between the individual and the world takes the form of a thin emotional connection, Musil argues, the emotional world of the Other Condition can be more appropriately compared to the total empathic participation of the experience of love.[19] What especially interests him is the peculiar bliss entailed in ecstatic states of love (*P* 189). This bliss (*Seligkeit*) is triggered by the disappearance of those feelings more directly connected to the struggle for survival that drives ordinary experience—hatred, egoism, envy, vanity, greed. These are however not the only feelings that are absent from the contemplative Other Condition:

> But also missing, as we have seen, are the feelings that appear as social reactions, and that are rooted in the objective attitude toward knowledge. Vanity, ridicule, and possessive feelings enter in here as well. The contemplative person has no conscience because this reaction is simply not possible for one who finds himself in a state of continuous ethical action. One thinks of the frequent predicate: "withdrawn" [*weltabgewandt*]. Let us say simply: Moral feelings. (*P* 190)

It may seem paradoxical that the contemplative's state of continuous ethical action is triggered by the absence of conscience and moral feelings. Yet the moral feelings that prop up conscience constitute the internalization of the moral principles in which society shrouds its injunctions and are little more than the reification of an original ethical intuition. Conscience stands in opposition to the ethical state because it is presumably anchored in that same subject/object partition of reality that pertains to the dimension of knowledge, calculation, purpose, desire—in other words, to ordinary life.

It is important to note that Musil's account refrains almost completely from any positive characterization of the Other Condition, which is instead described negatively as the undoing of fundamental distinctions in ordinary experience. Precisely this 'negative' approach holds the key to Musil's affinity for Kant. Upon closer look, in fact, the distinctions employed by Musil appear modeled after Kant's discussion of the disinterestedness of aesthetic pleasure: "It is a matter of evaluating differently. The opposition egoism-altruism loses its meaning; likewise, the opposition good-evil. In its place we can put the pair: enhancement-diminution" (*P* 187). The suspension of considerations of interest, whether as the involvement of the faculty of desire (in the opposition egoistic/altruistic) or as the participation of the will (represented through the polarity good/bad) engenders the bliss associated with the Other Condition. These terms closely echo the categories Kant enjoined in discussing the disinterestedness of the judgment of taste, the first of four essential features that characterize aesthetic judgment. In the "Analytic of the Beautiful" Kant defines the pleasure produced by the judgment of taste as disinterested because it does not create an interest in the object, that is, a desire to enter into a relation with it, but rather precipitates the individual into a state of contemplation (*CJ* 38–39, 43–44). The pleasure associated with the beautiful is qualitatively different both from the "pleasant" (*CJ* 39–41), which arouses the individual's desire by promising to please the senses, and the "good" (*CJ* 41–43), which pleases because it awakens the moral interest of reason. Both in the pleasant and in the good the pleasure relates to the actual existence of the object in view of the interest that the faculty of desire has in it, while in the beautiful, pleasure is elicited through the object's form, which merely functions as the trigger for the free play of the faculties of imagination and understanding. It seems that Kant's discussion of the disinterestedness of aesthetic judgment provides a frame for Musil's characterization of the Other Condition as a contemplative state of continuous ethical action that occurs in the absence of considerations of utility and morality. Specifically, Musil's narrative relocates the Kantian account from a strictly transcendental paradigm to the plane of empirical psychology congenial to Musil. Disinterestedness thus comes to denote for Musil a condition marked by the retreat of instrumental reason, which controls the ordinary relation to the world.[20]

The insights derived from this fragment can serve to complement the description of the Other Condition offered in the film essay. Aesthetic experience grants intermittent access to an alternative affective modality, which appears as a state of pure ethical activity marked by the suspension of desire and will, and by an ineffable bliss. It is presumably this tapping into a pure, nonconceptualizable condition that triggers a reshuffling in the individual's perception of the world, favoring the emergence of alternative accounts of experience. Art's ethical task resides in engendering the emergence of these accounts, both as the writer's imaginative activity of devising novel models for human experience and as the recipient's ability to glimpse alternatives to the way things are.

The essays discussed so far have focused on the experiential side of art as a bridge to an alternative modality of feeling related to ethics. Musil further explored the psychological processes involved in the making of the artwork in an essay from 1931, "Literati and Literature: Marginal Glosses," which enlists a promising theoretical paradigm, gestalt psychology, to present the artwork as a unique totality of meaning suspended between the intellectual and the emotional faculties. Musil sought to specify in this way his original idea of a distinctive aesthetic interplay between feeling and the intellect. Significantly, the gestaltist framework also brought him closer to Kant's understanding of the judgment of the beautiful as triggered by the free play of the intellect and the imagination.

The essay opens with a witty discussion of the "literatus" (*Literat*), the hip but presumably shallow man of letters commonly held to be the parasitic double to the authentic writer, the *Dichter*.[21] The capriciousness and versatility of the literatus, Musil suggests at first, seem to be well attuned to his double profile as an individual "whose intellect plays with his feelings, or whose feelings play with his intellect" (*P* 72). It soon becomes clear that the wry discussion of the literati in these opening remarks offers a pretext for addressing more general issues relating to the practice of literature, for the distinctive play between intellect and feeling, which the literatus ostensibly exhibits, is at the heart of the nicht-ratioid thinking that drives all art and literature, according to Musil. One of the issues the text proposes to tackle is how to ground these claims in the firm terrain of scientific research. To this aim Musil enjoins the psychological framework of gestalt theory, which presents all perception as organized around 'forms' (*Gestalten*).[22]

These are relatively stable configurations that predate any structuring intervention of consciousness. Just how central the concept of the gestalt is for Musil's argument on literature becomes clear when one takes a closer look at the explication of gestalt offered by the text:

> The concept of "gestalt" is the scientific basis for this interpenetration of form and content. It signifies that out of the juxtaposition or sequence of elements given by the senses, something can arise that can be neither expressed nor measured by them. As one of the simplest examples, a rectangle can be said to consist of its four sides and a melody of its sounds, but also of their unique internal relations, in the position of the sides in relation to each other, and of the notes to each other. This constitutes the gestalt, and expresses something that cannot be explained on the basis of the expressive possibilities of the individual component parts. As one can also see from this example, gestalt figures are not completely irrational, since they allow comparisons and classification, but they still contain something individual and unique. One could also say, to use an older term that will continue to be used as well, that they are a whole; but it must be added that they are not an additive whole, but in their moment of origin they bring into the world a special quality that differs from that of their elements. (*P* 83–84)

Gestalten generally account for the human ability to perceive objects as meaningful wholes before the intervention of consciousness. They are constellations of elements that allow for limited comparisons and classifications, thus supporting the formation of routines, of intellectual and emotional patterns in a process of "constructing formulas" that is indispensable for mastering even the simplest task of everyday life (*P* 84). On the other hand, as the examples of the rectangle and the musical melody show, they cannot be fully reduced to the elements that constitute them, for the unique relations entered by their components bestow on them an irreducibly singular quality that cannot be grasped by the mere addition of their parts. This is why they elude neat categorizations without being utterly random or irrational. Musil is adamant about emphasizing the appeal of this model of perception over traditional theories of subjectivity. As he notes, it does away with the presumption of a cohesive thinking subject and instead embraces the optimistic notion of a decentered self constituted by disparate "achievement complexes" (*P* 86). This very insight into the ultimate disunity of the individual is productively deployed to account for the peculiarity of aesthetic form. As Musil argues, the gestalt of the artwork makes fruitful the individual's dividedness by filling the crevice separating the sensual/emotional from the mental components:

> Gestalt and form too display precisely this peculiar position halfway between corporeality and spirit. Whether one is looking at a few expressive geometric lines or the ambiguous repose of an old Egyptian visage, what presses outward, so to speak, from the materially given is no longer merely a sensory impression, nor is it yet a content of clearly defined concepts. One might say: it is corporeality that has not entirely become spirit, and it appears that this is precisely what excites the soul: for by their adherence to the external world the basic experiences of feeling and perception, as well as the abstract experiences of pure thought, nearly exclude the soul. (*P* 86)

As Musil argues in this passage, the gestalt of aesthetic objects, which signifies the very entwinement of form and content in the artwork, inhabits a distinctive space between the elementary sensual impressions produced by the object's material being and the more abstract level of conceptualization. Precisely this middle position occupied by a corporeality that has not yet entirely turned into spiritual content liberates a mental/spiritual element ("the soul") located in a distinctive introspective space. This element is usually obliterated by the connection to outer reality, which is required both at the elementary level of sensations and perceptions and at that of abstract thinking. What is an artwork, then? As a gestalt, it is a situated, singular totality of meaning, not generalizable but also not utterly arbitrary. It is subject to the general processes of perception, yet also differs from them in that it remains suspended between material and conceptual structures, severing the link to outer reality that is necessarily established both in simple perceptions and in knowledge. This liminal position in between faculties induces an introspective, contemplative state, which is what grounds art's peculiar status at one remove from experience, as formulated in the film essay.

Musil's idea of the artwork as suspended in an interim space between intellect and feeling contains an unmistakable reference to Kant's free play of the intellect and the imagination in the judgment of taste. In the Kantian model, imagination (the faculty of sensibility) and understanding (the intellectual faculty) fail to proceed along the habitual schematism that produces knowledge, engaging in a free play that triggers a state of contemplation.

The ability of the two faculties to enter this free play provides the grounding for taste as an a priori principle of judgment.[23] For Musil aesthetic objects linger in a space between the sensible and the conceptual, a space that opens up when the suspension of ordinary routines severs the link to outer reality, inducing a contemplative state. Based on this parallel, both for Kant and for Musil aesthetic experience is a condition suspended in an interim sphere of faculties that lets some special meaning emerge. The correspondences do not end here, however, for Musil's increasing references to Kant in the 1930s testify to the fact that he was also appropriating the (in a broad sense) ethical notion of judgment and taste, which underlies Kant's aesthetic play of faculties. Key to unraveling this connection is Musil's attempt at solving a thorny problem in his understanding of literature, which revolves around the issue of the artwork's exemplarity.

The exemplary quality of artworks is briefly discussed in the final section of the "literati" essay, which brings up the familiar theme of the literary object as offering a unique and exemplary account of experience. However, nothing in the essay's gestaltist framework seems to substantiate the claim that artworks are endowed with exemplary force (*P* 89). Upon closer inspection, Musil's notion of the singular, exemplary artwork appears to be fraught with contradictions. What does it mean, exactly, that a unique artwork lays claim to possessing exemplary value? Does its character as a model not jar with the assertion of its singularity and uniqueness? Musil's awareness about the inconsistencies lurking behind his understanding of exemplarity is most explicitly reflected in a fragment from 1936, which reproposes the theme of literature as offering exemplary narratives that contribute to a "teaching about life."[24] It is however significant that the terms "teaching about life" and "exemplary narratives" can no longer be used without qualification in this text: "I once called literature a teaching about life by means of examples. Exempla docent. This is too much. It offers the fragments of a teaching about life" (*GW* 7, 971). As these remarks suggest, the teaching literature imparts is not a comprehensive system of wisdom that could eventually be reconstructed and fixed once and for all. It rather consists of fragments gathered in an endless process of investigation ("The solution to these questions is found at the end of infinite processes," *GW* 7, 971). This self-correction shifts the emphasis to the artwork's fragmentary character, particularly to its lack of a systematic relation within the network of literature, which is consistent with the claim about the artwork's singular quality. It however also exposes an inconsistency that appears to have menaced the idea of the exemplary artwork all along. In ordinary language the term "example" denotes the particular instance of a general content. Musil seems to at first follow this common use of the term, suggesting that the examples provided by literature represent the particular illustration of an abstract teaching on life. The reference to the artwork's fragmentariness, however, undermines this reading in that it implies that literature's "teaching about life" can never be satisfactorily reconstructed and articulated. The inconsistency at issue can be restated as follows: How can we perceive the literary object as providing the example for a general case we cannot adequately articulate? On the one hand, Musil insists on the utter individuality of the artwork as an account of experience enclosed within a specific historical horizon and addressing a contingent situation that cannot be inserted into general paradigms of interpretation. On the other, he maintains that the unique accounts produced within art purport to be not just any accounts but rather models that lay claim to possessing exemplary value. But where is the exemplarity of these examples grounded, one wonders, if not in general paradigms of interpretation to which the examples structurally point? What common ground do the artist and his audience have to share for an artwork to be recognized as exemplary?

In the 1930s, Musil sought and found an answer to these questions in Kant's understanding of exemplarity. In a diary entry written between 1937 and 1941, he noted Kant's famous dictum on the mutually exclusive domains of knowledge and art, explicating it further by adding that "science strives for the general, art for the exemplary," a claim that paraphrases a statement from the third *Critique.*[25] While (scientific) knowledge aims at formulating general rules and laws, this passage suggests, art strives for exemplarity. Exemplarity, as understood by Kant, seems to provide Musil with a framework for outlining art's cognitive potential in contrast to science's generalizing gesture. The investigation of art's distinctive potential for knowledge, as consigned to the concept of exemplarity, is intimately related to the epochal transition, in the course of the eighteenth century, from a normative understanding of art as a medium for the imitation of reality based on rational principles to a paradigm that presents the artwork as the outcome of an original, imaginative process, which is bound to explode the epistemological confines of reason.[26] At stake is art's ability to provide authoritative accounts of contingent and singular experience without forcing it into the general categories of interpretation associated with scientific knowledge and conceptual thinking. Kant counts among the most lucid thinkers of this transition, which he sought to account for in his

Critique of Judgment. He redefined exemplarity as the paradoxical property of aesthetic judgments to demand universal recognition in spite of their singular and incomparable quality—in Kant's own words, "as the example of a universal rule that we cannot state" (*CJ* 74). Precisely Kant's understanding of art as providing examples for a rule that cannot be articulated pointedly captures Musil's predicament. In Kant's aesthetics, the paradoxical exemplarity of artworks bears witness to the existence of taste as an immanent (a priori) principle of judgment that is not guided by concepts. I submit that Musil's exploration of exemplarity within a Kantian framework led him to also conceptualize aesthetic judgment as the site of a self-referential principle of orientation, which is quintessentially ethical in nature and cannot be articulated conceptually.

An analysis of Kant's discussion of exemplarity in the third *Critique* can help foreground the stakes of Musil's move. The question of exemplarity is related to one of the apparent contradictions that underlie Kant's notion of judgment. At issue is the following well-known antinomy: Although aesthetic judgments are singular and nongeneralizable, they nonetheless lay claim to universal recognition.[27] Kant accounts for the ability of singular aesthetic judgments to demand general approval by pointing to the specific exemplary quality that can be attributed to artworks. Their exemplarity is not rooted in a conceptualizable and generalizable teaching one could draw from the artwork but rather resides in the artwork's ability to point to the source from which it was created, a source that must be universally shared, as Kant assumes. This source is taste, that is, the subjective principle of the faculty of judgment (*CJ* §34). Specifically, taste denotes the capacity of the understanding and the imagination to engage in a free play that does not generate knowledge, which is the habitual product of these cognitive faculties: "Only where the imagination in its freedom awakens the understanding and is put by it into regular play, without the aid of concepts, does the representation communicate itself, not as a thought, but as an internal feeling of a purposive state of the mind" (*CJ* 138). The ability of the two faculties of knowledge to enter a free play provides the grounding for what Kant defines as the a priori principle of judgment, that is, its self-referential, autarchic means of orientation in the absence of the support provided by concepts. Taste thus indicates the ability of the faculty of judgment to orient itself according to an immanent principle grounded in the harmonic play of understanding and imagination, in an experience that does not produce knowledge but rather the feeling of a purposive state of the mind. Precisely this feeling lies at the heart of Kant's paradoxical notion of exemplarity.

That the artwork is exemplary means that it invites the recipient to tap into the same source from which the artist drew by eliciting the same purposive play of intellect and imagination that presided over its production.[28]

Jean-François Lyotard has incisively described the stakes of Kant's discussion of taste for today's philosophical debates. According to Lyotard, the all-important question around which the "Analytic of Aesthetic Judgment" revolves concerns the formulation of judgment's criteria for orientation. The issue is how judgment, and by extension all thinking, can steer itself in the absence of external points of reference, which Kant could no longer assume given his repudiation of metaphysics. That is, how can one judge properly before knowing what proper judgment is? How can thinking distinguish good from bad judgment if it is not previously given a criterion for doing so? The answer offered by the third *Critique,* Lyotard maintains, is that thought steers itself according to the feeling it has of itself while thinking.[29] In his reading of Kant, the free play of the understanding and the imagination in aesthetic judgment produces a pleasure that enables thinking to grasp itself in the act of thinking. Hence taste is the sensation that thinking has of itself while in operation.[30] It reassures thought of its self-referential mode of operation not by means of a conceptualizable insight but through a purposive feeling.

The ethical implications of this understanding of taste can hardly be overstated. In Lyotard's reading, the feeling elicited by the judgment of the beautiful holds the key to the immanent principle of orientation available to thinking. Taste becomes the site for thought's ability to discriminate between consistency and inconsistency, truth and untruth, desirable and undesirable behavior. This ability is not grounded in some principle located outside of experience but in an immanent criterion of judgment. Although this criterion cannot be raised to the level of knowledge, it nevertheless makes itself "felt," quite literally, in aesthetic experience, that is, in the free play of the faculties of knowledge outside of knowledge, which characterizes the judgment of the beautiful. This understanding of taste as an ethical medium that dispenses with the assumption of outside reference points is what is at stake in Musil's appropriation of Kant's notion of exemplarity. Musil made his debt to Kant explicit in a speech from 1937, which advances a notion of stupidity that appears as the exact reverse of Kant's harmonious play of faculties. By exploring the dangers that arise from the incongruity at the heart of stupidity, Musil outlined a notion of "capability" or "soundness" grounded in a faculty of judgment that operates according to self-referential coordinates. The final section of this chapter explores the quintessentially ethical character of the notions of taste and judgment Musil adapted from Kant in order to reconstruct the positive moment of orientation entailed in aesthetic experience.

Musil's articulation of aesthetic judgment in the 1930s grew out of his desire to understand the roots of the totalitarian developments in Germany and Austria. Musil had been residing in Berlin during the tumultuous months leading to Hitler's appointment to the Reich chancellorship in January 1933. He had a chance to witness firsthand the eradication of democratic institutions perpetrated by the National Socialists. In May 1933 he decided to permanently relocate to Vienna with his wife Martha, who was of Jewish descent.[31] Musil loathed the ideology of National Socialism. He was repelled by its contempt for individual liberties and mobilization of what Nietzsche had called the 'horde instinct.' He abhorred the National Socialist worship of authority, vulgar display of power, and flirtation with violence in the name of a fuzzy transvaluation of values. He likewise despised its peculiar mixture of atavism, anti-intellectualism, and pseudoscientific narratives, as well as its shrewd manipulation of affects in the cultural arena. Unlike many well-meaning opponents of National Socialism, however, Musil did not believe that pointing the finger at the movement's evil ideology was an effective means of resistance. Hypostatizing National Socialism as an intrinsically evil phenomenon was at odds with his belief that evil is not an absolute category but a contextual attribute, which arises from a specific constellation of factors. He thus thought it more productive to account for the broad historical and cultural constellation that had helped National Socialism to its breakthrough. The roots of National Socialism, but also those of the Austrian brand of fascism, went well beyond the appeal of specific ideological elements, such as their ranting nationalism, Musil believed. As he noted in some remarks jotted down along with notes for the *MwQ*, the National Socialist success had been made possible by the Germans' inability to come to terms with the aftermath of World War I: "Germany's enthusiasm for National Socialism is proof that a firm mental and spiritual mind-set is what is most important to people. The war was the first attempt" (*MwQ* II, 1748).[32] The Germans' enthusiasm for fascism was for Musil a symptom of their inability to cope with the fractured physiognomy of modernity, which World War I had laid bare. This remark is reminiscent of the broad diagnosis of modernity Musil had offered in his essays from the 1920s, where he had warned against the menace posed by his contemporaries' inability to accept the newness of the modern world and by their propensity for embracing habits of thought the war had discredited. In particular, it was the Germans' continued and misplaced yearning for fixed reference points that in the end had brought about the calamity of totalitarianism, for National Socialism purported to provide that firm spiritual framework for which too many yearned.

Although Musil's essays from the 1930s make his condemnation of National Socialism and fascism abundantly clear, they also often contain a plea for refraining from politicizing the literary in the struggle against totalitarianism. His repeated appeals for acknowledging the mutual autonomy of politics and culture even in the face of the fascist threat were at times misunderstood as attempts at dodging the ugly political reality of his day,[33] yet they were in keeping with his conviction that the cultural sphere offered a privileged, autonomous space of reflection for examining the contemporary situation in a nuanced and incisive way. Placing culture in the service of one specific political ideology, even one unambiguously poised to fight fascism, would have obliterated this precious space of reflection. Precisely the totalitarian co-optation of cultural institutions in both Germany and Austria during the 1930s made it all the more important to uphold culture's autonomy, Musil believed.[34] He thus saw his own contribution to the struggle against totalitarianism in the endeavor to deliver a broad-based analysis of the causes that had led to its affirmation. This inquiry prompted him to assume the deterioration of an immanent principle of judgment in the German people,[35] a principle that was at once aesthetic and ethical. Musil illustrated this principle in a speech delivered in 1937 at the Austrian *Werkbund*, which was to become the last text published during his lifetime. It contains a subtle, yet unambiguous indictment of fascism, along with the description of its spiritual and cultural conditions of possibility, which Musil sought to synthesize in a perceptive account of human stupidity. Stupidity originated for Musil from a discordance described as relation between feeling and the intellect. It marked the deterioration of an immanent, self-referential principle of orientation based on the harmony of these faculties. In setting up his discussion by explicitly drawing on Kant's notions of judgment and taste, Musil underscored the quintessentially aesthetic quality of this principle of self-orientation, simultaneously pointing to Kant's third *Critique* as his frame of reference.

The essay "On Stupidity" constitutes one of the finest examples of the essayistic mode of reflection Musil championed. It starts as a whimsical inquiry into the meaning of a term denoting a plethora of human weaknesses and vices but soon develops into the quest for principles to distinguish sound from foolish behavior at a time that has witnessed the demise of all traditional criteria of judgment. The connection between the aesthetic and stupidity is initially established through an empirical observation. The resistance against art by a people that so ostensibly professes to love art, Musil notes, has always impressed him as stupidity. This remark refers to contemporary Austrians and Germans, whose lack of artistic inclination, Musil argues, manifests itself not just in bad times but also in relatively good ones, "so that it is only in degree that oppression and censorship differ from honorary doctorates, membership in learned academies, and the awarding of prizes" (*P* 268). The link to the turbulent political situation of the mid-1930s lies at hand. The violence and repression that haunt the present, these remarks suggest, are nothing but an acute expression of aesthetic ineptitude, an endemic condition that in less troubled times exhibits itself in the pomposity and presumptuousness of academic honors and awards. It is not immediately evident how this disorder would be related to a lack of artistic inclination. In trying to make the link between stupidity and art more specific, Musil first challenges the view that regards stupidity as a mere deficiency of the intellect. Quite to the contrary, stupidity affects both the intellect and feeling, and in this it is not dissimilar to "aesthetic enjoyment," which also involves both "judgment," understood here as a primarily intellectual faculty, and "feeling" (*P* 269). In a clever rhetorical move, the juxtaposition of stupidity and aesthetic judgment is corroborated by pointing to an analogous constellation in Kant's antinomy of taste. As in the judgment of taste, Musil maintains, the difficulty of circumscribing the notion of stupidity lies in having to make general statements about something that calls for generalization, yet eludes all generalizing pronouncements in virtue of its utter singularity. Put in the Kantian terminology of the antinomies, both for the beautiful and for the stupid there is no general concept under which all the particular cases could be subsumed. Hence the phenomena encompassed by the beautiful and the stupid do not allow for systematization or generalization. As a consequence, Musil declares himself unable to offer a "theory" or a comprehensive definition of stupidity and instead chooses to explore the range of use of the term, in the hope of drawing at least some conclusions from the phenomena under observation (*P* 270). His examples, which without exception describe relations of power, offer a sly commentary on the contemporary political situation. So, for instance, a simulated display of stupidity is often the only available defense to the underling, whose cleverness is a threat to the master (*P* 271). But a treacherous mix of stupidity, vanity, and abuse of power is also often the hallmark of groups of individuals who gain control of power and, as a collective, permit themselves to entertain modes of behavior which they would never engage in as individuals (*P* 272–73). Musil's examples uncover a complex interplay of presumptuousness, conceit, vanity, and failure to fulfill the raised expectations (*P* 273), whose practical consequences can be assessed in terms of "brutality" and "immorality" (*P* 275). This constellation does not arise from a mere weakness of the intellect, Musil insists, but is rather due to a "disturbance of the emotional balance" (*P* 275) caused by an upset relation between "affect" and "intelligence" (*P* 276).

The relation between stupidity, vanity, and underachievement, as well as the claim that stupidity does not merely denote an intellectual deficit, prove central to Musil's argument. The stupidity of vanity lies in awakening expectations it fails to fulfill. Its inability to rise to the standards it itself summons suggests a deficit in coping with the practical tasks of everyday life, which in turn makes stupidity appear the opposite of not just intelligence but also practical cleverness and "capability" or "soundness" (*P* 276). Within this broader practical perspective, Musil maintains, the proper opposite for the stupid is actually not the intelligent but the fit, capable, skillful, clever. With the introduction of "capability" as a more fitting antonym for stupidity, the discussion shifts from the enumeration of *examples* of stupidity to an analysis of what one could define as the *judgment* of stupidity itself, that is, of the circumstances under which someone or something is deemed stupid. Musil notes that such a judgment represents a broad, unspecific charge that something or someone fails to meet the demands of a specific situation (*P* 277). Precisely the broad scope of this charge prompts Musil to liken it to the behavior of an individual who falls prey to panic after being confronted with an overwhelming situation. As the panicking individual performs a series of random acts in the hope that one of them might actually be the appropriate one, so is the use of the unspecific epithet "stupid" equivalent to the use of a plethora of words and is thus comparable to the exuberance of actions and shooting in the dark of the panic state. The sort of heated overreaction that triggers the panicking behavior fails to engender the purposive actions called for by the given situation and instead produces conduct that appears "aimless, and indeed counterproductive."[36] Similarly, the excessive use of the charge of stupidity, Musil maintains, is often accompanied by a tendency to senseless destruction or flight (*P* 279).

The shift from the examples of stupidity to the actual judgment of stupidity prepares an important, startling reversal. Musil wittily describes the mix of wrath, impotence, and repressed aggression that frequently accompanies the charge of stupidity. The individual proffering this judgment often finds himself in an "oppressive condition of insufficiency" that foreshadows an imminent explosion of rage,

> and the explosion is then usually introduced with the profoundly transparent words that "something has finally become just *too* stupid" for one to take. But this something is oneself. In periods when energetic, sweeping action is highly esteemed, it is essential to also be reminded of what sometimes resembles action to the point of being mistaken for it. (*P* 280)

As the passage suggests, "insufficiency," the quality that had elicited the judgment of stupidity, finally comes to identify the state of the individual who utters that very judgment. In other words, the something that in its intolerable stupidity triggers such irate reaction turns out to be the very person who passes the judgment of stupidity. Much like for Kant's judgment of the beautiful, the stupid does not denote a property of the object deemed stupid but rather the state of mind of the individual who passes that judgment, or, as Kant would put it, it arises from the individual's reflection on his state of mind. For this reason, the unsuitability that the individual criticizes in his judgment of stupidity actually reflects back on the individual's own insufficiency, laying bare his inability to cope with the given situation.

This reversal marks a return to the situation of the present, disclosing what is really at stake in Musil's discussion. The allusion to current calls to decisive action contains an unmistakable reference to the tumultuous climate of the late 1930s. As Musil suggests, such appeals for decisive action, which are generally interpreted as pointing to a clear sense of what needs to be done, might instead indicate a fundamental inability to cope with the contemporary situation. That is, those who vociferously vent their discontent about a modern world marked by chaos and corruption and invoke a return to simple truths might actually be giving voice to their own inadequacy in dealing with the present, that is, to their own stupidity. Not surprisingly, Musil's observations at this point abandon the plane of individual experience to address the broader issue of the cultural and ideological crisis dogging the present. At stake is a progressive erosion of traditional concepts of humanity, wisdom, freedom, and reason that has precipitated the modern world into a state of panic (*P* 280). This crisis contains the germs of a new condition but also highlights the difficulties linked to the transition to the new. The desire to outline a conceptual framework that could facilitate this transition prompts Musil to at least attempt to articulate a "notion or partial notion of stupidity," albeit without denying the diachronic instability of concepts like "stupidity," "reason," and "wisdom" (*P* 281).

Musil draws on contemporary psychological theories to portray human intelligence as predicated upon the harmonious balance of intellect and feeling (*P* 282–83). This frame, he argues, allows the observer to identify two fundamental kinds of stupidity. The first one refers to the naïveté and weak intellect of the simpleton and is fundamentally harmless. To this kind of harmless weakness of the intellect Musil opposes the notion of a "higher," treacherous stupidity. This involves not so much a lack of intelligence as the programmatic failure of an intelligence that pretends to take up tasks that exceed its ability:

> The higher pretentious form of stupidity stands only too often in crass opposition to this honorable form. It is not so much lack of intelligence as failure of intelligence, for the reason that it presumes to accomplishments to which it has no right; and it can have all the bad characteristics of weakness of reason, and in addition all those characteristics brought about by every mind that is not in balance, that is misshapen and erratically active; in short, every mind that deviates from health. To put it more accurately: because there are no "normalized" minds, this deviation expresses an insufficient play of harmony between the one-sidedness of feeling and a reason that is not strong enough to hold it in check. This higher stupidity is the real disease of culture (but to forestall misunderstanding: it is a sign of nonculture, of misculture, of culture that has come about in the wrong way, of disproportion between the material and the energy of culture), and to describe it is an almost infinite task. (*P* 283–84)[37]

The higher kind of stupidity, this passage suggests, differs from the harmless one in that it additionally presupposes a pathological state of the mind. But how is one to provide a definition for this pathology, given the difficulty of determining once and for all what a healthy mind should look or behave like? Musil advances the notion of an "insufficient play" of faculties, involving an intellect that proves unable to curb a biased, narrow-minded feeling. The failure of the intelligence in the stupid—that is, in the individual uttering the judgment of stupidity—is to be traced back to this incongruity of faculties. It is important to note that this imbalance is the reverse of the charge against reason routinely leveled within cultural-pessimistic and vitalistic currents in the first decades of the century. The problem for Musil is not that rationality stifles the emotional sphere but rather that an excess of feeling is bound to overpower an unguarded intellect.

The characterization of stupidity as a pernicious imbalance between intellect and feeling finally lays bare the Kantian horizon that lies behind the puzzling connection between stupidity and artistic ineptitude established at the beginning of the essay. Stupidity and the lack of artistic sense are linked because they both stem from an upset relation between feeling and the intellect. Conversely, "artistic inclination" and "capability/soundness," understood as the ability to orient oneself in life and cope with the demands of the present, depend on a balance between the two powers. As it has by now become clear, the crux of Musil's discussion is the formulation of a principle that can account for the human capacity to make sense of experience and engage in purposive behavior without postulating the existence of external points of reference. This once again brings Musil close to Kant, particularly to the overall aims of his critical enterprise. In Kant's model, the free play of the faculty of sensibility and the intellectual faculty, which produces the judgment of the beautiful, conveys the sense of reality's overall purpose. The apprehension of nature's ultimate meaning does not depend on any external points of reference but is instead inscribed in the two faculties' ability to suspend their automatic routines and engage in a free play. While this experience remains inaccessible to cognition, it is nonetheless enough to ground meaningful behavior, according to Kant. Within Musil's quite different epistemological horizon, the imbalance of the intellectual and the sensible faculties triggers a judgment of stupidity, that is, an attitude that prevents the individual from making sense of experience, thus resulting in unpurposive behavior. Much like for Kant, for Musil orientation is not contingent upon the existence of reference points anchored in a realm on the outside of ordinary experience, whether metaphysical or mystical/religious, but is made possible by an immanent predisposition of the individual, indeed, by the ability of his or her faculties to enter a specific balance. This balance is aesthetic in Kant's meaning of the term; it is not mediated by concepts but rather announces itself through the peculiar feeling of a disinterested pleasure.

This Kantian parallel makes it easier to grasp the connection Musil establishes between his tentative notion of stupidity and the plights of the present. As Musil argues, there is a correlation between patterns of individual behavior and the way a society goes about dealing with the dilemmas posed by a new situation, although one must be leery of heedlessly exporting psychological categories and procedures into the analysis of complex societies. Yet in the case of stupidity Musil tentatively advances the hypothesis that a society might wind up imitating the individual's spiritual defects, for "the occasional stupidities of the individual can easily lead to a constitutional stupidity of the body politic" (*P* 285). Musil's analysis of stupidity seeks to account not simply for the occasional failure of an individual confronted with an overwhelming situation but also for the behavior of a whole people or society, whose "incapacity to find [themselves] in life" and diminished "capacity for objective behavior" (*P* 284) make them unable to live up to the demands of a time of transition. When applied to the situation of contemporary Germany and Austria, Musil's conceptualization of a collective form of stupidity suggests that his fellow citizens have panicked vis-à-vis the dilemmas produced by a rapidly differentiating modern world. They have forsaken the present as "unsuitable" and abandoned themselves to longing for outlived models of experience. Instead of facing modernity's contingency, they have engaged in an anachronistic quest for a permanent system of orientation that has resulted in unpurposive, indeed self-destructive, actions culminating in the establishment of totalitarian regimes. It follows that the catastrophe of National Socialism cannot be explained away as the irresistible rise of an unprecedented evil. The Germans' susceptibility to fascism rather lies in their upset sense of orientation that manifests itself in an artistic ineptitude, which is intimately connected to stupidity.

What can one do, then, to avoid the disastrous imbalance of intellect and feeling that makes one unfit to come to terms with a challenging situation? Given the impossibility of articulating an ultimate criterion to identify the "insufficiency" at the heart of stupidity, Musil cautiously advances the concept of the "significant" as an insight into the truth of a situation that arises from the right balance of the two powers and triggers purposive behavior. The "significant" does not stand for an infallible sense of what needs to be done. It is rather the outcome of circumspect choices made in a condition that is the specular opposite of that "general disproportion in which, today, emotions crush reason instead of inspiring it" (*P* 286). The choices made within this 'significant' horizon are not necessarily always the appropriate ones, yet they differ from 'stupid' decisions in that they remain open to criticism and self-examination. While Musil realizes that it is pointless to search for a closer definition of the meaningful, which, much like the stupid, eludes all attempts at generalization, he also insists that one can at least try to foster the virtues that favor the self-critical attitude at the heart of the "significant." He points to the vigilant exercise of "modesty" as indispensable for curing the ominous imbalance of feeling and intellect, which triggers the judgment of the stupid (*P* 286). Modesty presupposes that all of us, at times, are compelled to act while in a state of stupidity, that is, in an unpurposive, inappropriate manner, often due to our insufficient knowledge of a given situation. This however need not deter us from acting altogether,

> for because our knowledge and ability are incomplete, we are forced in every field to judge prematurely; but we make the effort, and have learned to keep this error within recognized limits and occasionally improve on it, and by this means put our activity back on the right track. There is really no reason why this exact and proudly humble judgment and activity could not be carried over into other areas as well, and I believe that the principle, "Act as well as you can and as badly as you must, but in doing so remain aware of the margin of error of your actions!" would already be halfway toward a promising arrangement of life. (*P* 286)

That individuals sometimes act in ways that are inadequate to meet the demands of a given situation is not necessarily an indication of that structural imbalance exemplified by stupidity. The point is to remain alert to the fallibility of one's judgments and to exercise a healthy modesty. Modesty, restraint in judging, the ability to respond constructively to critique and to practice self-criticism, this is what Musil cautiously prescribes to restore and preserve that healthy balance of intellect and feeling, which is at the heart of purposive behavior.

These suggestions may strike the contemporary reader as weak and ineffective given the magnitude of the totalitarian threat in 1937—Musil delivered his talk only a few months before Hitler marched on Vienna. One might wonder about the usefulness of constructing such an elaborate conceptual edifice to reach fairly commonsense conclusions like the above, which fall short of providing concrete strategies for fighting fascism.[38] Yet Musil's aim in this essay was not to offer specific means of resistance against totalitarianism, but rather to analyze the conditions of possibility of fascism in ways that would also account for the totalitarian potential inherent in other political ideologies, including that of its main antagonist, bolshevism.[39] The point was to consider the totalitarian developments in the early twentieth century—not just in Germany and Austria, but in Italy and the Soviet Union as well—from a perspective that would not become engulfed in the war of ideas waged by antagonistic ideologies but would instead examine the needs these narratives were designed to fulfill against the backdrop of the modern condition. For Musil, the totalizing claim of these narratives was predicated on an anachronistic longing for absolute points of reference and unifying accounts of experience. It was hardly surprising that once helped to the breakthrough, they would endeavor to violently eradicate the multifariousness and differentiation of the modern world in order to impose their totalitarian syntheses. Musil's response sought to address the yearning for comprehensive and unifying horizons that fueled such narratives. He insisted that the demise of traditional coordinates for orientation and Archimedean standpoints, which characterizes modernity, does not make ethics impossible, although it certainly undermines the traditional view of ethics predicated upon an immutable, all-encompassing metaphysical framework. In his eyes it was imperative to go beyond this anachronistic view to bring ethical reflection in line with the conditions of modernity. His idea of an immanent, nonconceptualizable principle of orientation consigned to the aesthetic coalescence of fundamental human faculties represented his contribution to this complex task.

In situating Musil's reflection on art within a Kantian horizon, I initially focused on the notion of a disinterested pleasure arising in aesthetic experience when the suspension of the individual's ordinary relation to reality allows for the momentary emergence of an alternative state of mind, which Musil called the Other Condition. By engendering the temporary bridging of ordinary state and Other Condition, art effects a reshuffling in the individual's entrenched perceptions of the world, favoring the articulation of alternative accounts of experience. These accounts are utterly singular, because they are embedded in a contingent historical horizon; yet they lay claim to exemplary value. Their exemplarity is consigned to an aesthetic sense modeled after Kant's taste, which presupposes the aptitude of the sensible and intellectual faculties to interact in a specific way. This aesthetic configuration is in turn the site of an immanent principle that allows individuals to orient themselves in life and perform purposive actions.

As Musil suggests in the final sections of the essay on stupidity, the aesthetic interplay of faculties does not merely account for individual conduct but can serve to explain the behavior of a whole people—although very cautiously and metaphorically, as it were. It thus displays a central ethical valence—ethics representing in this context the quest for a shared principle of orientation that allows one to make sense of experience and engage in meaningful behavior. This understanding of ethics in turn sheds light on Musil's characterization of the Other Condition as a state of continuous ethical action. Far from providing a source of communicable rules and precepts, the ethical resides for Musil in that interplay of intellect and feeling that is key to passing sound judgments and producing appropriate behavior in the face of contingent reality. Borrowing a formulation from Lyotard's reading of Kant, one can conclude that aesthetic experience bears witness to the steering moment of thinking, that is, to thought's ethical capacity for self-orientation. Notably, within this ethical horizon the insight into the lack of external reference points does not result in nihilism but rather triggers the quest for defining meaningful behavior within the framework of self-reference.

The aesthetic vision that unfolds in Musil's essays and diaries over two decades accords art, and especially literature, a privileged place as the proper medium of ethical reflection in modernity. Art is the appropriate domain for ethical inquiry because it functions as a bridge between the ordinary and the other conditions of experience.[40] Accordingly, Musil reserved his in-depth exploration of the ethical Other Condition for his most ambitious thought-experiment, *The Man without Qualities.* The novel imaginatively explores the aesthetic link between the two conditions, thus offering a self-referential testing ground for Musil's understanding of art's relation to ethics.

Whatever had he meant by telling Diotima that it was necessary to take control of the imaginary, or that other time, when he had said that reality should be abolished? . . . And what on earth had made him say to her that one should live like a character in a book?

—Musil, *The Man without Qualities*

5. Staging the Failure of an Aesthetic Utopia: *The Man without Qualities*

When, in the midst of a personal crisis, the novel's protagonist Ulrich finds himself asking the above questions, he gives voice to concerns that the reader has had for a long time, for a good deal of the narration up to this point has revolved around Ulrich's puzzling attempt to shape his life according to the literary logic of essayism. But what does it mean, exactly, that one should wipe out reality and take possession of the unreal? And how is the reader to understand the call to live like a character in a book? At the heart of these demands lies the modern experience of a dividedness articulated at the beginning of the century through an array of irreconcilable polarities—intellect and feeling, mind and body, rational and nonrational, ordinary life and art.[1] These polarities are inscribed in the two "trees of life" (*MwQ* I, 636) whose incommensurability lies at the heart of Ulrich's crisis. At stake is Ulrich's personal dividedness, which he has inherited from his adolescent counterpart Törless. On the one hand, there is the disjointedness and confusion of ordinary experience. On the other, an unfathomable, thoroughly moral 'other' condition that fleetingly emerges in moments of blissful illumination. Ulrich's query in the novel pointedly articulates the dilemma that arises from this split: How can one conceive of a fulfilled life, if meaning and purpose remain confined to a nonconceptualizable, utterly other side of experience—defined, for lack of better terms, as feeling, intuition, soul, or the irrational? In answering this question, the man without qualities finds himself following a path pursued by most contemporaries: To reinvest ordinary experience with meaning—to make it moral or reenchant it, as Max Weber would say—Ulrich believes that it is imperative to close the gap between the two realms.[2] The demands alluded to in the passage contain in a nutshell the life program Ulrich has forged in his attempt to heal this division. As expressed in the exhortation to live one's life like a character in a book, Ulrich at first seeks to overcome modern fragmentation by drawing on the aesthetic as the medium that offers an intermittent bridge between the two domains.

The perspective of two incommensurable trees of life makes conspicuous the symmetrical structure of the narration, for Ulrich's utopian endeavors in the novel are intimately connected to this split. That is, the two main sections of *MwQ* center around two symmetrical enterprises, each aiming to erase this troubling incommensurability by reducing one realm to the categories or experiential mode of its counterpart. While in the first book Ulrich must acknowledge the futility of his youthful attempt to translate the illuminations of the Other Condition into a conceptualizable ethos informed by the perspectival movement of literary imagination, the second book narrates the failure of his quest—contrary in direction to the first one—to plunge ordinary experience into the unfathomable state of ethical accord fleetingly disclosed within aesthetic experience. In other words, the first book recounts the endeavor of raising the Other Condition to the level of ordinary experience, while the second focuses on the attempt to plunge ordinary experience into the Other Condition.

Both enterprises are doomed to collapsing in the novel. While Ulrich's double failure was meant to bear witness to the unbridgeable divide between the two conditions, it would be ill advised to interpret it as the pessimistic diagnosis of an incurably diseased human condition. Quite to the contrary, the protagonist's debacles, including his foreshadowed suicide in some drafts, were to carry a constructive message for Musil, for they were to exemplify the futility of all contemporary dreams of a reconciled, thoroughly moral life. Furthermore, they were to confront Musil's contemporaries with the task of learning to live with the split that defines the modern condition. The realization that ordinary and ethical experience are incommensurable was to point to the need for reformulating questions of meaning and orientation within the frame of nonconceptualizable ethical experience. Thus the tale of the man without qualities affirms the reality of ethical experience while showing that it cannot become a foundation for ordinary life, because the ethical can be experienced only as a void in ordinary existence.

Within this frame, *MwQ* appears as the enactment of the aesthetic project Musil outlined in his essays. If considered from this vantage point, Ulrich's aesthetic utopias form a testing ground for the reflection on literature unfolding in the essays. While the aesthetic overtones of Ulrich's visions have not gone unnoticed, this study goes one step further in underscoring the centrality of literature for Ulrich's utopia.[3] If one pieces together the frequent, often enigmatic declarations offered by the man without qualities at different points in the narration—the appeal to live like the character in a book, or to realize a 'literary existence,' or to take possession of the 'unreal'—one obtains the profile of a quest to turn literature into the ethos that can bridge the divide between ordinary experience and ethics. Reading the first part of *MwQ* as an aesthetic utopia destined to fail helps one establish the parallel with the doomed utopia of the Other Condition narrated in the second part of the novel and see the symmetry between the two main clusters that make up the narration.[4] In staging the failure of Ulrich's aesthetic utopias, the novel also articulates the potentialities and limitations of art in modernity as the domain in which the two dimensions fleetingly touch. It offers itself as a self-reflexive commentary on the role of literature as a medium for ethical experience and on its relation to other life-spheres in a differentiated modern world.

The failure of Ulrich's utopia of the Other Condition is only foreshadowed in the chapters that constitute the second volume of *MwQ*. At Musil's sudden death in Geneva in 1942 the novel was left at the stage of a heavily incomplete fragment. It lacked not only an ending, but also a considerable part of the second volume.[5] An examination of Musil's literary estate shows that throughout three decades he remained fundamentally faithful to the plan of staging the collapse of Ulrich's utopias.[6] In several sketches Ulrich's failure was to coincide with the outbreak of the Great War, which is foreshadowed at the beginning of the second volume.[7] Over time Musil weighed different options in regard to specific characters and narrative developments; they appear to unfold in agreement with his overall plan of offering an innovative perspective on ethics as a result of the collapse of the protagonist's flawed utopias.[8] This understanding of Musil's project provides the frame for my reading of *MwQ*.

Viewing Musil's essayistic texts as the nonfictional articulation of an epistemological inquiry and aesthetic project that could find their realization only in the novel entails drawing a methodological distinction between the reflection unfolding in the essays and the thinking enacted in the novel. While the essays and the novel engage virtually the same issues, the thinking they harbor displays different features and follows a different logic. Mikhail Bakhtin's analysis of the novel's discursive universe provides a fruitful methodological frame for examining the modes of reflection enacted in the essays and in the novel. Of particular relevance are his notions of polyphony and heteroglossia, which denote the proliferation of voices and idioms that formally distinguish the modern novel for the Russian critic.[9] When considered in light of these Bakhtinian categories, Musil's essayistic texts appear to be carried by a monolithic authorial voice. That is to say, they display a fundamentally monological quality that allows for a minimal degree of ambiguity. The novel, by contrast, exemplarily embodies the Bakhtinian idea of heteroglossia in that it stages a cacophony of rivaling perspectives, entrusted not only to different characters but also to an extremely elusive narrating voice that often imperceptibly blends into the interior monolog of a character. As a result, the ideas that are unambiguously argued in the essays become caught in the refraction of competing discourses and perspectives when touched upon in the novel.[10] The unsolved and unsolvable ambivalence produced in the novel through this multiplication of voices is not a token for a presumed nihilistic horizon that would undermine the narration, however.[11] Rather it epitomizes an epistemological stance that no longer believes in the existence of a privileged perspective on the world and is instead committed to acknowledging its own partiality by continuously evoking competing standpoints.[12] Where the essays monologically articulate an aesthetic project aimed at acknowledging the contingency and lack of Archimedean standpoints of modern reality, the novel enacts this project by inscribing it onto a form driven by the proliferation of clashing discourses and perspectives.[13]

I must emphasize that my account imposes an order onto the novel that does not claim to be *the* order, that is, the most accurate, authoritative, or comprehensive one. The aim here is not to uncover the novel's primary structuring principle but rather to verify the hypothesis that the narration can be read as the enactment of the aesthetic project I have reconstructed based on Musil's nonfictional texts. This perspective construes a possible order, which however remains the principle around which *this* reading, and not necessarily the novel itself, congeals. In other words, the linearity and coherence of the reading proposed here—its simple-mindedness, as it were—are not those of the novel. At the same time, the selective, reductive operations this reading performs in attempting to make sense of Musil's text do not merely represent a subjective response to the text, one of many possible ways to go about it. In its attempt to make sense of the novel, this reading emulates the strategies the novel itself implements in its quest for making sense of the world. *MwQ* harbors a reflection that seeks to interpret experience while navigating in an ostensibly selective way the modern archipelago of ideological stances, perspectives, modes of being, dilemmas, desires, and dreams. This approach deliberately refrains from camouflaging the irreducible complexity of modern reality. The 'story' of the man without qualities thus offers itself as a pointedly partial, selective account of the modern world, its partiality being inscribed in the arabesque of stories, characters, themes, and reflections that complicate and often rival the narration centering around Ulrich. In a way, the novel's fictional relation to the world is formally mimicked in this reading's relation to the novel, for the necessary partiality of any account of modern experience, which the novel postulates and enacts, finds its correlate in the partiality and selectiveness of the present reading.

What prompted Musil in the 1920s and 1930s to write a novel set in Vienna during the fateful year before World War I? How could a narrative frozen in the gesture of looking back to a bygone time lay claim to enacting an aesthetic and ethical reflection projected into the future? Would a novel bent on summoning up a world irremediably lost in the cataclysm of the war not appear anachronistic and pointless when considered against the backdrop of rising totalitarianism in Germany and Austria? The charge of anachronism, of having produced a work out of sync with its time, was very much on Musil's mind. In a note from the late 1930s, Musil found himself compelled to admit that his broad fresco of prewar Austria had by that time become a historical novel. Yet he also insisted that the increasing historical remoteness of the events narrated did not substantially alter the book's character as a "contemporary novel developed out of the past" (*MwQ* II, 1767).[14] By depicting the prewar past, this note suggests, Musil aimed at shedding light on the postwar present. As he knew well, the claim that the prewar years may help one understand the postwar age would sound preposterous to most of his contemporaries, used to regarding the war as a radical historical caesura that had brought about the emergence of a wholly new age. The novel's reconstruction of the fateful year that ushered in the Great War aimed at debunking precisely this assumption. It sought to show that the roots of the postwar crisis lay in the unacknowledged resurgence of prewar mental habits and doctrines that the war had proven bankrupt. That is to say, the new world was not as new as contemporaries liked to believe. In fact, in many ways it strikingly resembled the old one, for instance, in its inability to confront the modern reality of highly complex, decentered societies. Musil believed that the same appetite for uncomplicated and totalizing narratives that had triggered the catastrophe of World War I also bolstered fascism in the 1920s.[15] Thus, the novel's depiction of the prewar years was to be a mirror for the postwar age, a mirror in which the postwar present could finally see its 'true' face and recognize the threats ensuing from its persistence in the very habits of thought that led to the disintegration of the prewar world. Indeed, Musil saw in prewar Austria "an especially clear case of the modern world" (*MoE* II, 1905), that is, a multiethnic state that, due to a series of historical contingencies, had most distinctly epitomized the plights of the modern condition. If anything wound up casting a semblance of anachronism on the narration, it is the circumstance that the establishment of dictatorships in Germany and Austria in the 1930s turned into tragic reality the threats Musil had meant to warn against.

Volume 1 of *MwQ* appeared in 1930 and contains two main sections ("A Sort of Introduction" and "More of the Same Happens").[16] It portrays the protagonist's growing awareness of a crisis that has haunted him for some time and narrates his involvement with an inept political initiative in the Vienna of 1913. The culmination of Ulrich's crisis coincides with the circumstance of his father's death, which also marks the end of this first main section. The thirty-eight chapters of volume 2 ("Into the Millennium [The Criminals]"), published in the edition of 1932 to 1933, introduce the narrative of Ulrich's reunion with his 'forgotten' sister Agathe and constitute the last authorized portion of the novel.[17] They were followed by an array of drafts and versions that at Musil's death were left at different stages of completion. These materials constitute twenty chapters submitted to the printer and subsequently withdrawn in 1937 or 1938, known as the "galley chapters." Musil's literary estate furthermore includes revisions of six of these chapters, on which Musil worked during the two years prior to his death in 1942, as well as attempts at a sequel to the "galley chapters" (dating from 1938 onward).

"With wonderful clarity he saw in himself all the abilities and qualities favored by his time . . . but he had lost the capacity to apply them" (*MwQ* I, 44). This admission by Ulrich in one of the novel's opening sections comes as a welcome revelation to the reader, who has been wondering how the novel's title might actually apply to the handsome thirty-two-year-old who promises to be the narrative's protagonist. By his own admission, the young man has been disproportionally blessed with all the gifts that warrant an individual's success in life—intelligence, wealth, social status. Yet he lacks a worthy purpose or a cause toward which to apply them, and this is tantamount to possessing no quality at all, as he himself acknowledges.[18] Ulrich is a wealthy bourgeois, the son of a well-connected scholar of jurisprudence in the still feudal world of 1913 Vienna. His varied talents have allowed him to undertake different careers, first as an army officer, then as an engineer, and, as the narration sets in, as a mathematician. His erotic life, which includes affairs with a chanteuse and the wife of a judge, seems to fit the cliché of the benignly dissolute Viennese male of the educated middle classes. Yet the first glimpse the reader receives of the young man evokes an unmistakable sense of purposelessness and paralysis. Ulrich is portrayed as he stands by the window of his elegant urban residence, idly trying to apply mathematical formulas to the hectic traffic of cars and pedestrians in front of his house (*MwQ* I, 6–7). As the narration unfolds, the characterization of the man without qualities as a Nietzschean free spirit committed to living out bold new models of humanity further complicates the picture of a man wrestling with a deep crisis. Following the Nietzschean dictum with uncommon lucidity and resolve, Ulrich has sought to discard outlived moral assumptions and to live his life according to provisional principles, hoping to usher in a generation of spiritual conquerors who will distill new coordinates for orientation. He has found in science's antimetaphysical bias and allegiance to experience the appropriate framework for this ascetic ideal. For Ulrich has glimpsed in science's unyielding empiricism and healthy relativism the source for a liberating "sense of possibility" toward the real. This "sense of possible reality" (*MwQ* I, 12) encompasses a vigilant sensibility for reality's nonactualized potentialities. It undercuts the claim of normative accounts of experience and the semblance of ineluctability of any given state of affairs. As such it engenders a deliberate utopianism that treats the real as an imaginative task, a fluid, open-ended becoming, which bold individuals are called to shape in a heroic assertion of volition and autonomy.

Yet the very scientific worldview Ulrich has striven to embrace foils any quest for purpose right from the onset, for science proves unable to provide a goal for life.[19] Worse yet, the scientific mind-set also invalidates all visions of a telos or a coherent unfolding of experience. Existence turns into a gaping space of unconstrained options and interchangeable possibilities open to multiple interpretations. This is the exact opposite of the bold new horizon of meaning Ulrich had heralded. By the same token, the scientific refutation of traditional notions of the self in favor of a concept of the individual as the intersection of impersonal forces and qualities seems to undermine human agency rather than prepare the advent of Nietzsche's spiritual conquerors. Ulrich's realization that his personal qualities "had more to do with one another than with him" (*MwQ* I, 157) makes it impossible for him to establish a meaningful relation to experience, plunging him into apathy and alienation. This explains why, at the beginning of the narration, the thirty-two-year-old mathematician is hardly the Promethean individual envisioned by Nietzsche and rather appears as a deeply divided man grappling with a profound crisis. But there is more to Ulrich's Nietzscheanism than the scientific ethos outlined above. The novel's first volume recounts Ulrich's endeavor to take stock of what one might define as his imaginative aesthetic adaptation of the Nietzschean mandate. Ulrich's scientific program has produced an aesthetic utopia based on the attempt to erase ordinary experience, faulted for its disjointedness and lack of intrinsic meaning, and to replace it with the rule of 'literary reality.'[20] His spiritual itinerary in the first book unfolds as a gradual recognition of the delusions inherent in this utopia. To find the roots for his crisis Ulrich decides to, in his words, take a year of sabbatical from life, that is, to step back from the life he has led so far in order to better scrutinize it. In Musil's playfully paradoxical design, this time off from life was to serve the purpose of engaging the man without qualities in a fresh confrontation with experience and to come to terms with his frustrated quest for purpose.[21]

At the beginning of his year off from life, Ulrich's confrontation with reality leads him to become involved with a hapless political initiative aimed at planning, five years in advance, the celebrations for the seventieth jubilee of Austrian emperor Franz Joseph in 1918. The "Parallel Campaign," as the initiative is immediately dubbed to reflect its aim to emulate the planned celebrations for the thirtieth anniversary of German emperor Wilhelm II, anchors the narration in the historical context of the waning years of the Habsburg monarchy. The irony inherent in the circumstance of Franz Joseph's death in 1916 is hard to miss, for the circumstance that the historical Franz Joseph would never live to see his seventieth jubilee bestows the pompous preparations and self-important deliberations linked to the initiative with a sense of futility that only reinforces the general impression of historical shortsightedness and political incompetence summoned by its participants. Ulrich is nonetheless fascinated with the initiative because he glimpses in it a chance for coming to terms with his own quest for purpose. As the reader learns from humorous interior monologs of the Campaign's mastermind Count Leinsdorf, the Campaign purports to find the idea that can best illustrate to other nations the pivotal role played by the Austro-Hungarian monarchy in world history.[22] At stake is the objective of identifying the purpose or reason of being of a whole multiethnic state, the declining and troubled monarchy, in the cosmic order of things.

Diotima, the ambitious wife of a high diplomat and proud supervisor of the initiative, brings to the point the anxieties and regressive nostalgias that drive the enterprise. In the project of finding "a crowning idea" (*MwQ* I, 109) suited to represent the depth of Austrian culture, she correctly identifies the objective of recovering a transcendent dimension that could heal the wounds inflicted by that degenerative development of the social body "known as civilization" (*MwQ* I, 105). Unwittingly rehashing tired commonplaces on the presumed struggle that opposes the corrupting forces of civilization to authentic culture, Diotima declares herself confident that the "Old Austrian culture" (*MwQ* I, 104) can offer a last fertile ground to reenact that original "unity of mankind," which is being subverted, perhaps irreversibly, by the modern reality of a plurality of incompatible perspectives and domains of experience (*MwQ* I, 189). Such dreams are however frustrated by the fruitlessness of the very first sessions of the Campaign. With every meeting a distraught Diotima must witness the extent to which the experts summoned to her salon prove incapable of perceiving the limitations of their specialized perspectives and instead reproduce the reality of irreconcilable vantage points and disparate endeavors that marks the modern world (*MwQ* I, 321). Just as the disillusioned young woman begins to toy with the idea of resigning her office in the Campaign and withdrawing into a distinguished existentialism, she is introduced to the man whose gaze onto the world promises to perform, at last, the miracle of restoring reality's lost unity. "What all others are separately, Arnheim is rolled into one"—this is how the title of chapter 47 sums up the ability of Paul Arnheim, a powerful Prussian industrialist and celebrated essayist, to embody the well-rounded, harmonious, universal spirit supposedly needed to heal the conflicts and divisions of the present.

Arnheim is the character that in the novel epitomizes the delusions and false consciousness of the quests for meaning enacted within the Campaign. He is modeled after Walther Rathenau, the prominent industrialist and minister of foreign affairs of the Weimar Republic, who fell victim to a right-wing attack in 1922.[23] Much like the historical Rathenau, Arnheim becomes the center of cultural debates thanks to his self-stylization as the harbinger of portentous solutions that promise to heal the wounds produced by the differentiated structure of modern societies. At stake is his purported "fusion of interests between business and the soul" (*MwQ* I, 422), a fantasy predicated on the implausible combination of the ruthless logic of capitalism with a hazy humanism. Arnheim's uncommon appeal lies however not so much in the power of his redemptive narrative as in his uncanny ability to play the talented dilettante who purports to mediate among the claims of disparate discourses:

> The basic pattern of his success was everywhere the same: Surrounded by the magic aura of his wealth and the legend of his importance, he always had to deal with people who towered over him in their own fields but who liked him as an outsider with a surprising knowledge of their subject and were daunted by his personally representing a link between their world and other worlds of which they had no idea. So it had come to seem quite natural for him to appear in a world of specialists as a whole man, and to have the effect of a harmonious entity. (*MwQ* I, 207)

Arnheim's gift lies in his capacity to serve as a mediator among the disparate language games that make up the modern world. In the eyes of the helpless specialists that crowd Diotima's salon he appears as a portentous mirror that reassembles the erratic splinters of the real into a coherent and intelligible whole, returning an image of unity and totality. But Arnheim's display of a harmonious self able to master divisions and mediate among conflicting demands belies a profound inner split that he cannot name, let alone manage. It erupts with force in his love for the beautiful Diotima, which he seems unable to steer or contain and which effectively debunks his fiction of wholeness and self-mastery. This experience promises the emergence of an 'other' emotional realm, which entices with an ineffable promise of innocence and happiness but is also disquieting in that it defies all attempts at conceptualization and thus cannot be manipulated or controlled.

Arnheim's experience exemplarily dramatizes the twofold splinteredness that plagues the individual in modernity. In the first place, there is the alienation produced by a disjointed modern reality, in which the individual is confronted with disparate life-spheres that raise often incompatible demands—humorously illustrated by the Babylon of languages and discourses that coexist in Diotima's salon. Ordinary experience so defined, in turn, stands in opposition to a deeper, apparently more authentic realm that does not submit to conventional linguistic and conceptual structures, but emerges fleetingly within ordinary life in ineffable moments of love and mystical rapture—it is not hard to recognize in this realm Musil's idea of the Other Condition.[24] Arnheim exemplifies the problems that ensue from conflating the splinteredness of modern life with the more fundamental split that opposes ordinary experience and the Other Condition. The industrialist's cultural pessimism, much like that of the historical Rathenau, appears predicated on the clever exploitation of this confusion through a strategy that hastily points the finger at rationality as the disruptive force that presumably produced modernity's divisions. At the same time, the nonconceptualizable domain becomes identified with the locus of a pristine irrationality. These arguments have allowed Arnheim to fashion himself into the prophet of a trendy anti-intellectualism bolstered by patriotic appeals to save the "German spirit" from rationalism (*MwQ* II, 621). But the conflation of the two planes in Arnheim's *Weltanschauung* is not simply the product of a well-meaning, though conceptually murky, investigation. As the narrating voice renders Ulrich's interior monolog, "There was a con game in this union between the soul and the price of coal, a union that at the same time purposefully served to keep apart what Arnheim did with his eyes wide open and what he said and wrote in his cloud of intuition" (*MwQ* I, 304). In his cultural critique of a present corrupted by rationalism and mechanization Arnheim conveniently forgets that he owes his very fortune to the exploitation of the rationalizing drive at the heart of Western civilization. The strident discrepancy between the pancultural effusions of Arnheim the intellectual and the ruthless practices of Arnheim the industrialist is all too obvious. Arnheim preaches one thing and does the opposite, for in the modern world he can retain his position as the powerful tycoon of a flourishing electric concern only if he stays clear of the preposterous fusion of capitalism and socialism he recommends to others.[25]

Yet Arnheim is not a cardboard figure, a mechanical personification of the harmful tendencies of his time. The empathy and grace with which he is portrayed in the novel—as a man of great vanity and conceit, but also of uncommon intelligence and sensibility—reflect Musil's intricate attraction to the historical Rathenau, whose work he had reviewed. Arnheim in many ways represents a foil and counterpart for Ulrich, a formidable man with qualities who helps define Ulrich's lack of qualities without necessarily making it desirable. As such, he helps to bring to the point the roots of the malaise that haunts the modern individual. At issue is Arnheim's uncommon talent "for being, at times, convinced against [his] own convictions, splitting off a part of [his] mind and stretching it to form a brand-new wholehearted conviction" (*MwQ* I, 424). Such a compartmentalization of one's inner life, the narrator observes, is not so much a sin of civilization as a necessary requirement for functioning in the modern world, indeed, by shutting off the cacophony of disparate perspectives on any given issue and forming convictions that will lead to concrete actions. If Arnheim's dividedness poses a problem, this does not lie in the dividedness itself, that is, in the circumstance that modern life produces incoherent individuals who succeed in coping with the demands of disparate life-spheres only at the price of compartmentalizing their inner life. Instead, it lies in the denial of compartmentalization that is entailed in Arnheim's insincere display of a harmonic self. This denial—the product of a misplaced longing for unity and order—draws on a hazy mysticism and a virulent critique of rationality, which purport to address the longing for transcendence of modern individuals, while in effect foiling any constructive confrontation with the modern reality of differentiated life-spheres and the ethical dilemmas it produces.

Within the economy of the narration, Arnheim's character helps put in perspective the now self-deluded, now plainly disingenuous endeavors whose proponents rival each other for recognition during the Campaign's meetings. What they all have in common is the fixation on a presumably redemptive idea, which the narrator humorously describes as an illusory fixed point in which the state of equilibrium of the world and that of the self seem to miraculously coincide:

> Such fixed points, where the center of a person's equilibrium coincides with the world's center of equilibrium, may be, for instance, a spittoon that can be shut with a simple latch; . . . or the adoption of Oehl's system of shorthand, so effective a time-saver it can solve the problems of society once and for all; or conversion to a natural mode of living that would halt the present random destruction of the environment; not to mention a metaphysical theory of the motions of celestial bodies, simplification of the administrative apparatus, and a reform of sex life. (*MwQ* I, 147)

The discrepancy between these projects' ostensive objectives and the narrowly defined ideologies that inhere in the means deployed to achieve them—how is Oehl's shorthand system really going to solve the social question?—show how the Campaign's endeavors are predicated on an intransigent "reduction of the universe into the solid and pragmatic constituents of a stable world view," as Thomas Harrison has termed it.[26] This reduction potentially breeds violence, for it tends to acknowledge only those segments of the real that fit into its schemes, while seeking to discount or even eradicate those elements that exceed it. In other words, the problem is not so much that the strategies devised by the Campaign participants are patently inadequate to achieve the goals they propose to set for the initiative. Rather, it is the very dream of unity and reconciliation at the heart of their projects that proves to be hopelessly at odds with the complex reality of modernity. One could recall here the more ambitious projects of key Campaign players, for instance Count Leinsdorf's plan to restore the monarchy's lost cohesion by revamping the image of a fatherly emperor and undoing the dynamics of modern politics, or General Stumm's search for the secret principle that holds together a civil society besieged by countless centrifugal forces.[27] It is hardly surprising that the optimism of the first few sessions soon gives way to an oppressive sense of futility. Belligerent appeals to put an end to the interminable debates that impair the initiative gradually displace the original objective to find an idea that would embody the world-historical meaning of the monarchy. The goal instead becomes to break the spell of inanity and futility that overshadows the Campaign by means of boisterous calls to action and manly deeds (*MwQ* II, 845). The vacuity of these appeals mirrors the senselessness of the war that will fulfill them. At the end of the novel's first volume, the outbreak of the Great War is the foreshadowed outcome of such appeals.[28] The novel's warning for the postwar present could not have been clearer. The catastrophe that uprooted Europe's pre–World War I order was endemic to it. It was triggered by a regressive yearning for comprehensive principles and by the inability to cope with the decentered reality of the modern world.

The platonic love story between the ambitious Diotima and the egotistic Arnheim helps keep Ulrich's and the reader's interest in the Campaign alive after the initiative's futility becomes humorously apparent in the novel's early chapters. Ulrich's fascination is not simply motivated by the enjoyment that the sight of Arnheim's inner confusion and vacillating self-confidence procures him. The industrialist's tribulations come to epitomize an elusive type of love that is the site of a transfigured relation to the world and that brings back memories of Ulrich's first erotic involvement with the wife of a garrison major. The premonition and frustrated longing for this unfathomable condition seem to be at the heart of the troubling dividedness of consciousness in modernity, for it is the juxtaposition of ordinary experience with this heightened state of being, as it surfaces in accidental moments of illumination, which makes everyday life seem worthless and inessential. As Ulrich describes his experience of the 'other' state,

> He had penetrated the heart of the world. . . . In-feeling linked living beings without space . . . his state of mind had nothing in common with dreaming. It was clear, and brimful of clear thoughts; however, nothing in him was moved by cause, purpose, or physical desire, but everything went rippling out in circle after ever-renewed circle, as when an infinite jet falls on a basin's surface. . . . Life's very shape was completely altered. Not placed in the focus of ordinary attention but freed from sharpness. Seen this way, everything seemed a little scattered and blurred, and being infused all the while with a delicate clarity and certainty from other centers. . . . And with the help of such tranquil experiences everything that usually makes up an ordinary life was endowed with a radical new meaning for Ulrich at every turn. (*MwQ* I, 131)

The moments of illumination consigned to the alternative condition promise the disclosure of a "radical new meaning" that would completely transfigure and fulfill ordinary life. However these illuminations remain utterly unintelligible and inconsequential when raised to the level of everyday experience, for they are untranslatable into conventional conceptual and linguistic structures. From this perspective, ordinary experience and the Other Condition appear incommensurable.

The split between the two conditions is inscribed in Ulrich's own divided consciousness. On the one hand, there is a practical Ulrich, who is persuaded of the necessity to accept the insight into the groundlessness and evanescence of human existence as it manifests itself in the realization that there is no converging point, no central, transcendent instance that holds together the impenetrable tangle of experience. On the other, there is a shadowy Ulrich who clings to the hope that the fundamental transience of life may not represent its ultimate truth (*MwQ* I, 164). The paradoxical situation Ulrich faces brings to the point the quandary of modern consciousness. Meaning exists and can be irrefutably experienced, yet it is not translatable into the categories of ordinary life and therefore remains inapplicable to it. Two options present themselves at this point. The first is to accept the divide between the ordinary and the other condition as irreversible and to develop strategies for making sense of experience while acknowledging the reality of a nonconceptualizable meaning. The alternative is to seek to overcome this split by making the two realms commensurable. This is the path Ulrich has taken in implementing his Nietzschean life program. The "sense of possibility" he has appropriated from the natural sciences has led to a utopian vision that translates the movement of literary imagination into an all-encompassing mode of experience ostensibly filled with unbroken meaning. This literary utopia is designed to bestow on ordinary life the quality of fulfilled meaning that pertains to the Other Condition. As the reader comes to realize, Ulrich's crisis in the novel's first volume is linked to the inevitable collapse of this aesthetic utopia.

Ulrich's literary utopia remarkably assembles the key elements of Musil's aesthetic project into an ethos and a life program. Chapter 62 details this transmutation by granting a glimpse into young Ulrich's scientific optimism and his view of life as a grand "laboratory" for experimenting with alternative modes of experience. Over time Ulrich's experimental utopia becomes modeled after the literary notion of the "essay," which, more than a specific genre, denotes the medium suited for ethical reflection in the modern period:

> It was more or less in the way an essay, in the sequence of its paragraphs, explores a thing from many sides without wholly encompassing it—for a thing wholly encompassed suddenly loses its scope and melts down to a concept—that he believed he could most rightly survey and handle the world and his own life. The value of an action or a quality, and indeed its meaning and nature, seemed to him to depend on its surrounding circumstances, on the aims it served; in short, on the whole—constituted now one way, now another—to which it belonged. . . . But Ulrich generalized this: all moral events take place in a field of energy whose constellation charges them with meaning. They contain good and evil in the way an atom contains the possibilities of certain chemical combinations. . . . In this way an open-ended system of relationships arises, in which independent meanings, such as are ascribed to actions and qualities by way of a rough first approximation in ordinary life, no longer exist at all. (*MwQ* I, 270)

The essayistic mode enables the observer to examine a fact from different perspectives without purporting to offer an exhaustive, conclusive account.

The essay thus stands in pointed contrast to the systematic pretensions of philosophical thinking, which levels out experience by forcing it into the universal grid of the concept. It is intimately related to the idea of a morality that no longer relies on the fiction of independent, iterable, essential meanings but likens human actions and qualities to the atoms caught in the variable dynamics of a field of force, which are charged with meaning based on the unique constellation of factors within which they are inscribed. As meaning can never be extricated from the context in which it is embedded, so moral judgments can never be uncoupled from the situation in which they are uttered. This is the view of morality that results from extending the imaginative precision practiced by the natural sciences to the domain of ethics. Within this framework, ordinary morality appears as the ossified relic of an endlessly fluid movement (*MwQ* I, 271–72).[29]

Ulrich finds the incessant, nongeneralizing and nongeneralizable movement of ethical reflection exemplified in the works of great essayists. Essayists write out of and typify a condition of perfect inner accord in a nonrepeatable moment. The essayistic mode is inextricably entwined with the situated perspective of the observer, "for an essay is not a provisional or incidental expression of a conviction capable of being elevated to a truth under more favorable circumstances or of being exposed as an error . . . an essay is rather the unique and unalterable form assumed by a man's inner life in a decisive thought" (*MwQ* I, 273). Acting so that one's action derives from a state of innermost agreement with oneself, a state exemplified by the essayistic mind set—this cannot be the object of an injunction, Ulrich concludes in his soliloquy, but is rather a condition, or, in his spacial imagery, a "region" to which the man without qualities is transported as a result of his attempt to reflect on it:

> But what gave him this insight was no longer thinking, nor was it feeling in the usual incoherent way: it was a "total insight" and yet again only a message carried to him from far away by the wind, and it seemed to him neither true nor false, neither rational nor irrational; it seized him like a faint, blissful hyperbole dropped into his heart. (*MwQ* I, 275)

The "total insight" Ulrich experiences remains impervious to distinctions such as right/wrong, reasonable/unreasonable—indeed, the conceptual coordinates commonly employed to grasp ethical reality. What carries over from this state is only the intimation of an unintelligible message and the bliss of a heightened condition of being.[30]

Sensing essayism's affinity with ethical experience, Ulrich has made it into the bearer of a will to live according to endless exploration and experimentation (*MwQ* I, 271). Precisely this last step marks a crucial difference between the notion of essayism and literary imagination put forth in Musil's essays and Ulrich's essayistic ideal. If in Musil's essays literary imagination emerges as the medium suited for grasping elusive ethical experience, then for Ulrich the movement of aesthetic imagination becomes itself the ethical imperative according to which one is called to shape one's life in modernity. Ulrich's objective entails turning the movement of literary imagination into a life program centered on the constant experimentation with alternative modes of experience. It is however significant that the very chapter that sings the praises of Ulrich's essayistic utopia also recounts its failure. As the man without qualities comes to realize, the project of turning the essayistic attitude into a will and a principle for appraising life blatantly disregards the nature of the essayistic perspective, for essayism does not lend itself to articulating absolute truths or convictions: "And as little as one can make a truth out of the genuine elements of an essay can one gain a conviction from such a condition—at least not without abandoning the condition, as a lover has to abandon love in order to describe it" (*MwQ* I, 275). Precisely what Ulrich values in essayistic reflection, namely, its elusive quality and respect for the particularity of experience, is also what in the final analysis defies his ambition to turn essayism into a principle or program for life. The condition that essayism discloses produces a state that has no development and no direction, as witnessed by essayism's inconclusive movement. Because essayism does not make any of the reflections or situations it engages with universally true or compelling, it also does not lend itself to distilling noncontingent truths or certainties. As stated in the passage above, if one demands convictions or certainties, one is compelled to step back from this condition into some other domain of experience. It follows that the program of an essayistic life finds neither grounding nor support in the movement of essayistic reflection.

Ulrich's life program is grafted onto Musil's model of literature as the modern domain that integrates essayistic imagination to provide singular, meaningful accounts for situated experience. Essayism epitomizes the movement of an aesthetic imagination that infuses reality with meaning by means of rigorously singular accounts. It embodies the potentialities of literature as the domain that in modernity allows one to make sense of life while relinquishing the dream of a transcendent, absolute meaning. This entails that meaning is not extracted out of experience as its essential quality but is rather construed and attributed to it. As Nietzsche put it in what is perhaps the most famous line from *The Birth of Tragedy*, life can only be justified as an aesthetic phenomenon (*Basic Writings* 52). Within this frame, literature offers itself as a vital domain for confronting the modern insight that any meaning—whether generated within literature or within other domains—stands in an extrinsic relation to the experience it seeks to illuminate. Because meaning is always fundamentally artificial, constructed, selective with respect to the endless experience on which it is grafted, there always remains a gap between the accounts the aesthetic construes and experience itself. But one is compelled to ask, how does this gap affect the quest for engendering and sustaining a fulfilled life? The example of early German Romanticism is telling in this regard. Faced with the discrepancy between an existence hopelessly enclosed within an immanent horizon and a system of meaning production constantly reminded of the extrinsic, transient quality of this meaning, the early Romantics vowed to reclaim precisely what up to Kant had counted as the blemish of aesthetic imagination, namely, its artificial, man-made quality. In virtue of its artificiality, art configures itself as the medium in which humans can autonomously refurbish that unity and totality of experience the modern world lacks.[31] But this program is inextricably bound to the logic of aesthetic imagination; it remains confined to the medium of art. Because it ignores the different dynamics at work in other domains of experience, it is not transferable to them. It can perhaps be realized in a domain detached from ordinary life, as was the Jena house that for a brief period of time harbored the radical life experiment of a handful of thinkers imbued with the spirit of Romanticism and idealism. But as the breakup of the Jena group showed, the reality of the aesthetic does not represent a starting point for grounding or reforming ordinary reality. If at all possible, it can only displace it. The problem with this endeavor is that it potentially hypostatizes literature into the domain from which ordinary life can be overturned to make room for the more desirable experience presented within art, in a move that denies ordinary existence its right to existence, as it were. This is the path Ulrich has taken in turning the movement of essayism into a life program carried by the demands to abolish reality and realize a 'literary' life. In recognizing the futility of this dream, Ulrich gains insight into the roots of the crisis that has haunted him for a long time. At stake is the recognition of the necessary divide that separates art, and literature in particular, from life.

It is not until after the novel's main narrative turn—Ulrich's encounter with his estranged sister Agathe—that the man without qualities comprehensively outlines the advantages of literature over other domains of life. In looking back on his failed literary utopia, Ulrich tells his sister that his life lacks a specific idea, an all-encompassing horizon of meaning:

> by connecting no idea or every idea with myself, I got out of the habit of taking life seriously. I get much more out of it when I read about it in a novel, where it's wrapped up in some point of view, but when I'm supposed to experience it in all its fullness it always seems already obsolete, overdone in an old-fashioned way, and intellectually outdated. (*MwQ* II, 977)

Life appears interesting and relevant when observed from the consistent perspective of a book, but becomes intolerably passé when experienced immediately in its multifariousness, redundancy, and incoherence. As Ulrich pointedly puts it, "these happenings in our lives have less life than a book, because they have no coherent meaning" (*MwQ* II, 977). It is the finite horizon of a coherent meaning that bestows life on the events narrated in a book, that is, that imparts them with that meaning, which events in ordinary life consistently fail to display. One can conclude that the quality that makes literature superior to life resides precisely in the consistency and meaningfulness of its accounts, in the fact that, unlike life itself, they stand under a recognizable 'lasting idea' (*MwQ* II, 977). If lived experience is marked by the lack of such a comprehensive horizon, then the coherence of literary accounts is what makes literature 'unreal,' because it makes it stand in opposition to reality's basic physiognomy.

Ulrich's literary vision is extensively articulated in a conversation in which the man without qualities endeavors to help a distraught Diotima sort out the moral dilemmas arising from her relation to Arnheim. Ulrich's suggestions do little to dispel Diotima's confusion, but are quite revealing of his life program: "So I propose . . . that we try to love each other as if we were characters in a novel who have met in the pages of a book. Let's in any case leave off all the fatty tissue that plumps up reality" (*MwQ* I, 625). Living—in this case, loving—like a writer's character entails purging reality from the paraphernalia of everyday existence, from all that is accessory, inessential, distracting. Living in this essential mode entails living according to a constantly shifting truthfulness that assumes diverse, unpredictable guises based on the unique configurations of experience. As Ulrich maintains, "There is no detaching an idea in a book from its context on the page" (*MwQ* I, 626). As one cannot distill general truths from the unique experience presented in an artwork, one cannot condense this truthfulness in precepts for conduct. This life program amounts to restoring "the original condition of life itself" (*MwQ* I, 627), for in this transfigured state any deed is made thoroughly moral by its utterly self-consistent quality. However, this program first requires abolishing ordinary reality. For, as Ulrich explains, where an obstinate everyday life fails to display a coherent meaning, the only remaining option is to overturn it altogether and to take possession of the unreal ("we must try to recover unreality. Reality no longer makes sense," *MwQ* I, 627).

Concrete directives for the goal of abolishing reality are inscribed in the subversive quality of literary imagination. In an antagonistic exchange with Walter, Ulrich's childhood friend and the frustrated apostle of a shopworn humanism, the man without qualities portrays aesthetic imagination as the force that can revolutionize the established understanding of human experience by replacing the conventional notion of history ("the history of the world") with an emancipatory "history of ideas" (*MwQ* I, 395). If conventional history remains locked within the anachronistic assumption of a purpose arising from the irresistible necessity of events, the "history of ideas" capitalizes on the modern awareness about the contingency and constructed nature of meaning. What sustains it in its ambition to debunk the semblance of necessity of the real is that spirit of a "negation of life," which forms the hallmark of the literary: "Extract the meaning out of all literature," Ulrich challenges an outraged Walter, "and what you will get is a denial, however incomplete, but nonetheless an endless series of individual examples all based on experience, which refute all the accepted rules, principles, and prescriptions underpinning the very society that loves these works of art!" (*MwQ* I, 399). By presenting accounts of experience that effectively undermine the institutions and value system of the society in which they are embedded, literary artifacts incessantly stage a 'denial of life,' laying bare the reification and inadequacy of the outlived models that constrain existence. From this perspective, Ulrich's "history of ideas" is just another formulation for the appeal to shape ordinary experience according to the spirit of literature—the demand, in Ulrich's own words, "that our existence should consist wholly of literature" (*MwQ* I, 397).

For once, Walter's objections put his friend's vision to a difficult test. Ulrich's grandiose plans, Walter charges, fail to acknowledge the different dynamics at work in the aesthetic world of ideas and in the real world—or, which is even worse, they purport to undo this difference altogether. This objective appears not only unrealizable but also dubious. As Walter rebukes his friend, "aren't you overlooking the fact that such a life-as-art, or whatever you'd call it, unimaginable as it is to begin with, would make philosophy and art quite superfluous; it means one thing only, the end of art!" (*MwQ* I, 398). Fashioning art into the all-encompassing horizon of human existence means undercutting the reality of differentiated domains of experience and annihilating the aesthetic as a specific domain of meaning. Indeed, it means the end of art. Where Ulrich glimpses the fulfillment of human life, however, Walter sees a gaping void. It is telling that, in disarticulating the ramifications of his friend's vision, Walter is able to put his finger on a conspicuous omission in Ulrich's plan, which relies heavily on the surfacing of illuminations, inspirations, and ecstatic visions that dispense with conventional moral valuations. The issue is how to induce this condition, how to seize it and make it permanent. Because if this is not possible, then one must ask with Walter, what happens when the illuminations fail to occur? As Ulrich's friend maintains, in the absence of such blissful states all that is left is an individual at the mercy of his drives and appetites (*MwQ* I, 400). Precisely the impossibility of deriving some model of conduct from this condition is at the heart of Ulrich's paralysis and existential plights.

Ulrich's literary utopia appears sustained by an ambiguous aspiration to merge art and life —an aspiration that undergirds key moments of aesthetic reflection within German culture, from Schiller's adaptation of Kantian aesthetics at the end of the eighteenth century to the revolutionary agenda of avant-garde movements in the early twentieth century.[32] His vision appropriates art's ability to unsettle experience and turns it into a program, fashioning art into the site on the outside of ordinary existence from which a whole, pristine life can be summoned up. The aesthetic thus ceases to be a specialized domain to become the horizon that encompasses the totality of existence. This, in turn, means the end of art as a distinct sphere whose meaning is at a par with the meaning produced within other domains of experience. Ulrich's chiliastic fantasies appear to be clearly inimical to the differentiated structure of modernity. The Nietzschean program of embracing with scientific ruthlessness a disjointed and contingent experience paradoxically gives birth, via the model of essayism, to an ethos aimed at wiping out reality as we know it. It presupposes the complete denial of ordinary existence, for it is not to be developed out of everyday experience but can be attained only by stepping out of it.[33] Ulrich's dream effectively reproposes the fantasies of a *tabula rasa,* of a thoroughly new beginning that engrossed collective imagination at the beginning of the twentieth century. It is a vision that is sustained by a yearning for unity and totality, which is not dissimilar to the fundamental impulse at the heart of the Campaign's projects.

It is during one of the Campaign meetings—already pervaded by a persistent sense of failure—that the man without qualities engages in a comprehensive reassessment of his aesthetic utopia and of the reasons for its failure:

> And everything that, as time went on, he had called essayism, the sense of possibility, and imaginative in contrast with pedantic precision; his suggestions that history was something one had to invent, that one should live the history of ideas instead of the history of the world, that one should get a grip on whatever cannot quite be realized in practice and should perhaps end up trying to live as if one were a character in a book, a figure with all the inessential elements left out, so that what was left would consolidate itself as some magical entity—all these different versions of his thinking, all in their extreme formulations against reality, had just one thing in common: an unmistakable, ruthless passion to influence reality. (MwQ I, 646)

The visions listed in this passage all stem from the assumption that one can live ethically by translating features of literary imagination into a way of life—an assumption that links literary imagination to an ineffable condition of being associated with ethics. Though animated by a spirit that is fundamentally inimical to the reality of ordinary experience, these visions seek to act upon it—namely, by recasting it entirely. They originate from only one side of his self, that active side driven by an irresistible "urge to attack life and master it" (*MwQ* I, 646). As Ulrich comes to realize, the root of his plights lies in the fact that his demand to reconcile the two sides amounts to an impossibility (*MwQ* I, 647).[34] The second to last chapter of the novel's first volume recounts Ulrich's symbolic walk home after a showdown with Arnheim, which compels the man without qualities to take stock of his time off from life and of the impossible visions it has produced (*MwQ* I, 712). The available options include, significantly, writing a book about his failed endeavor:

> It flashed through his mind that Gerda had urged him to write a book about it. But he wanted to live without splitting himself into a real and a shadow self. He remembered speaking to Section Chief Tuzzi about

writing. . . . He remembered saying casually that he would probably have to either write a book or kill himself. (*MwQ* I, 722)

Writing a book about his failed literary utopia is one of only two options available to the man without qualities at this point. It would allow him to at least inscribe his experience into a fictional horizon of meaning. At the same time, it would be tantamount to reaffirming the split between literature and life, meaning and ordinary experience, a real and a shadowy self. Ulrich's utopia has been about overcoming this dividedness, and the man without qualities appears reluctant to accept it. Yet the only alternative to embracing the fundamental split of existence is suicide. In other words, because the split that marks existence cannot be bridged, the only possible way to rebel against it is to cancel oneself out of existence, in the most radical act of denial an individual can perform. A major narrative turn allows the man without qualities to defer his decision. At home he learns of the sudden death of his father. The ensuing journey to his home town marks the beginning of the novel's second volume. On this circumstance he is reunited with his forgotten sister Agathe and surrenders to the temptation of reenacting with her that unfathomable experience of love that lies at the heart of the Other Condition.

The novel's first volume ends with Ulrich's realization that his attempts at seizing the intuited ethical horizon failed because they were rooted in only one side of experience, the aggressive, dynamic realm of "violence" that makes up ordinary life. The novel's second book unfolds as an inquiry into the juxtaposed, elusive realm of "love," the domain to which meaning seems to have fled in modernity. In the loving relation to his sister Agathe, Ulrich glimpses the possibility of reconciling the two trees of life by plunging ordinary experience into the Other Condition. Yet the siblings' attempt at permanently anchoring their lives in the Other Condition gives rise to an impossibility, which is analogous to that produced by Ulrich's failed literary utopia—namely, the demand that ordinary experience be altogether erased. The collapse of the siblings' adventure appears inevitable and exemplifies the unsustainability of any call to live a thoroughly moral life in the modern period.[35] Yet this failure does not represent Musil's last word on the thought-experiment enacted by the siblings, for the import of their enterprise lies primarily in the self-referential investigation of art's relation to ethics, which their experiment makes possible. The novel tentatively portrays the 'other' realm of ethical experience as an exalted emotional condition grounded in the perception of an original, undifferentiated substrate of feeling before feeling enters the self-divisions that form the foundation for ordinary life. Aesthetic experience offers itself as the medium that enables humans to fleetingly perceive this otherwise unfathomable foundation of feeling within ordinary existence. The siblings' exploration of the Other Condition thereby configures itself as an inquiry into aesthetic experience itself.

The analysis of feeling pursued in crucial chapters Musil withdrew from publication in 1938 highlights the epistemological paradoxes in which the novel's inquiry became caught. Musil's unpublished papers leave the impression that the difficulties that hampered his writing in the last years did not originate from his losing faith in the overall project but rather from a specific epistemological dilemma he faced. The problem is that the empirical analysis of feeling undertaken in these drafts seems to merely produce insight into the cognitive impenetrability of the Other Condition. The myriad of drafts and competing versions that endeavor to circumvent this epistemological deadlock document that Musil was confronting the fundamental dilemma of literary practice, a dilemma he had been grappling with since *Törless.* This is the challenge of presenting within the medium of language an experience that eludes ordinary conceptual and discursive categories. Musil attempted to overcome this difficulty by recasting his exploration of ethical and aesthetic experience within the frame of a symbolically dense scene, which will be analyzed in the last section of this chapter.

In the first chapters of the second volume the siblings' unfolding relation makes the plot revolving around the Parallel Campaign recede into the background. Ulrich and Agathe are brought together after years of separation by the circumstance of their father's death. The forgotten sister immediately appears as a variation of Ulrich's own self.[36] Like her brother, she oscillates between states of spiritual numbness and a painful sense of self-division; like him she is incapable of coping with the banality of ordinary life and often retreats into apathy.[37] At the heart of Agathe's alienation lies the frustrated demand to live "'in complete harmony' with herself" (*MwQ* II, 811). Ulrich recognizes in this demand his own desire to heal the wounds of his split consciousness. He finds in Agathe an interlocutor who does not content herself with suggestive theories on morality but rather compels her brother to scrutinize the conduct engendered by his moral vision. Hence she calls attention to the dilemmas entailed in his suggestive morality "of the next step," based on which each action is judged not according to an immutable system of values but rather in relation to the step one takes afterward. Ulrich is compelled to recognize that this thinking not only permanently defers judgment in an endless series of steps but also engenders behavior that appears random and indefensible (*MwQ* II, 799).[38] In an ironic turn, the forgotten sister forces Ulrich into the position of a defender of conventional upright conduct, thus questioning the novelty of his presumably outlandish moral visions. When an irritated man without qualities self-righteously admonishes Agathe that one cannot 'just do' things, for random acts only bear witness to a deranged personality, his sister can easily point to the inconsistency in her brother's position; he wants to brand her actions as wrong but simultaneously lacks a criterion for distinguishing between right and wrong (*MwQ* II, 1037–41).While purporting to overcome the fixation with right and wrong of Western morality, Ulrich's vision requires an intuitive distinction between admissible and inadmissable behavior that does not appear less arbitrary than the moral categories it seeks to replace.

Struggling to find a principle that could dispel the threat of randomness, Ulrich attempts to clarify to his sister and to himself the distinction between arbitrary behavior and a conduct sustained by the movement of a quintessentially moral imagination. Moral imagination is rooted in an ineffable, unchanging condition in which every deed and every feeling are made thoroughly moral: "morality is the subordination of every momentary state in our life to one enduring one" (*MwQ* II, 944). This permanent condition is nothing other than that elusive state of bliss and accord with one's self disclosed within rare occurrences of mystical love.[39] Humans are given to glimpse the condition that grounds this love in the elusive experiences mediated through art, Ulrich believes. A humorous conversation with a fellow scientist met at a trolley stop prompts the man without qualities to ponder the constitutive character of aesthetic experience, in a reflection that echoes central tenets of Musil's film essay.[40] Boasting about the vacation she will soon spend in the Alps, Ulrich's acquaintance Dr. Strasil prides herself on rehashing trite views on the role played by nature and art as depositories of authentic experience in a world plagued by shallowness and the absence of lasting reference points. Her medley of prejudices and commonplace assumptions provides a humorous foil for Ulrich's own reflection on art. As he silently rebukes his fellow scientist, aesthetic experience is not an emotional cocoon filled with edifying messages but is instead grounded in a heightened level of feeling. This peculiar condition of feeling, Ulrich believes, induces a healthy 'stirring,' a quickening and regeneration of the emotions that help to preserve the malleability of feeling in ordinary life. Aesthetic experience induces this stirring by lifting the individual out of "his tangle of rational intentions, which involve him with countless alien objects" and into "a state wholly without purpose" defined by absence of any mental or physical activity ("a quiescence, a dying away of all activity," *MwQ* II, 942). In this condition feeling reaches its peak of purity and intensity.

Ulrich's psychological account of aesthetic experience highlights a crucial quality of the Other Condition, namely, its utter inertia and absence of activity. Precisely the lifeless quality of this condition casts an ambiguous light on Ulrich's ambition to appropriate it for his daring moral visions. His claim that one needs to anchor every deed in this condition in order to make life thoroughly moral (*MwQ* II, 1113) assumes a paradoxical connotation, for it calls for grounding conduct in a state defined by inertia, that is, in a state that cannot produce any behavior. It seems appropriate in this regard that the siblings refer to this condition as the "Millennium," the permanently deferred mythical territory which will be entered at the end of time but can never be attained in ordinary life. The man without qualities is aware of the paradox entailed in this vision. If a thoroughly moral life can only be a life entirely grounded in this condition, the individual who would attempt to ground his life in this state would be compelled to give up "the unequivocal" of ordinary experience and plunge into "twilight. Into fog and nonsense. Into unarticulated boredom" (*MwQ* II, 836).[41] Humans long to permanently ground their lives in the blissful state which they take to be the foundation for meaningful life; yet the permanent realization of this condition appears unnatural. As Ulrich acknowledges, to insist that one act on the basis of this undivided reality, out of one's innermost accord with oneself, is at bottom an utterly 'unreal' demand, because it denies the modern reality of individuals caught in an infinite network of relations, beliefs, and desires:

> What he was thinking amounted to taking leave of most of his living relationships; he had no illusions about that. For today our lives are divided, and parts are entangled with other people; what we dream has to do with dreaming and also with what other people dream; what we do has sense, but more sense in relation with what others do; and what we believe is tied in with beliefs only a fraction of which are our own. It is therefore quite unrealistic to insist upon acting out of the fullness of one's own per-

sonal reality. Especially for a man like himself, who had been imbued all his life with the thought that one's beliefs had to be shared, that one must have the courage to live in the midst of moral contradictions, because that was the price of great achievement. (*MwQ* II, 950)

There must be something wrong with the demand to lead a fully moral life, Ulrich concludes, if it calls for effacing human existence as we know it. This is why the actual challenge faced by ethical reflection in the present lies in rejecting such a demand and in learning to cope with the moral contradictions of modern reality. And yet Ulrich is unable to shake the longing for the unnatural condition disclosed in the ecstatic experience of a mystical love. The incestuous love between the siblings seems to be an instance of such mystical experiences.[42]

The unnatural trait of the siblings' relation symbolizes the abnormality of an experiment that is bound to undermine the foundations of ordinary experience. As intimated in the title of the novel's third section ("The Criminals"), the siblings' attraction constitutes a crime from the perspective of ordinary experience, its criminal quality being inscribed in the taboo of incest. By subverting the relations between kins of blood, incest disrupts the structure of the family, thereby threatening the very fabric of Western societies. Yet it is precisely the extraordinary experience of an unnatural love that enables Ulrich to discern in the sexual polarity that opposes man and woman a cipher for the two different conditions in which humans participate. If the polarity of the genders enacts the fundamental split of human experience, love stages its reconciliation, promising to heal the individual's inner divisions, in fact, to restore the individual's wholeness by means of the union with an opposite that is actually one's double, or one's negative foil (*MwQ* II, 1021–22).[43] Through its dialectic of sameness and otherness, love stages within ordinary experience the quest for the ineffable double of ordinary experience, namely, the Other Condition, and for a reconciliation of the two realms.

This understanding of love carries paradoxical implications. As one of two realms of experience, love stages a reconciliation of the two juxtaposed trees of life. Yet this reconciliation fleetingly occurs within an ordinary experience that remains irreducibly split. In this regard it appears hardly surprising that 'pure' love, that is to say, a successful and lasting reconciliation of the two domains, can only be glimpsed as a hypothetical case but never be fully realized. Hence love must become mingled with extraneous elements to manifest itself in ordinary life, such as sexual desire. Whereas sexual attraction entails interested desire for an object that fulfills a biological need, pure love distinguishes itself for its fundamental disinterestedness.[44] Ulrich finds the disinterested moment of 'pure' love most clearly embodied in the "need for sibling love, an addition to ordinary love, moving in an imaginary direction toward a love unmixed with otherness and not-loving" (*MwQ* II, 985). The affection between siblings satisfies the condition of disinterestedness because it is not based on erotic attraction but on an original oneness inscribed in the siblings' identity of blood, which overrides the differences marking distinct individuals. As a bond between two different beings that are not originally different, love stages the reconciliation of the antinomies that haunt the modern individual—mind and body, intellect and feeling, ordinary and other condition. "Anyway . . . love, if that is love, is an exceptional case, and can't serve as a model for everyday action" (*MwQ* II, 1021). Though it can be glimpsed as a hypothetical case, the condition of accord with oneself enacted by love cannot be sustained and therefore cannot provide a model for ordinary experience.

Yet precisely the siblings' unfolding relation seems to challenge Ulrich's conviction about the unattainability of pure love. Captivated by the promise of an ecstatic existence inscribed in their mutual love, the siblings engage the fantasy of the "siamese twins," a game of make-believe that pushes the ideal of sibling love to its utmost extreme. More than simple siblings or even twins, the "siamese twins" epitomize the dream of unity in difference, of an affective relation in which the two poles are distinct yet physically united, two beings and one at the same time—"the unseparated but not united" (*MwQ* II, 1201). In such a paradoxical relation to Agathe, Ulrich is able to finally experience a sense of wholeness and to regain his self-love: "Now I know what you are: you are my self-love! . . . I've always lacked the right sort of love for myself that others seem to have in abundance. And now . . . by some mistake or by fate, it has been embodied in you instead of myself!" (*MwQ* II, 975). One can only love oneself, that is, be reconciled or at peace with oneself, if one sees oneself mirrored in an 'other' who is not really other.[45]

The ideal of love as an infinite dialectic of sameness and otherness forms a central theme that early German Romanticism articulated, drawing on the philosophy of idealism. Jochen Hörisch has illustrated the interplay of self-reflection and reflection in an Other that provides the frame for the siblings' dialogic relation by linking it to the modern emergence of reflection as the movement of a consciousness that for the first time grasps the absolute absence of external points of orientation in which it could ground its operations.[46] Confronted with insight into its contingency and lack of transcendent grounding, consciousness splits into a self and an other in order to gain knowledge of itself within the medium of reflection. This split allows the self to become aware of itself and thus forms a fundamental precondition for the individual's self-relation. In the folds of reflection, the two components establish their distinct identities, that is, their mutual alterity, while at the same time recognizing that they are not truly other. The perception of this unity is, however, contingent upon the process of reflection. Unity can be perceived only as long as the two poles reflect each other, which presupposes that the subject's yearning for a stable relation to itself must be permanently frustrated, given the structural endlessness of the reflexive process that makes self-relation possible.[47]

Within this frame, it appears only fitting that the dialog, the medium of infinite reflection of early Romantic poetics, would provide the stage for the siblings' unfolding relation in the novel. A short section in the galley chapters elucidates the fundamental interdependence between the 'inclination for love' and 'loquacity.' Upon calling attention to the dialogical nature of the siblings' relation, the narrator remarks that "in love, conversations play an almost greater role than anything else" (*MwQ* II, 1312). The dialogical component of love, the narrating voice continues, is related to the need for communicating the contemplative thinking that love itself awakens (*MwQ* II, 1313). That is, the feeling of love triggers the emergence of the contemplative Other Condition, a circumstance that also produces the urge for communicating this very connection. Because love is intimately tied to the urge for communicating its link to an alternate condition of being, the relation between lovers can develop only as conversation; indeed, it thrives in and through the dialog. As the quintessential medium of love's unfolding, the dialog tends to revolve around love itself and becomes its most appropriate mode of investigation: "What they spoke about, too, turned around love, always and somehow" (*MwQ* II, 1313). In other words, the communication engendered by love is pointedly self-referential. In the dialog as the mirror that enables this self-referential exchange the two poles become able to perceive their unity beyond mutual difference. Unity can be perceived only as long as this exchange takes place; only through the medium of an endlessly renewed dialog can the unity that underlies difference be seen. Within this framework, unity configures itself as a process, as a reality that can be grasped, paradoxically, only as long as difference is preserved. The only way to perceive unity is to reaffirm the split, as it were, to deny that the condition of unity can be sustained permanently. For this reason, the unity love promises appears as a hypothetical case and not as a realizable goal. This insight into the processual nature of love exposes the crucial flaw in the siblings' quest for making the Other Condition permanent. Because to attempt to live in the permanent contemplation of unity, as the siblings desire, would hypostatize the moment of unity and erase the difference that makes the perception of unity possible. Obliterating the otherness of the two poles does not produce the desired reconciliation but only destroys the difference that makes the perception of unity possible.[48]

"Intimation of the unity of life through love: touched upon" (*MoE* II, 1843)—in this way one of Musil's notes for the *MwQ* captures the ethical quality of pure love. The siblings' inquiry into love demonstrates that the intimation of a fundamental unity of existence lies at the heart of the ethical; however, unity can be perceived only as long as the divisions of existence are preserved. But what is perceived as being united? What is the substrate whose fleetingly perceived unity gives rise to the bliss promised by love? To address these questions the siblings' inquiry shifts to the empirical investigation of the feeling of love, which gives way to a more general examination of the domain of feeling within a psychological paradigm.[49]

With the hypothesis of a pure love that is not attainable in ordinary experience, the siblings' self-referential investigation is finally confronted with the predicament that generally haunts the novel's inquiry into ethics. How is pure or fulfilled love to be presented and investigated if it cannot be fully grasped in ordinary life? What is the appropriate way to carry out an inquiry into this feeling and relational modality? This epistemological dilemma is at first examined in long essayistic passages couched in diary notes written by Ulrich.[50] They unfold as a phenomenological investigation of the general mechanisms of feeling. The man without qualities comes to postulate that individual feelings arise when an originally unspecified emotional substrate differentiates itself based on the object with which it engages and the acts this relation engenders (*MwQ* II, 1275–76). This emotional substrate shines through in ecstatic love experiences. Ecstatic states are marked by an exuberance of feeling that sets them off from the sober intellectual state, which prevails in ordinary experience. This ordinary intellectual mode is made possible not by an absence of feeling, Ulrich notes, but by feeling entering a specific state of neutralization (*MwQ* II, 1297–99). That is to say, the ordinary distinction between an objective realm of knowledge and a subjective dimension of feeling appears as the result of a split internal to feeling itself, of a "division of labor" (*MwQ* II, 1300) that takes place when feeling enters its neutralized state. Ordinary experience is primarily enclosed within this dimension, yet it contains the experience of love as the reminder of that originally nonneutralized substrate of feeling that makes it possible. This is the reminder of a feeling that is not yet split between the two apparently irreconcilable components of intellect and feeling, or, alternatively, that can perceive its unity beyond the split. Precisely the perception of unity accounts for the blissful experience of accord with oneself that forms the core of the Other Condition.

The ethical ramifications of Ulrich's reflection on love and feeling lie at hand. As a relation centering on the simultaneous perception of unity and difference, love stages the primal unity of feeling before and beyond its self-divisions, thus bearing witness to the ultimate unity of human existence. The fleeting emergence of this feeling "in its greatest purity" (*MwQ* II, 942) is what in modernity has become functionalized in aesthetic experience as the medium of a rejuvenation of the emotional sphere. Ulrich's exposition also sheds light on the elusive character of ethical experience. In his account, knowledge arises as a by-product of the differentiation of feeling's indistinct substrate. It entails a self-division that obliterates the initial unity of feeling. It follows that the ecstatic moments marked by a momentary suspension of feeling's self-divisions cannot be grasped from within the realm of knowledge, because the split between subjective feeling and objective knowledge is a precondition for knowledge itself. Hence the ethical illuminations of the Other Condition are bound to elude the cognitive structures of ordinary life, which is itself a by-product of the split that makes knowledge possible.

Ulrich's insight into the cognitive inaccessibility of ethics gives rise to a familiar paradox. The man without qualities is compelled to conclude that all one can safely ascertain by means of conventional conceptual structures is that there is a distinction between the ordinary and the 'other' emotional condition (*MwQ* II, 1301–03, 1310). Ulrich's epistemological impasse in the diary chapters makes clear that the issue of the exploration of feeling, as well as the question of the attainability of an existence born out of an ecstatic feeling, must be engaged in a form that is not exclusively dependent upon cognitive and discursive strategies which elude this realm. This consideration most likely prompted Musil to completely recast this portion of the narrative, embedding the discussion of feeling in a chapter that recounts the siblings' ecstatic dialogs as they unfold in their father's garden. The illustration of two juxtaposed realms of experience, ordinary life and the Other Condition, is inscribed in the spacial symbolism of the scene, which also exemplifies the role of art as the perspective that allows one to grasp their relation within ordinary experience. In thematizing art's function as a link between the two domains, this central scene spells out the conditions of possibility for the text's mode of operation, bringing to the fore the self-referential character of the inquiry the novel pursues.[51] It seems therefore appropriate that I conclude my discussion of the novel with a reading of this central chapter, "Breaths of a Summer Day."

The chapter opens with a portrayal of the siblings enjoying a mesmerizing summer day in the garden of their father's house. Captivated by delight in the blossoming of nature and with the sentiment that binds them, they believe themselves to be close to experiencing "the Millennium" (*MwQ* II, 1328).[52] Agathe in particular is depicted as she attempts to free herself of all thoughts and emotions in order to realize the state of mystical dispossessment associated with the Other Condition, "but it quickly proved as impossible to completely silence the impulses of thought, senses, and will . . . and after a few efforts she completely abandoned the attempt" (*MwQ* II, 1329). The conversation that ensues with her brother revolves around the alternate condition that just eluded her. This appears not as an alternative reality but rather as a different modality of experience, one that is filtered through an ecstatic feeling.[53] The two domains of experience are here associated with "different registers of emotion" (*MwQ* II, 1330), namely, that of an ordinary feeling driven by a motion that never finds rest or fulfillment, on the one hand, and, on the other, that of a mystical feeling which "resonates constantly but never achieves 'full reality'" (*MwQ* II, 1331). In some drafts the discussion of feeling is followed by a highly allusive description of the garden and its connection to the outer world.[54] The garden of the siblings' ancestral house is an enclosed space whose intersecting paths force the walker into a circular movement, which in its aimlessness and lack of progression recalls the movement of contemplative thinking: "The paths soon turned back upon themselves. The state of mind induced in both of them by walking on these paths eddied in circles, as a rising current does behind a dam" (*MwQ* II, 814).

In this pointedly asocial realm, an *ortus conclusus* marked by the suspension of the categories of ordinary experience, Ulrich becomes immersed in the contemplation of his sister, which plunges him into the 'other' state.

In one draft this experience is portrayed as an anomalous concentration of feeling that fails to find an outlet (*MoE* II, 1330–31; *MwQ* II, 1386). From the waning perspective of ordinary life Ulrich perceives this accumulation and congestion of feeling as a journey into death: "nonetheless he now felt not without distrust that when he directed his glance at Agathe and let it drink from the sight of her, an uncanny weakness of the will, a silent descent into the region of sleep, of death, of the image, of immobility and impotence spread in him like a dreamy substance" (*MoE* II, 1331). Ulrich cannot help but perceive the descent into this state as a queer condition at the borderline between the "greatest happiness" possible and "pathological behavior" (*MoE* II, 1330). As though unconsciously driven by the urge to break the spell of this abnormal state, the siblings repeatedly go near the edge of the garden in their circular walks, stopping by the fence that delimits their asocial realm. Through it they are able to see the ordinary reality of the street from the estranged perspective of disengaged observers (*MoE* II, 1336). The position by the fence grants the observer a vantage point onto reality that is simultaneously connected to and separated from it. It enables the siblings to step out of ordinary life without being completely severed from it, "for in the way this fence separated them from the world while also connecting them with it . . . it reminded them of the fundamental qualities of human love" (*MoE* II, 1337).

The fence becomes a cipher for love in virtue of its function as the link that unites while also separating the enclosed space of the garden from the outer world. Like love, it symbolizes the fundamental condition of human existence, that of being torn between two incompatible yet related modes of being. A variant of this passage in a parallel draft makes this relation explicit:

> but the name that, while in that condition, they had given the fence because of its metaphorical quality, and hence the name for the whole place in which they were because of the advantages of its location, "The unseparated and not united," this name had since then gained even more relevance for them. Because they were themselves unseparated and not united and thought they could intuitively recognize that everything else in the world was also unseparated and not united. . . . It is a reasonably self-effacing truth . . . that the world, by the way it is, constantly lets another world shine through, which it could have been or should have become; so that everything that grows out of its activities is mixed up with demands that would only be understandable in another world. (*MoE* II, 1350–51)

By recognizing the fundamental "unseparated and not united" quality of human existence epitomized by the fence, the siblings are given to realize that the reality humans are familiar with contains fissures through which the unintelligible demands of an 'other' reality are allowed to emerge. At stake are not two distinct worlds facing each other, though, but rather two different modalities of feeling through which perceptions and emotions are filtered and organized. These ground different ways of relating to the world, indeed, different images of the world. Put in the nonfigural terminology of the diary chapters, one could say that the unsettling perception of division and incompleteness that haunts a humankind firmly rooted within a neutralized state of feeling derives from the intimation of an ecstatic, undivided existence that promises to unfold within a nonneutralized emotional condition. Standing by the fence, the siblings are given to see the common roots of the two realms, which leads them to describe the fence itself as "unseparated and not united," that is, to portray it in terms of the existential truth it enables them to see. The fence becomes a cipher for the paradoxical state of separation and union of the two realms because it is itself the "challengingly ambiguous structure" (*MoE* II, 1337) that connects to *and* separates from the world. For this reason, it also represents the only position from which an observer can see both domains. Significantly, the passersby on the street are unable to see the siblings who watch them from behind the fence. The perspective of the street, that is to say, of ordinary life, does not allow them to glance into the garden's asocial realm. By the same token, moving away from the fence plunges one into a deathlike state that becomes oblivious even to itself, as Ulrich discovers. The standpoint by the fence appears therefore as the most desirable position, because it is the only position from which unity can be glimpsed. It is the position that engenders ethical experience itself, that is, that allows one to perceive the unity consigned to an unfathomable condition without completely diving into the void of this condition, a move which would wind up obliterating all recognizable perceptions, including the sought-for perception of unity. It is therefore understandable that the siblings are continually attracted to the fence, as the vantage point that makes perspicuous both the unity of human experience and the necessary divisions in which this perception of unity is grounded.

The 'image' of the fence holds further insights into the nature of ethical experience. When compared to the enclosed realm of the garden and the surrounding outer world, the fence appears to be a mere borderline separating two territories. Like all borders, it has no spacial extension, no territory of its own. This lack of extension is significant, for it suggests that the fence is not a place in which one could dwell, much less ground one's life. By the same token, one cannot anchor one's life in the vision of unity the fence affords. At the fence Ulrich and Agathe clearly recognize that they have only two options: they can either go back to the street, that is, to ordinary life, and learn to live with its messiness and incoherency or, alternatively, they can carry out their extreme experiment, taking up the challenge of an ecstatic, self-oblivious mode of existence. It is hardly surprising that a powerful sense of self-delusion looms large as the siblings decide to pursue their dream of an alternate mode of existence in the garden. As especially Ulrich realizes, this choice does not arise from the confident belief in the possibility of an alternative life but from his revulsion for that ordinary existence to which he is unable to adjust. Nothing other than his fundamental "contempt for life" has allowed his sister to become the emblem for an "extreme and last promise," Ulrich admits to himself in the garden (*MoE* II, 1334).[55] His self-doubts as he prepares to carry out his utmost experiment with Agathe foreshadow the inevitable failure of this enterprise.

Identifying the garden and the street as ciphers for the juxtaposed domains of ordinary experience and the Other Condition begs the question about the fence's own symbolic valence. The image of a device that links two realms in virtue of its lacking a territory of its own recalls a central trope of Musil's essay on film, which portrays aesthetic experience as an extensionless bridge connecting ordinary life and the Other Condition. The essay portrays aesthetic experience as the psychological mechanism that allows the individual to span for a moment the gap between ordinary experience and the Other Condition because it is not an autonomous condition in itself. In the text's figurative language, it is a bridge that lacks a territory of its own. These relations are clearly reinscribed in the spacial symbolism of the siblings' garden. Here the fence becomes another image for the aesthetic bridge, portraying art as the threshold that connects and simultaneously separates two domains. At the threshold of art, the touching of these two realms is permanently renewed, as their difference is reasserted. Art becomes the condition of possibility for ethical experience in modernity as the fence at which two incommensurable modalities of feeling touch. The self-referential implications of this portrayal of aesthetic experience lie at hand. In presenting art as a fence uniting and separating two incompatible modes of being, this scene spells out the conditions of possibility for the novel's own investigation. In this way, the novel presents itself not only as an inquiry into ethical experience but also as an inquiry into the preconditions that make the investigation of ethical experience possible within the medium of the aesthetic. In other words, by means of this highly symbolic scene the novel not only sets out to define the nature of ethics but also thematizes the relation between aesthetics and ethics as a question of the novel's own relation to its 'object' of inquiry. It specifies this relation by presenting the aesthetic as situated at the intersection between ordinary experience and the Other Condition.

This is where my reading of *The Man without Qualities* ends. This choice is not meant to suggest that the "Summer Day" chapter, the text on which Musil was working the day of his death, represents an ideal or symbolic conclusion for the novel.[56] Musil's unpublished materials rather suggest that after this scene the various narrative strains were to precipitate toward some sort of resolution—the militarist turn of the Parallel Campaign, the evolution of Clarisse's insanity, Moosbrugger's planned escape from the mental asylum—and come together at the end in the cataclysm of the war.[57] This chapter nonetheless provides a fitting end to my discussion of the novel in more than one respect. On a narratological level, it adumbrates the reasons for the failure of Ulrich's and Agathe's utopia, foreshadowing the possible resolution of the main narrative strain in the novel's second volume. The anticipated collapse of the siblings' attempt to plunge ordinary experience into the Other Condition also establishes a symmetry between the two volumes of the novel, confirming the futility of all attempts at healing the fundamental split between ordinary life and ethical experience. More important, the "Summer Day" chapter clearly addresses the three interlocking questions around which the novel's investigation revolves, namely, What is ethical experience and how does it relate to ordinary life? What is art's connection to the ethical? What role can art play in the modern period? The siblings' dialogs in the garden contribute to specifying ethical experience as the noncognizant perception of a fundamental unity of existence grounded in an unfathomable substrate of feeling. Art, as the fence between two incompatible modalities of feeling, offers a medium for letting this ethical intimation surface within ordinary experience, while reaffirming the split between the ordinary and the 'other' emotional modalities. Hence art configures itself as the domain in which the ethical as the perception of the unity of existence can be pursued, albeit not as a retrievable, intelligible horizon that could encompass the whole of life. Far from offering the last site for recomposing a totality of meaning, the aesthetic is portrayed in this chapter as the medium for acknowledging the modern split of ordinary and ethical experience. This represented for Musil a crucial step in dismissing the ominous dream of a reconciled, thoroughly moral life.

Postscript: Fragments of an Inductive Ethos

This study began with the hypothesis that Ulrich's question about the good, or just, life constitutes the primary frame of reference not only for the kaleidoscopic narrative unfolding in the *MwQ* but also for Musil's lifelong aesthetic and cultural inquiries in his diaries and essays. My discussion of Musil's fictional and nonfictional texts was guided by the presumption that they articulate a specific hypothesis about the nature of ethics and its relation to art in the modern period. Musil had outlined this inquiry already in his prewar writings but only fully developed it in response to the cultural and political challenges of the interwar period. Weaving insights gained from contemporary psychological theories into a network of Kantian images, Musil described ethics in terms of an alternate emotional modality that is incompatible with the ordinary one but intermittently surfaces within the experience of art. The *MwQ* configures itself as a thought experiment aimed at testing just this understanding of art and ethics. The novel shows what happens when one tries to realize a thoroughly moral life by attempting to bridge the gap between the distinct modalities of feeling that undergird the ordinary and the ethical realms of experience. It thus stages two specular endeavors, each aimed at reducing the one realm to the experiential categories of the other. Musil hoped that a demonstration of the troubling consequences of these experiments would help liquidate the dream of a reconciled, moral life that haunted his contemporaries.

I believe that Musil truly attributed his novel with the performative, iterable properties of a scientific experiment. The experimental nature of his aesthetic endeavor invests even Ulrich's and Agathe's projected failure with a positive valence. After all, one needs to carry out an experiment in order to find out whether it will succeed or fail; failure is an integral part of the experimental procedure. The novel can itself be seen as an experiment to be repeated by every reader, much as Wittgenstein's famed ladder in the *Tractatus* should be climbed in full by every individual wishing to understand the logical possibilities and limitations of language. In Musil's case, the experiment is designed to test the potential and limitations of art and ethics in modernity. In keeping with the Wittgensteinian image, one could add that it is fine to discard the novel's ladder after having climbed it. Thus Musil considered the possibility of sending his main character to die in the Great War after Ulrich had acknowledged his failures.[1] Within this frame it hardly appears pessimistic that the man without qualities was to be destroyed in the war along with the old order to which he belonged. The novel's constructive message was to lie not in the fate of its bourgeois hero but rather in the positive lessons to be drawn from his failures.

What are these lessons, however? After all, in the novel ethics turns out to be a cognitive void, the inexplicable yet very palpable emptiness that fills Clarisse's ring. The reader may wonder how Ulrich's 'question of the just life' is to be answered if the gap between the emotional modalities underlying ordinary life and ethics remains unbridgeable. Does this realization not invalidate anyone's quest for the good life? Musil's unpublished papers show that the novel's ultimate message was not to reside in some form of ethical nihilism. The collapse of the utopia of the Other Condition was to open the way for the utopia of an 'inductive ethos.' In Musil's own terms, this was a utopia "of real life" (*MoE* II, 1887), unlike the quest for the Other Condition, which was driven by Ulrich's 'denial of life.' The inductive ethos was intended to offer a venue for acknowledging and coming to terms with the disjointed reality of the modern world. As a mature version of the utopias of exactness and essayism pursued by Ulrich in the first book,[2] it was to represent the adequate ethos for that "inductive age" (*MwQ* II, 1749) ushered in by the collapse of the old order after World War I. Based on the pragmatic demand to formulate a "systematics of common life, a psycho-technology of the collectives" (*MoE* II, 1870), it was to confront the task of articulating coordinates for individual and collective experience from the open-minded perspective of an inductive empiricism. Musil's tentative remarks show that this inductive ethos was to operate according to a fundamental distinction between the collective realm, regulated by the "rational morality of a social, technical sobriety" (*MwQ* II, 1753), a technocratic vision informed by ideals of peace, justice, and general well-being, and the private domain of true ethical experience, an "exceptional realm of creativity and genius" (*MoE* II, 1879).[3] Musil did not possess a solid grasp of this utopian vision, but was rather exploring its ramifications as he was writing. His reflection at times displays a troubling elitist streak, which emerges, for instance, in the question of how to extend the genius morality articulated for individuals like Ulrich (and Musil himself, one could surmise) to the rest of a humankind drowning in the day-to-day struggle to satisfy immediate material needs. Here Musil feels compelled to distinguish between an inductive ethos for the multitudes, for which morality boils down to having regular access to food, shelter, and work, and an ethos for the few who, dispensed from such existential concerns, can concentrate on loftier visions (*MoE* II, 1885). The focus on a "genius morality" for the private realm suggests that Musil had trouble breaking loose from some assumptions of that very ideology of individualism he deemed obsolete.

Although it remains too tentative and rhapsodic to provide any concrete indications for our day, Musil's idea of an inductive ethos opens up important venues of investigation. While it does not dismiss the reality of ethical experience, this inductive attitude recognizes that the ethical cannot provide a unitary, intelligible horizon of meaning for ordinary life. It calls for relinquishing the dream of a thoroughly moral, reconciled life, which could transcend the messiness and ambivalence of modern experience. Instead it pleads for accepting as irreversible a modern condition defined by the dividedness of individual consciousness and the decenteredness of modern societies. What is more, it calls for acknowledging and seizing the emancipatory potential inherent in the modern condition thus defined. In the final analysis, Musil's ethos is carried by the realization that in modernity the question of the 'good life'—that is, of the coordinates for organizing and steering individual and collective existence—cannot be addressed from a purely *ethical* standpoint, but that it must become mingled with a host of *practical, pragmatic* considerations. What guides the inductive ethos is not the purity of a recognizable moral imperative but the hybrid reality of conflicting claims and perspectives of different spheres in the modern world.

This empirical pragmatism is permanently unsettled and rejuvenated by the subversive movement of aesthetic imagination. Art, and literature in particular, constantly challenge the status quo by presenting imaginative alternatives to the given. The authority of these unique models—their exemplarity, to use the term Musil appropriated from Kant—derives from art's ability to intermittently tap into the emotional modality of ethics. This is itself the site for an aesthetic judgment, which is consigned to the special interplay of intellect and feeling. It is a type of judgment that can produce purposive behavior in the absence of general principles of conduct. I believe that the appeal today of Musil's distinctive brand of modernism lies precisely in the open-ended, nonnormative quality of the ethical and aesthetic visions I have just outlined, as well as in the optimistic view of the modern condition that sustains them.

Notes

Introduction

1. In *Der Ring der Clarisse. Großer Stil und Nihilismus in der modernen Literatur,* 1984, trans. Christine Wolter (Frankfurt a.M.: Suhrkamp, 1987), Claudio Magris argues that Clarisse's hollow ring epitomizes the modernist quest of writers ranging from Knut Hamsun and Jens Peter Jacobsen to Robert Walser, Elias Canetti, and Italo Svevo. Magris 7. See also Magris's chapter on Musil, 269–316.

2. Jean-François Lyotard, "Answering the Question: What Is Postmodernism?" trans. Régis Durand, in *The Postmodern Condition: A Report on Knowledge* (Minneapolis: University of Minnesota Press, 1984), 79.

3. Habermas's oft-quoted phrase is found in his response to the "postmodern condition" Lyotard described in the homonymous study from 1979. Jürgen Habermas, "Modernity versus Postmodernity," 1979, *New German Critique* 22 (Winter 1981): 3–14. Lyotard's rejoinder in the essay quoted above sparked the contentious debates on the theoretical and political ramifications of the notion of postmodernity that opposed French and German theorists in the 1980s.

4. Lyotard, *Postmodern Condition,* 78–81.

5. Musil offered this characterization of his own work in a 1926 interview with Oskar Maurus Fontana. *GW* 7, 942.

6. Lyotard, *Postmodern Condition,* 82. Lyotard explicitly mentions Musil's work in his discussion of the postmodern demise of grand narratives. He situates Musil within what he terms the horizon of Viennese pessimism, in which he includes, fairly indiscriminately, Hofmannsthal and Kraus, Loos and Schoenberg, Mach and Wittgenstein (41). Significantly, Lyotard does not seem to draw on his direct familiarity with *The Man without Qualities;* his citations from Musil's novel stem from a commentary by J. Bouveresse (see note note 54, p. 90, and 136, p. 95).

7. The tendency of early modernism scholars to subsume modernist texts under a general category of interpretation, which is in turn presented as determining modernism's essential identity, also shaped the early phases of Musil criticism. For instance, it is typical for the early phases of Musil scholarship that the humanist values of harmony and reconciliation, as glimpsed in the existential quests of several characters in *MwQ,* are regarded as being at the heart of Musil's presumed modernist message. A case in point is Wilhelm Braun's reading of the siblings' exploration of the Other Condition. Braun starts from an understanding of modernism as the pursuit of the humanist quest for reconciliation, understood both as the longed-for recomposition of the inner dividedness that plagues the modern individual and as an attempt at reestablishing a harmonious relationship between the individual and the world. Wilhelm Braun, "Musil's Siamese Twins," *The*

Germanic Review 33 (1958): 41–52. The themes of balance and reconciliation are paradigmatically inflected in Wolfdietrich Rasch's thorough reading of the novel. Rasch views Ulrich's and Agathe's quest for the Other Condition as an attempt at mending the imbalance between rational and nonrational sides of human existence. Wolfdietrich Rasch, "*Musil. Der Mann ohne Eigenschaften,*" in *Der deutsche Roman. Vom Barock bis zur Gegenwart,* ed. Benno von Wiese (Düsseldorf: Bagel, 1965), vol. 2, 361–419. Irrespective of their diverging valuations of the utopia of the Other Condition in the second volume of *MwQ,* both Braun and Rasch draw on remarkably consistent assumptions with regard to the modernist discourse that in their eyes frames Musil's narrative and that they see driven by desire for recomposing the split that haunts individuals in modernity. For a history of Musil criticism see Christian Rogowski, *Distinguished Outsider: Robert Musil and His Critics* (Columbia, S.C.: Camden, 1994).

8. The postmodern debates favored the introduction of less dichotomizing categories for the appraisal of modernist texts and sparked renewed interest in Musil's work. This shift in the understanding of cultural and literary modernism is emblematically reflected in the appeal to expand and differentiate the categories deployed in reading modernist texts made by David Bathrick and Andreas Huyssen in their introduction to *Modernity and the Text: Revisions of German Modernism* (New York: Columbia University Press, 1989), 1–16.

9. For a brief overview of Musil's life, see Rogowski, *Distinguished Outsider,* 8–17, and the monographs by Burton Pike, *Robert Musil: An Introduction to His Work* (Ithaca, N.Y.: Cornell University Press, 1961), and Hannah Hickman, *Robert Musil and the Culture of Vienna* (LaSalle, Ill.: Open Court, 1984). See also David S. Luft's intellectual biography, *Robert Musil and the Crisis of European Culture, 1880–1942* (Berkeley: University of California Press, 1980). For the most comprehensive documentation of Musil's life and work see Karl Corino, *Robert Musil: Eine Biographie* (Reinbek bei Hamburg: Rowohlt, 2003).

10. Hugo von Hofmannsthal, *Reden und Aufsätze* I, *1891–1913,* ed. Bernd Schoeller (Frankfurt a.M.: Fischer, 1979), 60. My translation.

11. For a discussion of modernism's entwinement of cultural and scientific contexts within a European perspective see William R. Everdell, *The First Moderns: Profiles in the Origin of Twentieth-Century Thought* (Chicago: University of Chicago Press, 1997). For a philosophical perspective on the relations between aesthetics and science, see Art Berman's *Preface to Modernism* (Urbana: University of Illinois Press, 1994), 121–97, and Charles R. Bambach's *Heidegger, Dilthey, and the Crisis of Historicism* (Ithaca, N.Y.: Cornell University Press, 1995), 21–55. For a discussion of the so-called spirit of 1914, i.e., the nationalistic surge that resulted in the unprecedented mobilization of prominent German intellectuals and artists in favor of World War I, see Wolfgang J. Mommsen's *Imperial Germany 1867–1918: Politics, Culture, and Society in an Authoritarian State,* trans. Richard Deveson (London: Arnold, 1995), 205–16.

12. As Lukács writes: "The circle within which the Greeks led their metaphysical life was smaller than ours: that is why we cannot, as part of our life, place ourselves inside it. Or rather, the circle whose closed nature was the transcendental essence of their life has, for us, been broken; we cannot breathe in a closed world. We have invented the productivity of the spirit," Georg Lukács, *The Theory of the Novel,* 1920, trans. Anna Bostock (Cambridge, Mass.: MIT Press, 1971), 33.

13. Far from painting reason as an all-corrupting force that should be combated, Lukács's account presents it as the faculty that quintessentially defines the human condition. Because they were originally endowed with reason, humans were destined to leave the Garden of Eden that was Greek antiquity and begin their troublesome journey on earth. Much as in the Christian narrative, this journey contains within itself the promise of redemption, albeit displaced into an aesthetic realm that has yet to come, and perhaps feebly announced itself in the groundbreaking works of Dostoevsky.

14. LeRider's study focuses in particular on the subversion of gender identity and the perceived threat emanating from Jewish identity articulated in *fin de siècle* narratives. Jacques LeRider, *Modernity and Crises of Identity: Culture and Society in Fin-de-Siècle Vienna,* trans. Rosemary Morris (New York: Continuum, 1993). For analyses of turn-of-the-century Viennese culture, see Carl Schorske's *Fin-de-siècle Vienna: Politics and Culture* (New York: Knopf, 1980), Allan Janik and Stephen Toulmin's *Wittgenstein's Vienna* (New York: Simon & Schuster, 1973), and Jens Rieckmann's *Aufbruch in die Moderne. Die Anfänge des Jungen Wien* (Königstein / Taunus: Athenäum, 1985).

15. Bahr appropriated this phrase from Ernst Mach's *Analysis of Sensations.* See Hermann Bahr's *Dialog vom Tragischen* (*Dialog on the Tragic*), especially the section "Das unrettbare Ich" ("The unsalvageable self") (Berlin: Fischer, 1904), 79–101.

16. See Fritz Mauthner's *Beiträge zu einer Kritik der Sprache* (*Essays on a Critique of Language*) (Hildesheim: Olms, 1967) and *Gottlose Mystik* (*Mysticism without God*), (Dresden: Carl Reissner, 1924). For an analysis of neomystical currents in German culture at the turn of the century, see Uwe Spörl's *Gottlose Mystik in der deutschen Literatur um die Jahrhundertwende* (Paderborn: Schöningh, 1997).

17. See in particular Chandos's wistful description of moments characterized by the merging of self and the world, which he longingly describes as a lost "condition of almost perpetual intoxication" in which the whole of existence appears as "one vast unity"; Hugo von Hofmannsthal, *The Lord Chandos Letter,* trans. Russel Stockman (Marlboro, Vt.: Marlboro Press, 1986), 16–17 and 43.

18. Musil's vision resonates with Dominick LaCapra's warning against conflating the concepts of absence and loss in the endeavor to cope with apocalyptic, traumatic events. LaCapra argues that most cultures harbor an anxiety about the absence of ultimate foundations and metaphysical grounds. To properly deal with this insight, it is imperative that this absence not be conflated with the loss produced by

a traumatic event of unfathomable magnitude. His criticism of some contemporary attempts at coping with the trauma of the Shoah echoes Musil's critique of his contemporaries, whom he chided for conflating the historical trauma of World War I with the contemporary, insufferable insight into the impossibility of metaphysical certainties. Dominick LaCapra, "Trauma, Absence, Loss," *Critical Inquiry* 25 (1999): 696–727, especially 701–02.

19. For recent readings that stress the timeliness of Musil's understanding of contingent modernity and acceptance of decentered subjectivity, see Alice Bolterauer's *Rahmen und Riss. Robert Musil und die Moderne* (Wien: Praesens, 1999); see also Stefan Jonsson's discussion of Musil's productive undoing of outlived notions of subjectivity and identity in *Subject without Nation: Robert Musil and the History of Modern Identity* (Durham, N.C.: Duke University Press, 2000).

20. A case in point is Cedric E. Williams's remark that the siblings' mystical adventure offers an escape from the isolation in which Ulrich's "sense of possibilities" and mathematical precision have plunged him. Williams not only emphasizes the escapist overtones of this endeavor but also correlates them with Musil's presumed mystical temptation, which Williams accounts for by suspecting an undeclared sympathy for fascism in Musil. This correlation appears utterly unwarranted, as it flies in the face of Musil's well-documented, unambiguous denunciation of National Socialism in several essays and diary remarks from the 1930s. Cedric E. Williams, *The Broken Eagle: The Politics of Austrian Literature from Empire to Anschluss* (London: Elek, 1974), 166–67 and 184–85.

21. While this line of interpretation may well be successful in corroborating a specific notion of (poetic) language, the atemporal views of language and the literary, which it presupposes, are so removed from Musil's own idea of literature as a historical, socially embedded phenomenon that their contribution to a deeper understanding of Musil's aesthetic endeavor appears doubtful at best. See, for instance, Hans-Georg Pott's reading of Musil's novel as an "endless text" in *Robert Musil* (Munich: Fink, 1984), 162. See also Gerd-Theo Tewilt's contention that the Other Condition must be regarded as a phenomenon constituted by and in language in *Zustand der Dichtung. Interpretationen zur Sprachlichkeit des "anderen Zustands" in Robert Musils "Mann ohne Eigenschaften"* (Münster: Aschendorff, 1990), 171. See also Giorgio Agamben's discussion of Musil as the epitome of a critical project that investigates the void which opens up when thought confronts the impossible scission between poetry and philosophy, ecstatic-inspired language and rational-conscious thought, in *Stanzas: Word and Phantasm in Western Culture,* trans. Ronald L. Martinez (Minneapolis: University of Minnesota Press, 1993), xvii–xix.

22. Stanley Corngold, *Complex Pleasure: Forms of Feeling in German Literature* (Stanford, Calif.: Stanford University Press, 1998), 19.

23. It is important to point out that this reshuffling is not triggered by the release of another of rationality, which would serve as the guarantor of authenticity

and truthfulness, as in Surrealism. Rather, it is consigned to a special unison of ordinary human faculties, the emotional and the intellectual.

24. Corngold, *Complex Pleasure,* 12.

25. In this regard Peter Bürger suggests that staging the failure of the Other Condition was a means for Musil to denounce contemporary quests for unity and totality. According to Bürger, this failure was to prepare the way for the acknowledgment that in modernity the foundation of ethics lies in the very ability to cope with the undecidability of the fundamental questions. Peter Bürger, "Literarische Form als Denkform: Musils 'Der Mann ohne Eigenschaften,'" in Peter Bürger and Christa Bürger, *Prosa der Moderne* (Frankfurt a.M.: Suhrkamp, 1988), 422–37, here 437.

26. On the rise of a new intellectual stratum in Western societies, see Jürgen Habermas's momentous *The Structural Transformation of the Public Sphere,* trans. Thomas Burger (Cambridge, Mass.: MIT Press, 1989), especially section 6, on the transformations of the public sphere's political function in the twentieth century (181–235). For a sociohistorical perspective on cultural and aesthetic discourses in Germany at the beginning of the twentieth century, see part 3 in Volker Berghahn's *Imperial Germany, 1871–1914* (Providence: Berghahn, 1994), 132–89. See also Musil's own take on the erosion of the intellectual's and writer's autonomy and social status under the pressure of a new-media market dominated by capitalistic practices, as reflected in an essay from 1923, "How Does One Help Writers?" "Wie hilft man Dichtern?" (*GW* 8, 1112–16).

27. See Part 1, "Tempted by Distance: Intellectuals and the Grey Republic" in Barnouw's *Weimar Intellectuals and the Threat of Modernity* (Bloomington: Indiana University Press, 1988), 11–42.

28. Barnouw observes that Weimar intellectuals were too often blind to the paradox of the circular self-definitions they were providing, based on a notion of masses whose presumed, innate good sense was treated as an article of faith, but who at the same time needed the intellectual's guidance to become able to draw on this presumed goodness. Ibid., 21. From a perspective that also takes into consideration the changing role of the intellectual throughout the post–World War II period, Peter Uwe Hohendahl has called attention to the double bind entailed in the intellectual's self-empowerment. While intellectuals have defined themselves in terms of a critical discourse that sets them off from immediate material and political interests, they have also insisted on maintaining control over the production and dissemination of this discourse, which, then, becomes their property, power base, and source of legitimation. Peter Uwe Hohendahl, "The Scholar, the Intellectual, and the Essay: Weber, Lukács, Adorno, and Postwar Germany," *The German Quarterly* 70.3 (Summer 1997): 217–32, here 228–29.

29. See Peter Gay's classic study *Weimar Culture: The Outsider as Insider* (New York: Harper & Row, 1968), particularly chapter IV, "The Hunger for Wholeness: Trials of Modernity," 70–101, which draws attention to the entwinement of

nostalgia for wholeness and uncompromising repudiation of politics that defined much of Weimar intellectual climate.

30. Starting from Max Weber's thesis of a "disenchanted modernity," which the German sociologist saw as emblematic for the historical process of rationalization that led to the collapse of metaphysical accounts of experience and the compartmentalization of life-spheres in modern societies, Norbert Bolz has spoken of a paradoxical quest for reenchanting the world in the thinking of key modernists like Benjamin, Bloch, Jünger, Heidegger, and Lukács. According to Bolz, the radicalization of the idea of disenchantment pursued by these thinkers, as it appears most manifestly in Benjamin, was to usher in a paradoxical reversal by facilitating the retrieval of an unimaginable, new horizon of meaning, which would in turn allow humans to reinvest existence with a permanent, unifying meaning. An important building block in Bolz's argument is his contention that these intellectuals were motivated by and acted upon an "exodus impulse," that is, the desire to withdraw or pull out of present reality rather than confront it in its ambivalence and messiness. Norbert Bolz, *Auszug aus der entzauberten Welt: philosophischer Extremismus zwischen den Weltkriegen* (München: Fink, 1989), 7–11. Anson Rabinbach echoes Bolz's assessment in his probing review of intellectual responses to the events of World War I from the perspective of their apocalyptic and messianic expectations. Rabinbach points to the mood of world repudiation and of intolerance for the present, seen as tainted by an unredeemable past, which drives the modernist dream of a *tabula rasa* or a radical new beginning—expressed, for instance, in Heidegger's summoning of a 'groundless ground.' Anson Rabinbach, *In the Shadow of Catastrophe: German Intellectuals Between Apocalypse and Enlightenment* (Berkeley: University of California Press, 1997), 2–5.

31. Jochen Schulte-Sasse, "Modernity and Modernism, Postmodernity and Postmodernism: Framing the Issue," *Cultural Critique* 5 (Winter 1987): 5–22; here 11–12.

32. A comment from the diaries captures Musil's attitude toward Thomas Mann: "Creative writing is not merely description but, in the first instance, interpretation of life. . . . If one interprets it by using the concepts and prejudices that people apply, then refines these a little as Th[omas]M[ann] does, then one becomes the teacher, philosopher, etc. Far be it from me to overlook the high degree of certainty, composure, and suchlike, which such a procedure bestows on one" (*D* 481–82).

33. For Musil's engagement with Rathenau, who provided the model for Paul Arnheim in *The Man without Qualities,* see chapters 2 and 5.

34. Zygmunt Bauman, *Legislators and Interpreters: On Modernity, Postmodernity and Intellectuals* (Ithaca, N.Y.: Cornell University Press, 1987), 115–16. While I find Bauman's characterization of intellectual positioning and self-consciousness within modernism compelling, I do not share his unsympathetic assessment of modernist intellectuals. For Bauman, modern/modernist intellectuals are defined by their clinging to a monolithic notion of culture as a realm that will enable

the intellectual/legislator to impose a unifying order upon the inexhaustible multiplicity of the life-world. This modernist attitude is pitted against a postmodernist stance that has shed the claim to a privileged, totalizing perspective and has learned to valorize and respectfully interact with the plurality and relativity of views in contemporary societies. Bauman's discussion of modernism and postmodernism must be seen in the context of the debates on postmodernity in the mid-1980s.

Chapter 1

1. These are key terms in the poetic program Maeterlinck lays out in the essays collected in *The Treasure of the Humble,* 1896, trans. Alfred Sutro (London: Allen, 1897). See the excerpts from Maeterlinck's collection of essays in Musil's diaries from 1904–05 (*TB* I 134–35).

2. For the impact of Maeterlinck's Symbolist poetics on turn-of-the-century literature in the German-speaking countries, see Spörl, 142–58.

3. In this respect see Jürgen Habermas's reconstruction of the unfolding of Western aesthetic discourse since the nineteenth century, which in his eyes revolves around the understanding of art as the "other" of reason, in *The Philosophical Discourse of Modernity: Twelve Lectures,* trans. Frederick G. Lawrence (Cambridge, Mass.: MIT Press, 1987). Habermas's central claim is that at least since Nietzsche aesthetic reflection has given up hope in art as the medium for expanding the scope of reason beyond its instrumental applications and into a truly communicative, emancipatory modality—an endeavor Habermas sees most consistently attempted in Schiller's reappropriation of Kantian aesthetics; see his excursus on Schiller, 45–50. Modern aesthetic reflection since Nietzsche, which for Habermas includes thinkers as diverse as Adorno and Foucault, Luhmann and Lacan, has tended to stylize art into the "other of reason." This formulation entails that art is not simply reason's critical consciousness but also and especially a modality of being alternative to reason and grounded in myth, that is, in an archaic, preconceptual, prerational mode of being, which lures with its promise of a decentered subjectivity freed by the bonds of cognition and purpose, from all imperatives of utility and morality (see especially chapter 6, "The Entry into Postmodernity: Nietzsche as a Turning Point"). For Habermas, the critique of reason entailed in this conceptualization of the aesthetic sphere winds up forfeiting the emancipatory project of the Enlightenment while at the same time opening the gates to an irrational vitalism that is politically regressive in nature.

4. Musil had started work on the novel in 1903 while working as an assistant at Stuttgart's Technical University.

5. The novel was published by the Wiener Verlag in 1906. The review that launched Musil's career as a writer appeared in the Berlin newspaper *Der*

Tag on December 21, 1906. It is reprinted in Karl Corino's "Robert Musil und Alfred Kerr. Der Dichter und sein Kritiker," in *Robert Musil: Studien zu seinem Werk,* eds. Karl Dinklage, Elisabeth Albertsen, and Karl Corino (Reinbek bei Hamburg: Rowohlt, 1970), 240–45. See Corino, 246–47, for the novel's immediate reception.

6. For a discussion of the theme of *décadence* in Musil and Nietzsche, see Regina Baltz-Balzberg's "Antidekadenzmoral bei Musil und Nietzsche," in *Robert Musil: Theater, Bildung, Kritik,* eds. Josef Strutz and Johann Strutz (Munich: Fink, 1985), 204–26.

7. Friedrich Nietzsche, *The Case of Wagner,* in *Basic Writings of Nietzsche,* trans. and ed. Walter Kaufmann (New York: Modern Library, 1968), 626. Nietzsche's characterization of decadence closely recalls an analogous formulation by the French critic Paul Bourget, whose essays on the decadence Nietzsche knew well.

8. See Musil's reference to Huysmans's "hothouse" in *D* 93. On D'Annunzio see *D* 13–14 and 86–87.

9. For a probing description of Germany's growth between 1870 and 1914 and its social and cultural impact, see "Chapter II, Berlin" in Modris Eksteins's *Rites of Spring: The Great War and the Birth of the Modern Age* (New York: Houghton Mifflin, 1989), 55–94. For the Nietzsche reception in Germany between 1890 and 1918, see Steven E. Ashheim's *The Nietzsche Legacy in Germany, 1890–1990 (*Berkeley: University of California Press, 1992).

10. See Weber's momentous articulation of modernity's disenchantment in "Science as a Vocation" in *From Max Weber: Essays in Sociology,* trans. and ed. H. H. Gerth and C. Wright Mills (New York: Oxford University Press, 1946), 129–56, here 139. See Weber's discussion of the modern differentiation of spheres in his "Religious Rejections of the World and their Directions," ibid., 323–59.

11. For an outline of the crisis of philosophical discourse at the beginning of the twentieth century, see Werner Schneiders, *Deutsche Philosophie im 20. Jahrhundert* (München: Beck, 1998), 9–47.

12. See Nietzsche's second essay in his *Unfashionable Observations,* trans. Richard T. Gray (Stanford, Calif.: Stanford University Press, 1995), from 1874. Charles Bambach sees in the epistemological and disciplinary crisis at the onset of the twentieth century the breeding ground of concerns that still dog poststructuralist thinking. According to Bambach, these concerns can be traced back to the seemingly insoluble dilemmas faced by the human sciences, which saw their metaphysical foundations undermined by the irresistible ascent of the skeptical criteria of truth and knowledge developed within the natural sciences. The terms for this crisis become especially clear when one examines the difficulties of historicist reflection in the decades between 1880 and 1930. Bambach perceptively argues that the dilemmas confronting historicism grew, on the one hand, out of its self-imposed imperative to articulate standards of precision, verifiability, and

accountability comparable to those of the natural sciences and, on the other, out of the impossibility of satisfactorily adapting these standards to the realm of particular, situated, transient experience that pertains to historical inquiry. It is this quandary that framed the debates around materialism, positivism, scientism, and naturalism in the latter decades of the nineteenth century and fueled the attempts at formulating a specific methodological approach for the *Geisteswissenschaften* by Heinrich Rickert and Wilhelm Dilthey as well as the momentous rearticulation of ontology and historical being within the philosophy of Martin Heidegger. See the introduction and chapter 1 in Bambach's *Heidegger, Dilthey, and the Crisis of Historicism,* 1–55.

13. Mauthner, *Gottlose Mystik,* 11; my translation. For a discussion of Mauthner's philosophy of language against the backdrop of fin de siècle epistemology, see Katherine Arens, *Functionalism and Fin de Siècle: Fritz Mauthner's Critique of Language* (New York: Lang, 1984).

14. For an analysis of this phenomenon in the context of the Nietzsche reception at the turn of the century, see Ashheim, 51–84.

15. As it has been read, for instance, by Wilhelm Braun in "The Confusions of Törless," *The Germanic Review* 40 (1965): 116–31, here 116.

16. For a compelling analysis of the novel's narrative structure focusing on the devices deployed to deflect the charge of immoral behavior from the novel's protagonist, see Corngold, 103–20. For a discussion of the sexual problematic in Törless from the perspective of a psychoanalytic understanding of desire and language, see Andrew Webber, "Sense and Sensuality in Musil's Törless," *German Life and Letters* 41.2 (1988): 106–30, and Christian Dawidowski, *Die geschwächte Moderne: Robert Musils episches Frühwerk im Spiegel der Epochendebatte* (Frankfurt a.M.: Lang, 2000), 33–76. See also Peter Henninger's discussion of Musil's early fiction, *Der Buchstabe und der Geist: Unbewußte Determinierung im Schreiben Robert Musils* (Frankfurt a.M.: Lang, 1980).

17. See Hickman's reading of the novel in chapter 2 of her monograph.

18. Kerr quoted in Corino, "Robert Musil und Alfred Kerr," 243–45.

19. For a discussion of Mach's psychology within the context of the theories that revolutionized the field of psychology at the turn of the century, see Judith Ryan, *The Vanishing Subject: Early Psychology and Literary Modernism* (Chicago: University of Chicago Press, 1991), 6–22. For a contextualization of Mach's theories within late-nineteenth-century science and his influence on Viennese culture, see Manfred Diersch, *Empiriokritizismus und Impressionismus: Über Beziehungen zwischen Philosophie, Ästhetik und Literatur um 1900 in Wien* (Berlin: Rütten & Loening, 1973), 13–45, and Friedrich Stadler, *Studien zum Wiener Kreis: Ursprung, Entwicklung und Wirkung des logischen Empirismus im Kontext* (Frankfurt a.M.: Suhrkamp, 1997), 132–67. See also the section dedicated to "Machism" in Janik/Toulmin, 133–41.

20. See Hermann Bahr's *Dialog,* particularly the famed section on "The Unsalvageable Self," 79–101.

21. Otto Weininger, *Geschlecht und Character: Eine prinzipielle Untersuchung* (München: Matthes & Seitz, 1980), 199.

22. For instance, Musil did not find that Mach had made a convincing case on behalf of his radical atomism, which led to regarding sensations as the exclusive building blocks of knowledge, and of the monism it entailed, which negated any qualitative distinction between physical and psychical reality, the body and the mind. On this point, see the discussion of Musil's criticism of Mach in Hickman, 26.

23. Ryan, 20. See also her reading of *Törless* as Musil's working through a Machian problematic, 208–12.

24. Hermann Bahr, "Die neue Psychologie," *Zur Überwindung des Naturalismus. Theoretische Schriften 1887–1904,* ed. Gotthard Wunberg (Stuttgart: Kohlhammer, 1968), 53–64.

25. See the section on ecstasy in Bahr's *Dialog,* 131–39, especially 133–35.

26. Alfred Kerr pointed to the deceptive similarity between the two realms. Törless, he remarked, "loses his way in the tangle of sexuality . . . of those peculiar abominations that shimmer aside of the broad daylight of life just as that other hidden realm." Kerr, quoted in Corino, "Robert Musil und Alfred Kerr," 243. My translation.

27. Musil's dualistic vision of human experience has no metaphysical grounding, however. Mach's postulation of a radical monism was prompted by his conviction that any dualism ultimately leads to metaphysics. Musil certainly sympathized with Mach's struggle against metaphysics, yet he did not believe that dualism necessarily led to postulating a realm beyond the grasp of experience. This is a major point of contention between Musil and Mach. For a comparative analysis of Bahr's and Musil's reception of Mach, as well as Musil's further development toward gestalt theory, see Claudia Monti, *Musil. La metafora della scienza* (Napoli: Pironti, 1983), 29–51.

28. Hickman, 40.

29. Jerry A. Varsava, "Törless at the Limits of Language: A Revised Reading," *Seminar: A Journal of Germanic Studies* 20.3(September 1984): 203.

30. Musil critics have routinely regarded the issue of an imbalance between intellect and emotion as the root of Törless's tribulations. See, for instance, Hickman's suggestions that the problem in *Törless* is the "dualism of intellect and feeling" (36) or the "balance between intellect and emotion" (45).

31. Robert Musil, *Briefe 1901–1942,* vol. 1, ed. Adolf Frisé (Reinbek bei Hamburg: Rowohlt, 1981), 13. My translation.

32. What follows is an apt description of Törless's plight: "The self literally becomes split, it gains a double ground and through the murky glass of the first [self], which was up to now the only one, one sees mysterious movements without being able to interpret them." Ibid., 14. My translation.

33. For a brief overview of this cultural constellation, see Linda Dalrymple Henderson, "Die moderne Kunst und das Unsichtbare: Die verborgenen Wellen und Dimensionen des Okkultismus und der Wissenschaften," in *Okkultismus und Avantgarde. Von Munch bis Mondrian 1900–1915*, eds. Hellmut Seemann and Veit Loers (Frankfurt: Tertium, 1995), 13–31, especially 14–15.

34. On the neo-Romantic revival at the turn of the century, see Martin Lindner, *Leben in der Krise. Zeitromane der neuen Sachlichkeit und die intellektuelle Mentalität der klassischen Moderne* (Stuttgart: Metzler, 1994), 131–37.

35. A novelist, poet, and historian, Huch (1864–1947) was instrumental in rekindling her contemporaries' interest in the Romantic tradition through her own poetry and historical novels. Her two-volume monograph, published between 1899 and 1902, helped set the standards for the contemporary reception of Romanticism. At this point Musil was presumably familiar with the first volume of Huch's monograph, *Die Blütezeit der Romantik* (*The Blossoming Age of Romanticism*), which appeared in 1899 and was followed, in 1902, by a volume chronicling the decline of the Romantic movement.

36. In Huch's anthology, this contrast is mentioned in reference to a passage from Tieck's *William Lovell*, which Musil wrongly attributes to Novalis.

37. As Musil writes, somewhat cryptically, the moderns have proved unable to "throw the light of the spirit onto sensuality itself" but have rather engaged in "exercises that involve extemporizing on, and clever play with, sensuality" (*D* 87).

Chapter 2

1. The essay, "The Mathematical Man" (*P* 39–43), appeared in *Der Lose Vogel*, a monthly periodical published by Franz Blei and Kurt Wolff in Leipzig.

2. Musil's account reflects contemporary developments in mathematics and the natural sciences. The flourishing inquiries into the theoretical underpinnings of mathematics in the nineteenth and early twentieth centuries shook scientific inquiry at its foundations. At issue is especially the insight into the impossibility of ultimately grounding basic mathematical assumptions and axioms by means of necessary, rational principles and the ensuing awareness that mathematics's historical scaffolding represents just one of the possible theoretical edifices that can be imagined. For a discussion of the impact of mathematics on European modernism, see Everdell, 30–46 and 177–92. See also Linda Dalrymple Henderson's study of the influence of non-Euclidean geometries on cubist, futurist, and suprematist painting in France, Italy, the United States, and Russia, *The Fourth Dimension and Non-Euclidean Geometry in Modern Art* (Princeton, N.J.: Princeton University Press, 1983).

3. Lepenies traces the successful bid for epistemological preeminence made by the experimental sciences in the course of the nineteenth century, which resulted

in the affirmation of a narrow and morally indifferent notion of truth. Faced with the irresistible ascent of highly proficient scientific disciplines, the human sciences found themselves put on the defensive and were soon compelled to take their cue from scientific discourse—a circumstance which Lepenies relates to the literary experiments of Balzac, Flaubert, and Zola. In the reshuffling of disciplinary positions which ensued from the retreat of the traditional "moral sciences," sociology emerged as a hybrid discourse bent on legitimizing itself by embracing scientific standards of precision and accountability. At the same time it was forced to acknowledge that it could itself never be an exact science in the way of the natural sciences, given the limited use of practices such as generalization and categorization in the analysis of historically situated phenomena. Wolf Lepenies, *Between Literature and Science: The Rise of Sociology,* 1985, trans. R. J. Hollingdale (Cambridge, U.K.: Cambridge University Press, 1988), especially the "Introduction," 1–15. For the articulation of a relation between the natural and the human sciences within conservative and nationalist circles in Weimar Germany, see Jeffrey Herf, *Reactionary Modernism: Technology, Culture, and Politics in Weimar and the Third Reich* (Cambridge/New York: Cambridge University Press, 1984). For a historical analysis of the cultural constellation in the Second Reich up to 1918, see Wolfgang J. Mommsen, *Bürgerliche Kultur und künstlerische Avantgarde. Kultur und Politik im deutschen Kaiserreich, 1870 bis 1918* (Berlin: Propyläen, 1994).

4. Hickman, 68.

5. Karl Corino, *Robert Musil. Leben und Werk in Bildern und Texten* (Reinbek bei Hamburg: Rowohlt, 1988), 150.

6. Musil was actively engaged in the cultural and literary debates of his day. His first published essay, "The Obscene and Pathological in Art," from 1911, is a passionate plea against censorship in art (*P* 3–9). Another short essay, "Analysis and Synthesis," was published in 1913 in *Revolution* as part of a campaign that denounced the confiscation of one of the journal's issues by the police. *GW* 8, 1008–9.

7. Corino, *Leben und Werk,* 222.

8. Jacob Schaffner, *Die Neue Rundschau,* 1911, quoted in Corino, *Leben und Werk,* 179. My translation.

9. The moral outrage aroused by the novellas is exemplified by the assessment of a reviewer in the *Berliner Börsen–Courier:* "It is a sickly, tainted, nebulous atmosphere which I entered. . . . But I have the duty to warn from Musil those readers who do not enjoy the excessively strange, the highly abnormal, the wildly chaotic, the intellectually perverse, the absolutely sickly and hysterical in literature." Quoted in Corino, *Leben und Werk,* 179; my translation.

10. See in particular Kandinsky's "On the Question of Form" and Franz Marc's "Two Pictures" in *The Blaue Reiter Almanac,* 1912, second edition, ed. Klaus Lankheit (New York: DaCapo, 1989), 147–87 and 65–71, respectively. See also

Kandinsky's 1911 essay *Concerning the Spiritual in Art,* trans. M.T.H. Sadler (New York: Dover, 1977). The modernist understanding of art as a surrogate for waning religious narratives forms the culmination of an age-old process, which Peter Bürger has linked to the processes of rationalization and differentiation at the heart of the development of modern societies. These processes helped debunk the dogmatic assumptions of transcendence in traditional religion. At the same time they left those questions involving the meaning and grounding of experience unaddressed. Bürger argues that in modernity the gap left by the demise of traditional religious beliefs has increasingly been filled by a reflection that takes place within the domain of art conceived as an autonomous sphere that eludes the constraints of rational reflection and traditional philosophical speculation. In other words, in modernity issues concerning the sense of experience and the world are raised within an aesthetic domain that displaces religion from its traditional role. Peter Bürger, "Literary Institution and Modernization," first published in *Poetics,* 12 (1983), reprinted in *The Decline of Modernism,* trans. Nicholas Walker (University Park, Penn.: Pennsylvania State University Press, 1992), 3–18. On Musil's confrontation with the contemporary renaissance of mysticism, particularly his debt to Martin Buber, see Dietmar Goltschnigg, *Mystische Tradition im Roman Robert Musils* (Heidelberg: Stiehm, 1974).

11. "Essaybücher," *GW* 9, 1450–57.

12. Musil's essay is titled "Commentary on a Metapsychics" (*P* 54–58). Musil had made Rathenau's acquaintance a few months earlier, apparently at a soiree organized by Franz Blei (see *TB* I, 295; see also endnote 125a with a note by Martha Musil in *TB* II, 173). Already on this occasion Musil toyed with the idea of making Rathenau into a fictional character for one of his works. Indeed Rathenau served as the primary source of inspiration for the character of Paul Arnheim in *The Man without Qualities.* On Walther Rathenau's intellectual background and ambivalent vision of modernity, see Stern's sympathetic portrayal in *Einstein's German World* (Princeton, N.J.: Princeton University Press, 1999), 165–96. See also Dagmar Barnouw's more critical assessment, 44–77.

13. Corino notes that Rathenau reacted bitterly to Musil's criticism. Corino, *Leben und Werk,* 212.

14. The Berlin police chief Traugott von Jagow had confiscated a controversial issue of *Pan,* the bimonthly periodical founded by Wilhelm Herzog and Paul Cassirer in 1910, which contained excerpts from the newly published diaries written by Gustave Flaubert during his trips to Italy and Egypt. The censor had stepped in because of the sexually explicit content of the Flaubert excerpts. Traugott had furthermore prohibited the following issue of *Pan* due to the refusal of the editors to abstain from further publishing the contested diaries. See Frisé's commentary in *GW* 9, 1803–4.

15. "Quantifiability of Morality: The Writer's Morality" ("Quantificierbarkeit der Moral. Die Moral des Dichters") *GW* 8, 1307–8; and "Sought Morality" (Die gesuchte Moral), *GW* 8, 1305–7.

16. In this regard see Musil's portrayal of the Moosbrugger character in the *MwQ*. Moosbrugger is a compulsive sexual murderer whose deranged personality is the product of an explosive mix of suffered abuse, misogynistic neurosis, and Dionysian dissolution of the self.

17. See Musil's extensive excerpts from Rudolf Kassner's *Die Moral der Musik,* from 1905 (*TB* I, 481), which seem to have provided a foil to Musil's reflection on morality in this essay. See furthermore Musil's reference to Kassner's articulation of a relation between art and morality in a diary entry from around 1921–23 (*TB* I, 660).

18. For Musil's discussion of Mach's notion of function, see the last two sections (four and five) in his dissertation on Mach, *On Mach's Theories,* trans. Kewin Mulligan (Washington, D.C.: Catholic University of America, 1982), 44–80.

19. On the relation between literature and psychology, see both drafts of "Profile of a Program," an essay from 1912 (*P* 10–17).

20. The allegorical elements of the narration are underscored by some exquisitely farcical moments. One instance is the revealing gesture of the healthy writer, who spits in one ridge of Musil's cerebral cortex and absent-mindedly splatters his spit with his foot. Shortly thereafter the literary geologist chops off a piece of Musil's gray matter, crushes it with his hand, and blows it off (*P* 26).

21. In Musil's words:

> It [the essay] takes its form and method from science, its matter form art. . . . The essay seeks to establish an order. It presents not characters but a connection of thoughts, that is, a logical connection, and it proceeds from facts, like the natural sciences, to which the essay imparts an order. Except that these facts are not generally observable, and also their connections are in many cases only a singularity. (*P* 49)

22. On the relationship between essayism and science, see Marike Finlay, *The Potential of Modern Discourse: Musil, Peirce, and Perturbation* (Bloomington: Indiana University Press, 1990). Finlay relates Musil's notion of essayism to the epistemological evolution of the twentieth century. Drawing on the semiotic model developed by Peirce, she defines essayism as an infinite continuum of sign interactions within an infinite series of contexts, whose structural incompleteness and open-endedness contain an antidogmatic, utopian moment (46–55). See further Thomas Harrison's compelling discussion of Musil's notion and practice of essayism as a form of knowledge and a modality of writing that exemplarily respond to the specific challenges of the modern period in *Essayism: Conrad, Musil, and Pirandello* (Baltimore, Md.: The Johns Hopkins University Press, 1992), 148–88. For a discussion of essayistic writing within the Western tradition, see John A. McCarthy, *Crossing Boundaries: A Theory and History of Essay Writing in German, 1680–1815* (Philadelphia: University of Pennsylvania Press, 1989), and Wolfgang

Müller-Funk, *Erfahrung und Experiment. Studien zu Theorie und Geschichte des Essayismus* (Berlin: Akademie, 1995).

Chapter 3

Payne's translation of the passage in the epigraph is clumsy (*D* 208); I have therefore substituted my own.

1. See Zweig's famed memoirs *Die Welt von gestern,* published posthumously in 1942. Stefan Zweig, *The World of Yesterday: An Autobiography* (New York: Viking, 1943).

2. See in particular the preface and the central section of Eksteins's *Rites of Spring,* xiii–xvi and 139–238. Eksteins argues that the Germans' contempt for traditional rules of warfare was a direct consequence of their prewar willingness to challenge Western cultural, moral, and political norms—a willingness that had been nurtured by a culture enthralled with vitalism, primitivism, amoralism, and the cleansing force of violence. As is well known, World War I radically altered the Western understanding of warfare. Germany's military and political elites were principally responsible for changing the rules of engagement by way of previously inconceivable behavior, which included the violation of previously stipulated pacts of neutrality, the introduction of gas and unrestricted submarine warfare, and the breakdown of the fundamental distinction between combatants and noncombatants. The brutality of the total war inaugurated by Germany succeeded in driving a coil into shared models of behavior and humanity that had defined the civilization of the West for centuries. World War I helped clean the slate of centuries-old principles of interaction among sovereign nations as well as individuals, as Britain and France hurried to join in the barbarism they had decried in the Germans to beat them at their game.

3. This mood likened the void created by the collapse of the old order in World War I to a negative or "groundless" ground, in Heidegger's terminology, on which radical renewal could take place. For thinkers as diverse as Walter Benjamin, Oswald Spengler, and Georg Lukács, the very corruption of the present became a symptom for the inevitability of revolutionary change or transformation (Rabinbach, 2–4). For the historical background of cultural pessimism, see Fritz Stern's classic study, *The Politics of Cultural Despair: A Study in the Rise of the Germanic Ideology* (Berkeley: University of California Press, 1961); see also George L. Mosse, *The Crisis of German Ideology: Intellectual Origins of the Third Reich* (New York: Grosset & Dunlap, 1964), and Robert Wohl, *The Generation of 1914* (Cambridge, Mass.: Harvard University Press, 1979). For an examination of the sociopolitical and cultural background in the Austro-Hungarian monarchy and the Austrian republic, see William M. Johnston, *The Austrian Mind: An Intellectual and Social History, 1848–1938* (Berkeley: University of California Press, 1972); Walter

B. Simon, *Die verirrte Erste Republik: eine Korrektur österreichischer Geschichtsbilder* (Innsbruck: Multiplex, 1988); Friedrich Weissensteiner, *Der ungeliebte Staat: Österreich zwischen 1918 und 1938* (Vienna: Österreichischer Bundesverlag, 1990); and Michael P. Steinberg, *Austria as Theater and Ideology: The Meaning of the Salzburg Festival,* second edition (Ithaca, N.Y.: Cornell University Press, 2000).

4. For a discussion of Musil's short-lived involvement with Müller's and Hiller's activist program, see note 249 in *TB* II, 248–52.

5. The title of Musil's drama has also been translated as *The Enthusiasts.*

6. The essay in question is "Europeanness, War, Germanness" ("Europäertum, Krieg, Deutschtum") from September 1914. *GW* 8, 1020–22. For a discussion of Musil's political thinking between 1912 and 1922 as reflected through his early essays, see Daigger 1992.

7. See *TB* I, 475–484, 491–93, and 530–32, for Musil's extensive excerpts from Mann's *Reflections* and Chamberlain's *Foundations.*

8. Musil's essay, "Mind and Experience: Notes for Readers Who Have Eluded the Decline of the West," is based only on the first volume of Spengler's work, from 1918 (*P* 134–49).

9. "Symptoms Theater I" ("Symptomen-Theater I") was published in Efraim Frisch's *Der Neue Merkur* and is the first of three essays that were meant to offer a critical commentary on the bygone dramatic season (*GW* 8, 1094–1103).

10. As his diaries show, Musil owed this insight to Thomas Mann, who in a section of the *Reflections* had pointed out the irony entailed in the Expressionists' rejection of Impressionism. Expressionism, as one reads in Musil's abbreviated excerpt from Mann, disavows the Impressionist's rendering of philistine bourgeois reality, which it holds to be uncritically affirmative, and instead champions a notion of art based on the untainted, boundlessly creative eruption of the "spirit" (*Geist*) or the artist's soul (*TB* 483). Yet, Musil noted following Mann, at closer inspection the Expressionists appear to be following in a quintessentially Impressionist path in upholding the individual's impressions and emotions as the measure of truthful experience: "All of them (the Expr.sts) follow the impression of the moment, so they're Impr.sts" (*D* 253). More on the continuity between Impressionism and Expressionism can be found in a later essay, "Toward a New Aesthetic," from 1925. Here Musil comments on the "today widely disseminated false doctrines" that aim "at freeing the human spirit from reason [*Verstand*] and placing it once again in immediate relationship to creation." As he maintains, "today these efforts seem to express a yearning that first became important in connection with the related efforts of Expressionism. But if one looks a few decades further back, one sees that this critique of 'reason' in the name of liberating the 'soul' was already present at that time; even then it wanted to help 'soul' achieve more immediate expression than the empty term, caught in a conceptual tangle, allowed, and led the human spirit to freedom by all the side roads, just not by the main one. The real seeds of this striving for emancipation were already present in Impressionism . . . and had

been planted by the influence of German Romanticism, Emerson, and the mystical eclectic Maeterlinck" (*P* 200).

11. See also Musil's comments on Expressionism and immediacy in "Books and Literature" ("Bücher und Literatur," 1926): "Impressionism relied on some essence in the belief that art grants immediate access to the heart, in some physiologically unspecified way. Neo-idealism and Expressionism operated with a no less immediate 'intuition' of thinking, which does not entirely correspond to the thoughtfulness that is at stake" (*GW* 8, 1169).

12. The other two essays of Musil's 'dramatic triad' are "Symptoms Theater II" ("Symptomen-Theater II," *GW* 8, 1103–11) and "The 'Decline' of Theater" ("Der 'Untergang' des Theaters") (*GW* 8, 1116–31).

13. William E. Connolly, *Political Theory and Modernity* (Ithaca, N.Y.: Cornell University Press, 1993), 13–14.

14. Ibid., 14–15.

15. The translator renders here the term "immanent" of the original (*GW* 8, 1375) with the English "imminent," probably as a result of a misreading. I correct this error while retaining his translation of the passage.

16. See, for instance, Hartmut Böhme's early study on Musil as emblematic of the anomie of the bourgeois intellectual in the stage of advanced capitalism, *Anomie und Entfremdung: Literatursoziologische Untersuchungen zu den Essays Robert Musils und seinem Roman "Der Mann ohne Eigenschaften"* (Kronberg: Scriptor, 1974). See also Luft's characterization of Musil as representative of the mandarin intellectual caste of his time in the introduction to his monograph.

17. The professional politician and the activist represented for Musil the two main forms of political engagement. He viewed both with slight contempt. In his eyes, the politician captures the essence of politics as "a) representation of interests b) relation of ideologies to interests" (*MoE* II, 1856). That is to say, he manipulates the elements of existing ideologies to uphold the interests of his constituencies and maintain himself in power. The activist is instead fired by pure ideological zeal and is not driven by a conscious calculation of self-interest. In a diary entry from 1920, Musil groups together Dadaists, Expressionists, anarchists, nihilists, Communists, monarchists, new Catholics, and Zionists as examples of activism. What they all have in common, he argues, is ascetic ardor and the obdurate commitment to a cause, a redemptive and apocalyptic stance which recalls the passion of early Christian martyrs (except, as Musil ironically notes, that the martyr's sacrifice is now replaced by far less truculent discussions that unfold in the nebulous atmosphere of newspapers and magazines; *TB* I 382–83). The fanaticism of the activist culminates for Musil in the uncompromising fervor of the revolutionary, who represents an utterly harmful type. The revolutionary's harmfulness lies in his all-or-nothing attitude and determination to always take the high road. This translates into a fanatical desire to realize abstract ideals without taking into account the messiness of their implementation: "He flies, yet cannot walk; he swims under water but

cannot breathe the air. That which for an important person is personal fate, a path blazed with difficulty through objections he has set up himself, is, for him, style. The creative person is—with respect to the issue of life and death, for example so constituted that both scales are heavily weighted and only an excess surplus weight is needed to tip the balance, the 'ultra' is either aflame for the inviolability of every hair on the human countenance, or he condemns thousands to destruction with a mental pen stroke" (*D* 270). The determination to hold on to absolute demands and never enter compromise is formalistic and becomes empty gesture, because it fails to commit itself to pondering the consequences of the revolutionary's actions in a given situation. Psychologically, the flip side of the revolutionary's abstract pathos is a self-righteous contempt for the needs of real people who might stand in the way of the realization of the ideal. Revolutionary pathos thus engenders a radical politics that breeds violence and destruction. Hence it proves unable to come up with constructive alternatives to what it fights. See also Musil's comments on Ulrich's relation to politics in *MoE* II, 1871–72.

18. The translator misreads here "capitalism" for "socialism." Cf. Musil's original formulation in the *Tagebücher:* "Die Frage des Sozialismus lautet nicht . . . " (*TB* I, 639).

19. Musil's debt to Nietzsche in his assessment of human nature can hardly be overstated.

20. For instance Hickman, 102–3.

21. See Musil's retrospective assessment in *TB* I, 960, according to which the play represents such an innovative dramatic form that one should have imaginatively created (*gedichtet*) its actors as well. The play was well received when it appeared in print in 1921; it was awarded the Kleist Prize in 1923. At the same time it was immediately recognized as being difficult to stage. The humiliating flop of its only production during Musil's lifetime, in Berlin in 1929, was an immense disappointment to Musil. Musil never ceased to reflect upon the reasons for the misfortune of a text in which he had placed great hope.

Chapter 4

The second passage in the epigraph is taken from a draft of the last lecture Musil delivered in Vienna in 1937, titled "On Stupidity" (*P* 268–86). It is found in *Der literarische Nachlaß,* CD-ROM, eds. Friedbert Aspetsberger, Karl Eibl, and Adolf Frisé (Reinbek bei Hamburg: Rowohlt, 1992), iii/4/115, p. 3.

1. Neo-Kantianism encompassed various attempts at reviving Kant's transcendentalism, primarily in epistemology and ethics, between the 1880s and the 1950s. It arose as a response to the crisis of philosophical discourse unleashed by the collapse of Hegelianism in the German universities, which had proven unable to meet the challenges posed by the relativistic epistemological paradigm that

propelled the natural sciences after 1850. For a discussion of the impact of Neo-Kantianism on philosophy and cultural theory, see Klaus Köhnke, *The Rise of Neo-Kantianism: German Academic Philosophy between Idealism and Positivism,* 1986, trans. R. J. Hollingdale (Cambridge, U.K.: Cambridge University Press, 1991) and Thomas Willey, *Back to Kant: The Revival of Kantianism in German Social and Historical Thought, 1860–1914* (Detroit, Mich.: Wayne State University Press, 1978).

2. Unlike Kant, Musil never provided conclusive definitions for key terms like intellect or understanding (*Verstand*), reason (*Vernunft*), and feeling (*Gefühl*). He regarded these terms as heuristic categories and used them consistently but was not interested in defining their content or range of use once and for all, which would have amounted to yielding to what Nietzsche disparagingly called "the will to system." In reconstructing the Kantian subtext in Musil's reflection, I will follow his terminological practice, pointing to possible influences where appropriate.

3. This formulation is taken from Jürgen Habermas's *The Philosophical Discourse of Modernity,* in which it appears as a polemical reappropriation of the title of Hartmut's and Gernot's Böhme's study on the development of structures of rationality in Kant's age, *Das Andere der Vernunft: Zur Entwicklung von Rationalitätsstrukturen am Beispiel Kants* (Frankfurt a.M.: Suhrkamp, 1983). Musil seems to in many ways foreshadow Habermas's critique of an aesthetic discourse prone to rejecting rationality in the name of an irrational concept of art. At the same time, Musil would not and could not endorse the prescriptive impulse that sustains Habermas's notion of communicative rationality as the normative grounding of modernity. In fact, Musil's concept of reason does not allow for normative claims and remains more flexible and open ended, if less specific, than Habermas's.

4. Musil most certainly encountered Kantian philosophy at the latest during his Berlin studies. For a discussion of Musil's studies in Berlin, see Gesine Bey, "'Bei mir laudabile.' Zu Robert Musils Berliner Studienjahre," *Wissenschaftliche Zeitschrift der Humboldt Universität zu Berlin* 38.6 (1989): 655–66. See also Corino, *Robert Musil: Eine Biographie,* 219–34 and 309–17. Works on Kantian philosophy he consulted include *Klassiker der Philosophie,* edited by Richard Falckenberg, and Johannes E. Erdmann's *Entwicklung der deutschen Speculation seit Kant* (*TB* I, 75, II, 50). Early on, in a diary note from around 1918 to 1921, Musil voiced the need for a better grounding in the aesthetic of Kant: "the examination of Kantian aesthetic thus indispensable" (*TB* I, 455). A diary entry from around 1937 suggests that he never seriously engaged the tradition of philosophical aesthetics, in part because of his antipathy toward the reductive systematic thinking he associated with it. It is nevertheless notable that in this context he singled out the judgment of taste as an area which he thought deserved closer investigation: "But my life so far has lacked any confrontation with academic aesthetics, e.g., with the concept of judgments of taste" (*D* 452).

5. There are two main reasons for the relative neglect of Musil's debt to Kant in the scholarship. In the first place, if one combs Musil's erudite diaries and essays for direct references to Kant's philosophy or his texts, one will find that they are often brief and at times deceptively superficial. When compared to the lengthy passages Musil dedicated to other thinkers in his diaries, including Ellen Key, Thomas Mann, Ludwig Klages, and Edmund Husserl, and taking length as a gauge of intellectual engagement, one could conclude that Kant was not among his major influences. In addition, one must reckon with Musil's declared aversion to systematic philosophy, which found in Kant's transcendentalism one of its absolute high points. It seems that there could be little affinity between Musil and Kant, particularly when one considers Musil's critique of the misguided reception of Kant's ethics, which turned his ethical imperative in the legitimation of the Germans' obsequiousness to authority. See for instance Musil's abbreviated allusion to the deployment of Kantian terms as a means of legitimizing National Socialist totalitarianism in his excerpts from an essay by Wilhelm Sauer, which discusses the juridical and social fundaments of National Socialism (*TB* I, 853; II 636, note 143). At the same time, see also Musil's early plea for reading Kant correctly, that is, for properly contextualizing his philosophical enterprise (*D* 19). Thomas Söder's study of *Törless* provides an example of the ways in which Musil's references to the harmful reception of Kant within German culture have been misunderstood. Söder argues that Musil's first novel contains a repudiation of Kantian philosophy as the epitome of that Western will to system that marks the intellect's triumph over the imagination and forces reality into a reductive epistemological grid (see in particular his chapter "Kant aus der Sicht Robert Musils" in *Untersuchungen zu Robert Musils "Verwirrungen des Zöglings Törless,"* (Rheinfelden: Schäuble, 1988), 89–122. David Luft has offered a more nuanced reading of the role of Kantian philosophy in Musil's first novel, noting that Törless's rejection of Kant arises as a reaction to the "perfunctory acceptance of Kant or mathematics as complete reductions of reality" (39). Ulrich Karthaus's reflections on the affinities between Kant's and Musil's concepts of the imagination repropose the theme of a subordination of the imagination to the intellect, which dominated the early phases of Musil scholarship. Ulrich Karthaus, "Der Mann ohne Eigenschaften und die Phantasie. Überlegungen im Anschluß an Kant," *Musil–Forum* 7, (1981): 111–17. Christian Dawidowski traces Kantian resonances as he grounds Musil's aethetics in the primacy of desubjectivized perception and a postontological understanding of decentralized reason. Dawidowski's analysis is framed by the resurgent interest in an aesthetics of the sublime, which began with the postmodern debates, and focuses primarily on Musil's early fiction. Dawidowski, 186–215.

6. The fragment, from around 1921/22, is titled "The Writer and the Times" ("Der Dichter und diese Zeit") (*GW* 8, 1349–52).

7. The essay, "Books and Literature" ("Bücher und Literatur"), consists of two related segments published, respectively, in October and November/December 1926 (*GW* 8, 1160–80).

8. For Musil's belief in the central function of reading in the experience of literature, see also *D* 250: "Creative writing is not an activity but a condition. . . . Reading is transmission of this condition."

9. Musil's discussion of criticism recalls the early-Romantic idea of a literary process that is consigned to the endless work of criticism, which Walter Benjamin illustrated in his masterful study of Romanticism, *The Concept of Criticism in German Romanticism,* 1920, in *Selected Writings,* Vol. 1: 1913–1926, ed. Michael W. Jennings (Cambridge, Mass.: Harvard University Press, 1996), 116–200. As Benjamin shows, the Romantics' concept of criticism was indebted to the notion of reflection, which they productively adapted from the philosophy of idealism. It is important to point out that this idealistic framework is utterly missing in Musil's characterization of criticism. See in this context Musil's concise definition of art, which contains a clear disavowal of any type of systematic aesthetics: "Scientific aesthetics searches for the universal building block from which the edifice of aesthetics might be erected. But, for us, art is that which we come across under that name. Something that is simply there and that has no need of laws whatsoever, a complicated social product" (*D* 245).

10. In a diary entry dedicated to the nonratioid realm from around 1918–21, Musil specifies these different modes of observation by drawing on the polarity between causal determination and singular motivation (*D* 255–56). Whereas the scientist, in particular the psychologist, examines human behavior with the aim of determining general patterns and isolating a limited number of types based on causal explanations, the writer explores the singular entwinement of motives, reasons, and influences that move an individual to a certain act, his goal being not to explain it in a deterministic way but to find the unique grounds that account for situated human experience. Musil is here confronted with the difficulty of defining the singular events that underlie the nonratioid. As he observes, facts and experiences that are uniquely individual can nonetheless be inserted in statistical accounts or lend themselves to psychological generalizations. That is, they can be fitted in the domain of the ratioid, provided one leaves out some or all of the traits that make up their uniqueness. Precisely the exceeding dependence of the distinction ratioid/nonratioid on the given criteria of observation prompted Musil to rethink the polarity altogether by shifting the emphasis from the nature of the facts under observation to the observer's ability to consider a phenomenon from different angles. In pondering the idea of a "nonratioid method," Musil observed that "in principle, perhaps, there is no nonratioid realm at all; or, speaking more cautiously, we cannot imagine any. But there remains the difference in method or behavior" (*D* 255). The ratioid thus becomes identified with a procedure of observation that allows for assessing an object according to its suitability for integration in an abstract system of laws and regularities, whereas the nonratioid calls for emphasizing the object's factuality, that is, its constitutive individuality before any attempt at systematization (the "pre-logical," *D* 255). Musil finds his distinction

between causal and poetic confirmed in a 1914 study by psychologist Hugo Münsterberg, who was concerned with drawing a distinction between a causal and explanatory psychology on the one hand, and a hermeneutic, humanistic study of the psyche on the other. While the first type of inquiry seeks to objectivize experience, humanistic psychology endeavors to grasp it in its singularity. As Musil concludes, "the separation in categories of objects I performed is thus foreign to [Münsterberg]. I must take into consideration that it is not just a matter of ratioid or non-ratioid object, but that often what's at issue is simply the choice between ratioid and non-ratioid context!" (*TB* I, 521). Musil never came to a definitive characterization of the binary ratioid/nonratioid. Throughout Musil's writings these terms denote alternatively domains of experience, states of mind in the individual, or modes of thinking. Over time, this distinction was in part supplanted by the distinction between an "ordinary" and an "other" condition of the mind.

11. Béla Balázs, *Der sichtbare Mensch oder die Kultur des Films* (Wien: Deutsch-Österreichischer Verlag, 1924). For an in-depth discussion of Balázs's theory of cinema against the background of the "cinema debates" of the 1920s and in its significance for Musil's essay, see Arno Russegger, *Kinema Mundi. Studien zur Theorie des "Bildes" bei Robert Musil* (Vienna: Böhlau, 1996), 37–60. Musil's discussion in this essay revolves around silent film—in Germany the first sound feature movie, Fritz Lang's *M,* was released in 1929.

12. Musil is here careful not to endorse arguments of cultural pessimism. As he insists, the circumstance that art disrupts our formulaic modes of experience should not be understood as a condemnation of allegedly reified experience. Quite to the contrary, the tendency to master experience by forcing it into a preformed grid of interpretation is an essential requirement for coping with a complex world. That experience follows formulaic patterns should not be regarded as evidence for the degeneration of a more authentic experiential modality, as deplored within cultural-pessimistic and neomystical currents (*P* 200–1).

13. Lucien Lévy-Bruhl, *Les fonctions mentales dans les sociétés inférieures* (Paris: Alcan, 1910).

14. Musil developed his idea that a continuous dwelling in the Other Condition amounts to a psychological disorder by drawing on Ernst Kretschmer's investigation of the psychopathologies of feeling in *Medizinische Psychologie* (Leipzig: Thieme, 1922).

15. Kant himself employed the image of a missing bridge to describe this situation in *Critique of Judgment:*

> The realm of the natural concept under the one legislation and that of the concept of freedom under the other are entirely removed from all mutual influence which they might have on one another (each according to its fundamental laws) by the great gulf that separates the supersensible from phenomena. The concept

> of freedom determines nothing in respect of the theoretical cognition of nature, and the natural concept determines nothing in respect of the practical laws of freedom. So far, then, it is not possible to throw a bridge from the one realm to the other. (*CJ* 32)

Subsequent references to Kant's third *Critique* will likewise be indicated in parentheses by the abbreviation *CJ* followed by page number. All references are to Immanuel Kant, *Critique of Judgment,* trans. John Henry Bernard (New York: Hafner, 1951).

16. See especially the last section in Kant's final draft of the introduction to the *Critique of Judgment.* By presupposing a final purpose in nature, Kant argues, reflective judgment provides the mediating concept between nature and freedom, the sensible and the supersensible:

> The understanding, by the possibility of its *a priori* laws for nature, gives a proof that nature is only cognized by us as phenomenon and implies, at the same time, that it has a supersensible substrate, though it leaves this quite *undetermined.* The judgment, by its *a priori* principle for the judging of nature according to its possible particular laws, makes the supersensible substrate (both in us and without us) *determinable by means of the intellectual faculty.* But the reason, by its practical *a priori* law, *determines* it; and thus the judgment makes possible the transition from the realm of the natural concept to that of the concept of freedom. (*CJ* 33)

My understanding of Kant's notions of taste and judgment in this chapter is in part indebted to Paul Guyer's commentary of the third *Critique.* Unlike Guyer, however, I must take Kant's arguments at face value as the subtext for Musil's developing notions of taste and judgment. For this reason, some important aspects of Guyer's explication of the third *Critique,* for instance his discussion of discrepancies between Kant's notions of aesthetic response, taste, and reflective judgment, are not taken into account in this chapter. See especially "The Theory of Reflective Judgment," in Paul Guyer, *Kant and the Claims of Taste,* 1979, second edition (Cambridge/New York: Cambridge University Press, 1997), 29–59.

17. See in this regard Kant's characterization of judgment as a "middle term between the understanding and the reason" (*CJ* 13).

18. This line of inquiry reflects Musil's intensive engagement with Ludwig Klages's *About the Cosmogonic Eros* (*Vom kosmogonischen Eros*) (München: Georg Müller, 1922), a psychological-philosophical treatise on love Musil extensively excerpted in the early 1920s (*TB* I, 615–23). Klages's culture-critical study identifies in an erotic experience uncoupled from the sexual drive the source for an ecstatic condition of wholeness, which is predicated on shedding the shackles of consciousness and rationality and on embracing an intuitive form of thinking sustained by nongeneralizable images and analogies. It might seem odd that a paladin

of reason like Musil would draw on the work of a contested philosopher like Klages, which in many ways embodied the anti-intellectualism and cultural pessimism Musil abhorred. Yet Musil was intrigued by the description of ecstatic states of feeling in Klages's suggestive treatise and drew on it for his own investigation of the Other Condition. Klages was personally acquainted with Musil's close friend Gustav Donath and his wife, Alice. The triangle that arises among three central characters in the *MwQ,* namely, Walter, Clarisse, and Dr. Meingast, is in part modeled after the intricate relationship between Klages and the Donaths. On Klages's influence on Musil's articulation of the Other Condition, see Adolf Frisé's commentary in *TB* II, 419, note 371.

19. Musil's reference to a preconceptual or nonconceptual mode is not meant to evoke the standard opposition between rationality and the irrational. Rather Musil relies on a broad notion of 'concept' as the relatively stable structure which shapes not only mental but also emotional processes. The nonconceptual mode, then, consists in the temporary suspension of these structures. It is important to note that Musil's notion of the 'concept' is not restricted to intellectual functions. As he notes, not only our intellect but also our sensory perceptions must be regarded as intellectual, for they are guided by preformed expectations—based on generalizations from previous experience—that serve as guidelines for the evaluation and categorization of subsequent experience. Within this frame concepts provide the necessary molds for shaping and organizing all experience, including sensory perceptions. They represent generalizations and abstractions that enter an osmotic relation with the experiences they organize, for they are incessantly modified by the very experiences they help shape. Far from stifling feeling and impoverishing emotional life, concepts are for Musil key to forming elementary pictures of reality and therefore to providing an indispensable tool of orientation (*P* 201).

20. A late diary entry (most likely from after 1938) shows that Musil became eventually aware of the affinity between his understanding of aesthetic pleasure and Kant's: "My early rebellion against disinterested pleasure and its legitimacy after all?" (*TB* I, 777).

21. Adolf Frisé notes that the text was intended as a contribution to a collection of essays honoring the sixtieth birthday of Musil's long-time friend Franz Blei. The project was however never realized, and Musil submitted the text for publication in *Die Neue Rundschau.* The original pretext is however still discernible in the witty defense of the "literati" in the essay's initial section. Musil presumably had in mind a defense of the flamboyant Blei, who was generally viewed as an emblematic incarnation of the pernicious "literatus." The final draft of the essay does not make any direct reference to Blei, though, and soon loses sight of the polemics on the literati to engage a broad exploration of the processes involved in the making of the literary artwork. See Frisé's remarks in *GW* 9, 1825–26.

22. Gestalt psychology grew out of some insights in Mach's theory of perceptions, whose relativism it sought to counter. Its principal representatives, M. Wertheimer,

K. Koffka, and W. Köhler, drew on the model of perception advanced in the 1880s by Christian Ehrenfels in response to Mach's psychological model. While concurring with Mach's dispensation of metaphysical categories in the study of psychological processes, gestaltists disavowed Mach's radical atomism in perception and relativism in knowledge. Taking issue with Mach's claim that reality emerges from imposing an ultimately arbitrary grid of interpretation upon the essentially undifferentiated flux of experience, Ehrenfels argued that perceptions are not completely arbitrary, that is, irrational, but are rather structured according to relatively stable forms that predate the intervention of consciousness. In other words, perceptions organize themselves according to structures/relations that do not overlap completely with the sum of individual perceptions of which they are made. These totalities display an irreducible singular quality and thus do not completely allow for generalization and systematization. Musil's acquaintance with gestalt psychology and critical stance toward Mach go back to the influence of his main advisor in Berlin, the influential psychologist and philosopher Carl Stumpf. Stumpf was critical of Mach's epistemological premises and favored the methodologically more rigorous approach taken by gestalt psychology. Musil's fascination with this psychological model lay in its potential for formulating a theory of knowledge that would not treat reality as an entirely arbitrary construct but at the same time would acknowledge the singularity and situatedness of perception, restricting the role of the rational component and emphasizing the contribution of the emotional sphere. For a discussion of Musil's debt to gestaltist theories, see Silvia Bonacchi, *Die Gestalt der Dichtung: Der Einfluss der Gestalttheorie auf das Werk Robert Musils* (Bern: Peter Lang, 1998). See also Monti, 55–129. On the development and impact of gestalt psychology, see D. W. Hamlyn, *The Psychology of Perception: A Philosophical Examination of Gestalt Theory and Derivative Theories of Perception* (London: Routledge & Paul, 1957). See also Anne H. Harrington, *Reenchanted Science: Holism in German Culture from Wilhelm II to Hitler* (Princeton, N.J.: Princeton University Press, 1996).

23. For a recapitulation of Kant's argument in the "Deduction of Pure Aesthetical Judgments," see section 35 on taste as the subjective principle of judgment, in particular the following passage:

> . . . the judgment of taste must rest on a mere sensation of the reciprocal activity of the imagination in its *freedom* and the understanding with its *conformity to law.* It must therefore rest on a feeling, which makes us judge the object by the purposiveness of the representation (by which an object is given) in respect of the furtherance of the cognitive faculty in its free play. (*CJ* 129)

As Kant explains, the free play of imagination and intellect is what grounds reflective judgment. It denotes the type of judgment not guided by concepts but by reflection of the individual on his emotional state. This distinguishes the judgment of taste from a logical judgment, which instead entails subsuming the manifold content of the imagination under the unifying power of concepts for the production of knowledge.

24. The fragment is a draft for the preface of *Pre-Posthumous Notes (Nachlaß zu Lebzeiten),* a collection of short prose texts Musil published in 1936 (*GW* 7). For Musil's early formulations of exemplarity, see a diary entry from 1918–21, in which Musil identifies the essence or function of literature with this phrase: "Exempla docent. Teach through examples" (*TB* I, 489).

25. *TB* I, 940. The context for this passage is Kant's famous dictum, according to which "There is no science of the beautiful, but only a critique of it; and there is no such thing as beautiful science, but only beautiful art" (*CJ* 147). In the ensuing explanatory paraphrase, Musil draws on Kant's commentary, in section 34, on the scope of the critique of taste, which operates at the level of "art" when it provides empirical cases or examples, but necessarily moves to the level of "science" anytime it is called to spell out the conditions of possibility for taste as a faculty of knowledge (*CJ* 128). Around the same time Musil transcribed this same thought in a different notebook dedicated to gathering his ideas on literature:

> Kant on art: 33/106 (a new world in space and time)
> Art strives for the exemplary 33/107. (*TB* I, 779)

26. I am referring here to Meyer Abrams's famed thesis concerning the shift from Neo-Classicism to the aesthetics of Romanticism in *The Mirror and the Lamp: Romantic Theory and the Critical Tradition* (New York: Oxford University Press, 1953). Tzvetan Todorov has offered a compelling rereading of this thesis that highlights the issue of language as a medium of representation. As he argues, at the end of the eighteenth century the demand that language be made to conform to the poetic object in the process of imitation wound up exploding the rationalist categories of neoclassical poetics, giving rise to the self-referential understanding of art that marks early Romantic aesthetics in Germany. Tzvetan Todorov, *Theories of the Symbol,* 1977, trans. Catherine Porter (Ithaca, N.Y.: Cornell University Press, 1982).

27. This is because they are, on the one hand, accompanied by a pleasure that is imputable to everyone, as though it were objective, that is, triggered through a property of the object that elicited the judgment, and thus could be grasped by means of concepts, of a knowledge to be shared universally (*CJ,* §32). On the other hand, aesthetic judgments cannot be supported by rational proof, for they are utterly singular and thus do not allow for comparison. This is why Kant maintains that one can argue about taste, that is, agree or disagree over someone else's judgment; at the same time, one cannot dispute it, that is, cannot reason about taste by means of rational proof. As a result, it is not possible to articulate an objective principle of taste, which would provide the artist with conceptualizable guidelines for operation. This was the declared goal of the neoclassical poetics against which Kant polemicized. See the famous discussion of the antinomy of taste in *CJ,*

section 56 (183–84). For a detailed discussion of the relation between the notion of exemplarity and the antinomy just described, see section 32 of the third *Critique.* Kant's discussion of genius in section 46 ("Beautiful Art Is the Art of the Genius") sheds further light on his understanding of exemplarity. For a discussion of Kant's enterprise within the framework of contemporary philosophical disputes, see Frederick C. Beiser, *The Fate of Reason: German Philosophy from Kant to Fichte* (Cambridge, Mass.: Harvard University Press, 1987). An essay from 1922 witnesses to Musil's familiarity with Kant's arguments on the relation between genius and exemplarity. Musil enlists Kant's aid in addressing the phenomenon of generational style, by which he means the indiscriminate support for superficial trends he finds in the art's enthusiasts of his day:

> Kant says of the genius—which back then still meant the artist—that he produces 'exemplary' works, which inspire emulative following, and not imitation. The 'style generation' is always such a spiritual following; however not the sudden appearance of a new soul, but rather the flying over and dashing from all roofs of pigeons when someone stands on the empty square and scatters feed. (*GW* 7, 666)

28. Taste grounds a type of judgment that is called reflective, for it is not guided by a general concept under which particular experience could be subsumed but rather stems from the reflection of the subject on its own state as signaled by a feeling of pleasure or displeasure. In the production of knowledge, judgment proceeds in a manner that is primarily steered by concepts, the tool of orientation proper to understanding. In this mode of operation, which Kant calls determinant judgment, judgment presides over the subsumption of the sensory data of experience provided by the imagination under a priori concepts of the intellect. When a concept is not available, however, judgment is compelled to draw on a principle intrinsic to it, namely, taste, which is predicated upon the capacity of understanding and imagination to enter a free play that suspends the schematism of knowledge and instead elicits a specific feeling (*CJ* 129). See also section 40, "Of Taste as a Kind of Sensus Communis," *CJ* 135–38. Reflective judgment, more specifically the judgment of the beautiful in nature, is assigned a crucial role in Kant's critical framework, for it enables the subject to grasp the hint of God's comprehensive design for nature—not as conceptualizable knowledge but as a universally communicable feeling. The perception of nature's unfathomable purposiveness in aesthetic judgment serves as a temporary bridge between the otherwise incommensurable realms of theoretical and practical reason, nature and morality. This affords judgment its central place in the economy of the faculties and grounds the far-reaching ethical valence of taste as judgment's self-referential principle of orientation.

29. Jean-François Lyotard, *Lessons on the Analytic of the Sublime,* 1991, trans. Elisabeth Rottenberg (Stanford, Calif.: Stanford University Press, 1994), 31–32. Lyotard's broader argument in this analysis of Kant's third *Critique* involves a comparison between the experiences of the beautiful and the sublime for the subject,

though what really interests him is the experience of the sublime. As he argues, the sublime shatters the concordance intimated by the harmonious play of faculties in the judgment of the beautiful. This experience of disunity allows thought, quite paradoxically, to think (and not simply "feel") the absolute, which is the unpresentable truth of thought's self-referentiality and self-grounding. Kant's perhaps most accessible discussion of the issue of orientation is found in one of his popularizing essays, "What Is Orientation in Thinking?" ("Was heißt: sich im Denken orientieren?"), from 1786; in *Kant: Political Writings,* trans. H. B. Nisbet, ed. Hans Reiss (Cambridge, U.K.: Cambridge University Press, 1970).

30. Lyotard, *Lessons,* 43 and 89.

31. The publication of the first two parts of *The Man without Qualities* in 1930 had finally brought Musil the critical acclaim that had eluded him since his first novel. In Berlin he hoped to work out an arrangement with his editor Rowohlt that would grant him a livelihood during the time necessary to complete the novel. The establishment of the National Socialist dictatorship quickly undermined his recent success, as the National Socialists acquired control of the cultural market and proceeded to purge the once vibrant cultural scene of the Weimar Republic of the works of undesirable intellectuals and writers.

32. Along similar lines, see Musil's comments on the intellectual and spiritual climate that set the scene for National Socialism in *MoE* II, 1860.

33. See Rogowski's discussion of Musil's apolitical declarations in *Distinguished Outsider,* 16.

34. Musil's most explicit stance on National Socialism is found in an essay fragment from 1933, "Ruminations of a Slow-witted Mind," written as an immediate response to the Nazi's seizure of power (*P* 214–34). It was meant for publication in *Die Neue Rundschau,* but was never printed, probably due to the rapid deterioration of the political situation in Germany. Among the essays that explore the relation between literature and politics, see the acclaimed speech "The Serious Writer in Our Time," which Musil delivered in December 1934 at the Austrian Society for the Protection of German Writers (*P* 250–64). Musil's appeal for safeguarding culture's autonomy from politics, which he presented in a speech given at the antifascist congress for the Defense of Culture in Paris (in 1935), proved far more controversial. For Musil's stance on political engagement in the 1930s, see Dieter Schiller, "'Die Grenze der Kultur gegen die Politik.' Zu Robert Musils Rede auf dem Pariser Kongreß 1935 (mit Dokumenten)," *Zeitschrift für Germanistik* 3 (1988): 274–90; Bernd Hüppauf, "Musil in Paris. Robert Musils Rede auf dem Kongreß zur Verteidigung der Kultur (1935) im Zusammenhang seines Werkes," *Zeitschrift für Germanistik* I:1 (1991): 55–69; and Patrizia C. McBride, "On the Utility of Art for Politics: Musil's 'Armed Truce of Ideas,'" *The German Quarterly* (Fall 2000): 366–86.

35. In Musil's usage the term "Germans" generally denotes the German-speaking population in both the Weimar and the Austrian Republics, whom he saw as sharing a common cultural tradition.

36. The German formulation here carries an unmistakable Kantian resonance: "zwecklos, ja zweckwidrig" (*GW* 8, 1282).

37. The German formulation for "insufficient play of harmony" strongly evokes Kant: "ein ungenügendes Zusammenspiel" (*GW* 8, 1287).

38. In "The Politics of Stupidity: Musil, *Dasein,* the Attack on Women, and My Fatigue," in *Stupidity* (Urbana: University of Illinois Press, 2002), 61–93, Avital Ronell argues that Musil shrewdly describes fundamental aspects of the experience of stupidity, yet winds up dodging its political and ethical implications, while redirecting his discourse in ways that exhibit his presumed contempt for women. Ronell's discussion of Musil's essay presents itself as a singular experience of reading framed by Ronell's own oppressive/depressing awareness that one's own stupidity is possibly always on the lure. This awareness arises at the ambiguous junction between the stupefying experience of the limits of thinking, on the one hand, and the experienced violence of disciplinary and professional subjugation, on the other.

39. Musil's belief that bolshevism raised a totalizing claim not dissimilar to that of fascism brought upon him the wrath of the antifascist intellectuals who attended his speech at the 1935 Congress for the Defense of Culture in Paris. See Schiller, 277.

40. This is the meaning of Musil's statement in the diaries, according to which "What the poem is about is that which can only be expressed in the poem" (*D* 244).

Chapter 5

1. In her analysis of the symptoms of cultural crisis that pervaded the intellectual debates in the Weimar Republic, Dagmar Barnouw presents the problematic relation between these two 'trees of experience' as one of the central, though often misrecognized and misrepresented, issues: "What Ulrich and his author experience in Vienna in 1913 is the same failure to balance emotional and intellectual energies, to mediate between logically-empirically and emotionally directed thought—'empirischem Denken und Gefühlsdenken'—that helped to bring about the collapse of the Weimar Republic." Barnouw, 92.

2. For an insightful comparison between Musil's and Weber's understanding of the relation between the scientific and nonscientific mode of approaching experience, see Barnouw, 84–86.

3. Karl Heinz Bohrer focuses on the Other Condition as the representation of a radically contracted aesthetic utopia. Because in modernity it is no longer possible to articulate a utopian vision within ordinary temporal structures, utopian thinking becomes confined to the hollow—that is, devoid of content—space of aesthetic illuminations. Karl Heinz Bohrer, *Suddenness: On the Moment of Aesthetic Appearance,* 1981, trans. Ruth Crowley (New York: Columbia University Press, 1996), 197–203 and 218–33. Roger Willemsen has seen in the ecstatic illuminations at the heart of the Other Condition the epitome of an utterly 'other' aesthetic

space from which the inauthentic social order can be critiqued, that is, a last site of resistance against the cooptation of ubiquitous power. Roger Willemsen, *Robert Musil. Vom intellektuellen Eros* (München: Piper, 1985), 158. Both critics—though Bohrer more so than Willemsen—focus their attention on the Other Condition, which they do not examine in relation to the aesthetic utopias illustrated in the first part of the novel. See also Ulf Eisele's thesis that the novel is primarily about the conditions of possibility of literature in modernity, indeed, about the very impossibility of the literary project, in "Ulrich's Mutter ist *doch* ein Tintenfaß. Zur Literaturproblematik in Musils 'Mann ohne Eigenschaften,'" in *Robert Musil,* ed. Renate von Heydebrand (Darmstadt: Wissenschaftliche Buchgesellschaft, 1982), 160–203, here 192–93.

4. Albrecht Classen emphasizes the anticipatory character of the novel's first volume, which in his eyes prepares the utopian fusion of rationality and the nonrational at the heart of the utopia of the Other Condition; "Robert Musil, *Der Mann ohne Eigenschaften:* Der antizipatorische Charakter des ersten Buches," *Carleton Germanic Papers* 15 (1987): 1–16. For a similar reading that establishes the novel's continuity by seeing in the love between the siblings of part two the culmination of part one, see Philip Beard, "'Beginn einer Reihe wundersamer Erlebnisse': Prüfstein einer Umwandlung in Musils Gebrauch von Essayismus und Ironie," in *Robert Musil: Essayismus und Ironie,* ed. Gudrun Brokoph-Mauch (Tübingen: Francke, 1992), 105–14.

5. The novel's projected ending became the object of contentious debates in the early phases of Musil reception. A vicious controversy was spurred by the fierce attack launched by the novel's English translators, Ernst Kaiser and Eithne Wilkins, against the first comprehensive edition of *MwQ,* published in 1952 by Adolf Frisé. Frisé was a young writer and admirer of Musil who had come in contact with his widow in 1947. Upon Martha Musil's death in 1949, he was entrusted with the task of editing Musil's works. Being among only a handful of critics to be granted access to Musil's unpublished papers in the early 1950s, Kaiser and Wilkins unmercifully pointed to the flaws in Frisé's edition. To be sure, Frisé was ill prepared to tackle the maze of papers which made up Musil's *Nachlaß,* for he lacked training in the methodology of critical editorship. However, he also never claimed to have produced a definitive critical edition of *MwQ*. The hastiness of his enterprise was motivated by his desire to see the novel in print soon. Christian Rogowski suggests that Wilkins and Kaiser's attack was driven by their objective to discredit what they saw as Frisé's personal version of *MwQ*. In their eyes, the editor's willful arrangement of the novel's final chapters suggested a narrative solution Musil had discarded in his mature years. At the same time, Wilkins and Kaiser's claim that Musil leaned toward a positive outcome of the siblings' mystical adventure appears impossible to sustain in view of the previously unpublished materials that have become accessible today. Their thesis that the siblings' narrative was to culminate in an exalted mystical union devoid of any sexual content is today discredited,

having been shown to be the result of a methodologically flawed textual approach, which, ironically, is not dissimilar to the approach for which they censured Frisé's edition. The doubts surrounding Frisé's editorial practices, along with the divisive atmosphere produced by the dispute, contributed to poison the discussion around the novel's ending and overall structure to such an extent that several critics sought to avoid being dragged into what appeared to be a sectarian struggle by focusing their attention on individual themes or aspects and therefore refraining from attempting a comprehensive interpretation of the novel. For an assessment of the way in which this dispute affected especially the early phases of Musil scholarship, see Rogowski, 26–29. Thanks to the publication of Frisé's revised edition in 1978 and of the CD-ROM edition of Musil's unpublished papers in 1992, the difficulties linked to problematic editorial choices and an unmanageable literary estate are today dispelled. Musil's literary estate primarily comprises the drafts, sketches, and studies from different phases of composition and at various stages of completion, which Musil chose to take along to his Swiss exile. Regrettably, the materials Musil left behind in his Vienna apartment went missing during World War II. Rogowski, 57.

6. Wolfdietrich Rasch persuasively argues that Musil planned to represent positively Ulrich's "final situation" after the collapse of the utopia of the Other Condition; Rasch, 404–5. A decisive piece of evidence in this regard is found in an interview with Oskar Maurus Fontana from 1926, in which Musil asserts that the collapse of Ulrich's final adventure with his sister Agathe was to be followed by an espionage episode (*GW* 7, 939–42). This was to contain an omen for the impending war, for the narration was to end with the breakdown of the old order in the devastations of World War I. When asked if such an apocalyptic ending should be seen as bearing a gloomy prophecy for the present, Musil responded, with a wry allusion to Spengler's philosophy of history, that he wished his work would be read not as yet another example of those "declines of the West" that were so popular in his time but rather as a parody of one. Precisely the parodistic character of the final apocalypse was to contain the novel's positive message, as it were: "We need . . . a new morality. We cannot get by on the old one. My novel offers material for such a morality. It is an attempt at clearing the slate and the intimation of a synthesis" (*GW* 7, 942). After narrating the siblings' failure to 'seize' the Other Condition, Musil intended to portray the last session of the Parallel Campaign as clearly foreshadowing the outbreak of the war. Several notes from around 1932 testify to Musil's intention to drop the espionage subplot from the narration for the purpose, as he himself stated, of letting the outbreak of the war emerge more directly from the collapse of the utopia of the Other Condition ("Chapter sequence: drop or greatly shorten the chapters 'spying' and 'Agathe-men,' so that the war develops out directly from the negative Other-Condition attempt"; *MoE* II, 1856); see also analogous remarks from around 1929 and 1932, respectively, in *MoE* II, 1837 and 1851. Around 1932, most likely on the occasion of the publication of the first

installment of the second volume, Musil found himself pondering the narration's need for coherence and closure. In recapitulating the "fundamental idea" of the novel's second part, he alluded to plans to dramatize the failure of Ulrich's utopia with Agathe during a trip to Italy—indeed, a symbolic journey into the Other Condition:

> *Fundamental idea:* . . . What had been analyzed must somehow be summarized. . . . This coincides with Ulrich having in any event to build his life anew after the journey with Agathe, during which the "reserve idea" of his life has collapsed. So the connection to the ideas of Volume One and their new context is indicated from his point of view also. This, whatever may happen in between, is the content of the second half. (*MwQ* II, 1746–47)

The trip alluded to in this passage may be a variation of the famous fragment "Journey into Paradise" from the mid-1920s, which recounts the consummation of the siblings' erotic union during a trip to Italy (*MwQ* II, 1450–74). This journey was to usher in the definitive collapse of their adventure. Ulrich's need to rebuild his life after this failure was to give the author a chance to return to and summarize the ideas of the first volume, pointing to the continuity between the two and illustrating the kind of ethos viable in modernity. The idea of a failed journey into a mystical condition still dominates a group of notes drafted between 1934 and 1938. They appear to be remarkably consistent with Musil's early plans (see his 1926 interview with Fontana) and focus on the siblings' mystical journey into "the Millennium." This journey was to represent both the climax and the liquidation of the related utopias of the Other Condition and of "life in love." This latter utopian vision is alternatively defined as "the utopia of motivated life" (*MoE* II; 1925). As Musil notes, "The journey into the Millennium places the other two utopias in the foreground and disposes of them as much as possible" (*MwQ* II, 1753). All these sketches date to the years 1932/33–1941. Along these lines one reads in a related note: "The utopia of motivated life and the utopia of the Other Condition are disposed of beginning with the diary-chapters. What remains—in reversing the sequence—is the utopia of inductive thinking, that is, of real life! The book closes with it" (*MoE* II, 1887). The "utopia of inductive thinking"—the only utopia grounded in real life—was to bear the novel's positive contribution to the reorientation called for in the postwar years: "And here an attempt at a solution is intimated, which is different and more real than that of the Other Condition. *Summarize as that of inductive thinking*" (*MoE* II, 1877; note dates from after 1934). Other notes document Musil's desire to present the utopia of inductive thinking as the novel's constructive contribution. A note from around 1932 reads: "The utopia of the Other Condition is replaced by that of the inductive way of thinking" (*MwQ* II, 1749); and again: "The utopia of the Other Condition will be later replaced by that of inductive thinking" (written between 1930 and 1938/39; *MoE* II, 1907). Several remarks in Musil's notes suggest that this utopia was to incorporate some traits of the utopian visions that inform the first volume (the related utopias of exactness and essayism). The collapse of the siblings' mystical adventure is also mentioned in an extended outline for the closing session of the Parallel Campaign. While this sketch is not dated in Frisé's edition (*MoE* II, 1932–35), the CD-ROM edition of the *Nachlaß* situates it between 1935 and 1937 (*Nachlaß*, Mappe II/7/119).

7. See chapters 34–38 in the novel's second volume, which portray the gradual development of the Parallel Campaign from a peaceful enterprise into the breeding ground for those ideologies and initiatives that will lead to World War I. These chapters represent the last of the thirty-eight new chapters Musil included in the second edition of the novel, published in 1932/33. Some notes from the 1930s indicate that Musil planned for the war to be a stage for Ulrich's suicidal plans at the end of the narrative. See the section of the *Nachlaß* entitled "Concluding Portion" (presumably drafted after 1934): "The Parallel Campaign leads to war! . . . Ulrich at the end: knowing, working, being effective without illusions. Final result of the utopia of inductive thinking. He feels it, but does not dodge the mobilization" (*MwQ* II, 1755–56; the last two sentences are my translation from *MoE* II, 1902). A remark at the end of this long outline exemplifies the connection between Ulrich's involvement in the mobilization and his suicidal plans: "To write a book, hence suicide, hence to participate in the war" (*MoE* II, 1904). That Musil planned to narrate the suicide of his antihero is hardly surprising when one considers that in his notes Ulrich and Agathe are portrayed as the representatives of a human type rooted in a bygone era, indeed, that very age that was swept away by the war. As the hero of a past age, Ulrich chooses to go under with the world to which he belongs. A sketch entitled "Ulrich's Afterword, Conclusion," from January 1942, a few months before Musil's death, suggests somewhat different plans. Here Musil toys with the idea of an aged Ulrich who provides an epilog for his story, and thus, for the novel itself, from the perspective of his experience in World War II. This was to be a stratagem for spelling out the connection between the time at which Musil was writing (the Second World War) and the prewar past. This planned closing does not alter Musil's plan to stage the failure of the Other Condition (*MwQ* II, 1769–70). For a thoroughly documented discussion of Musil's plans for the novel's ending, see Walter Fanta, *Die Entstehungsgeschichte des "Mann ohne Eigenschaften" von Robert Musil* (Wien: Böhlau, 2000), 468–69 and 530–32.

8. Commentators have disagreed on how to evaluate the import of the protagonist's final fiasco within the economy of the narration. Some have interpreted the foreshadowed failure of Ulrich and Agathe's mystical enterprise as a cipher for the collapse of Musil's own aesthetic project in the novel. See for instance Duncan Large, "Experimenting with Experience: Robert Musil, *Der Mann ohne Eigenschaften,* " in *The German Novel in the 20th Century,* ed. David Midgley (Edinburgh: Edinburgh University Press, 1993), 125–26. Large sees Musil's failure as inscribed in the myriads of drafts and fragments in which the narration dissipates.

Drawing on Musil's understanding of literature as endless reflection, some critics have argued that the novel was destined to remain incomplete from the onset. See for instance Hans Jost Frey, "Musils Essayismus," in *Der unendliche Text* (Frankfurt a.M.: Suhrkamp, 1990), 256–61, and Peter V. Zima, "Robert Musils Sprachkritik. Ambivalenz, Polyphonie und Dekonstruktion," in *Robert Musil: Theater, Bildung, Kritik,* eds. Josef Strutz and Johann Strutz (München: Fink, 1985), 200–2. As the thesis goes, an ending would be at odds with the experimental and open-ended quality of the reflection the novel enacts. To be sure, incompleteness qualifies the specific kind of reflection that drives the narrative—as consigned to the perspectival movement of essayism and the clash of voices and standpoints it stages, as well as to the tapestry of characters and stories the novel weaves together. The presence of an ending to the narration would not, however, have detracted from this structural open-endedness.

9. See Bakhtin's analysis of polyphony and heteroglossia in "Discourse in the Novel," 1934, *The Dialogical Imagination: Four Essays,* ed. Michael Holquist, trans. Caryl Emerson and Michael Holquist (Austin: University of Texas Press, 1981), 259–422.

10. In this regard, see Maurice Blanchot's compelling discussion of irony as the device for decentering narrative perspective in the novel in *Le livre a venir* (Paris: Gallimard, 1959), 172–73. Along similar lines, see Theodor W. Adorno's examination of the medium of reflection in Musil's novel. By undermining the pure immanence of the novel's form, Adorno argues, reflection shatters the illusionary character of the narration, thereby undermining its monological claim to reality, as it were. Theodor W. Adorno, "Standort des Erzählers im zeitgenössischen Roman," 1954, *Noten zur Literatur, Gesammelte Schriften* 11, ed. Rolf Tiedemann (Frankfurt a.M.: Suhrkamp, 1974), 41–48, here 45.

11. The claim about the novel's nihilistic horizon is found in Zima, 195–96. It is persuasively countered in Finlay, 129–34.

12. Considering the clash of perspectives staged in the novel from the formal viewpoint of heteroglossia helps address the intricate issue of Musil's authorial relation to the novel. It is undeniable that the character of the man without qualities is to a degree the product of the author's narcissistic self-stylization, for Musil attributed Ulrich with a number of physical, psychological, and intellectual traits he either possessed or would have liked to possess. See, for instance, what critics consider to be the novel's earliest drafts, from around 1902; quite tellingly, the protagonists here are Robert and Gustl, Musil's childhood friend (*D* 25–35). By granting insight into the tangle of rivaling perspectives and discourses that make up the narration, the notions of polyphony and heteroglossia help the reader orient himself or herself in the novel's ideological labyrinth while circumventing the simplistic association of one character or stance with the "author's." To be sure, one can recognize in the novel the physiognomy of the project outlined by the comparatively uniform voice that drives reflection in the essays, and that I have attributed

to Musil. In the novel itself, however, there is no single character or perspective, not even the protagonist's, which can be regarded as the sole or privileged harbinger of the project sketched in the essays.

13. Compare, for instance, the diagnosis of the exhilarating years preceding the outbreak of the war offered in the essay "Helpless Europe" (*P* 116–33) and in the novel's introductory sections, especially 15 and 16. They touch upon many of the same issues, for instance, the contradictory cultural trends that defined the quest for meaning in the years before the war, the loss of a unified horizon of meaning, and the perception of modern life as accelerated and disjointed. In the essay these issues are discussed by a largely consistent voice that calls for the need to accept and cope with the new situation. By contrast the discussion in the novel is far more diffused. The issues at stake are refracted through Ulrich's personal experiences and are further mediated by the unintrusive voice of an ironic narrator who possesses a high degree of omniscience and smoothly trades positions inside and outside the characters' consciousness. On the novel's relation to the essays, see Musil's self-critical statement in a letter to Johannes von Allesch (from 1927): "Moreover fear of my old essays. I have now read through what immediately goes along [with the novel]. I don't agree with specific details, but in general I was actually pleasantly surprised: the pieces sound quite contemporary in spite of their age. Which is very important, because the longer essays draw on the same circle of ideas as the novel. They repeat each other in part and in the novel I repeat some things again; but I suddenly have the feeling that it doesn't hurt." Quoted in Marie-Louise Roth, *Robert Musil. Ethik und Ästhetik. Zum theoretischen Werk des Dichters* (München: List, 1972), 16. My translation.

14. See also Musil's remark in "Exposition of Volume Two of *The Man without Qualities*": "Above all, there is a continuity in that volume that permits the present period to be already grasped in the past one" (*MwQ* II, 1745).

15. This explains the novel's focus on the war, as articulated in some notes from the same time (1932): "The immanent depiction of the period that led to the catastrophe must be the real substance of the story, the context to which it can always retreat as well as the thought that is implicit in everything" (*MwQ* II, 1748).

16. The translation by Sophie Wilkins renders the phrase *Seinesgleichen geschieht* as "Pseudoreality Prevails." I offer a more literal rendering of the German, which to me is more in keeping with Musil's own understanding of this phrase:

> Note the title of the major portion of the first volume: [*Seinesgleichen geschieht.*] This means that in general today the personal givens of events are definite and delineated, but that what is general about them, or their significance, is indefinite, faded, and equivocal, and repeats itself unintelligibly. The person awakened to awareness of the current situation has the feeling that the same things are happening to him over and over again, without there being

a light to guide him out of this disorderly circle. I believe that this characterizes a major idea of the first volume, around which large parts of the material could be ordered. (*MwQ* II, 1745)

Musil stresses here the sense of alienation produced by the occurrence of events that lack a definite meaning and thus give the impression of the same thing happening over and over again. The term "pseudoreality" chosen by Wilkins implies an opposition between authentic and inauthentic reality that is not entailed in the German formulation.

17. Musil published an installment of the second volume in 1932–33 in an effort to keep the readers' interest alive after the success of the first volume. After his relocation to Vienna in 1933, his work on the novel was hampered by continued financial difficulties and worsening health. Austria's annexation to Germany in 1938 forced the Musils to find refuge in Switzerland, first in Zurich and then in Geneva, where Musil's work continued at an even slower pace.

18. For a discussion of the notion of "lack of qualities" (*Eigenschaftslosigkeit*) and an overview of the different layers of meaning it assumes in the novel, see Thomas Rentsch, "Wie ist ein Mann ohne Eigenschaften überhaupt möglich? Philosophische Bemerkungen zu Musil," in *Paradigmen der Moderne,* ed. Helmut Bachmaier (Amsterdam: Benjamins, 1990), 49–76.

19. Musil's portrayal of Ulrich's quandary recalls Max Weber's claim, in "Science as a Vocation" (1917), that science cannot have any inherent goal or meaning. To turn the logic of scientific reflection into an ethos, Weber maintains, means to disregard the modern differentiation of spheres of experience. From Max Weber, 143–47.

20. In examining the utopian "sense of possibility" the novel proposes, Michael Jakob suggests that Ulrich's vision must be read as a metacommentary on the potentialities of the literary medium (15). However, Jakob does not go so far as to read the whole tale that makes up the novel as a statement on the possibilities and bounds of art in modernity. Michael Jakob, "'Möglichkeitssinn' und Philosophie der Möglichkeit," in *Robert Musil: Essayismus und Ironie,* ed. Gudrun Brokoph-Mauch (Tübingen: Francke, 1992), 15.

21. As Musil himself wrote around 1929: "Thus *a main theme* for the whole is: confrontation of the man of possibilities with reality" (*MoE* II, 1881).

22. See Leinsdorf's ruminations in chapter 21 of volume 1.

23. See chapter 2 for my discussion of Musil's confrontation with Rathenau in an early essay from 1914, "Commentary on a Metapsychic" (*P* 54–58).

24. Compare the novel's characterization of Arnheim's experience of love as a transfiguration of ordinary reality and erasure of the boundary between self and the world (*MwQ* I, 418–19).

25. As the reader discovers at the end of the first volume, ulterior motives induced Arnheim to infiltrate the initiative. For all his purported fascination with

glorious Austrian culture and his platonic infatuation with Diotima, Arnheim is intent on exploiting the connections established in Diotima's salon to pursue a lucrative deal involving some coveted oil fields in Galicia.

26. Harrison, 68.

27. See, respectively, chapters 21 and 85 in volume 1.

28. As foreshadowed by the narration, the war appears as a last, ominous stratagem through which the Campaign's organizers seek to deflect attention from the bankruptcy of their initiative. By drawing on empty 'calls to action' (*MwQ* II, 882–83) the Campaign organizers hope to conceal their initiative's failure especially from hostile sectors of public opinion. Both the German nationalists and their Slavic counterparts suspect the Campaign to be a ruse to help their enemies to a breakthrough.

29. Essayism is a well-investigated aspect of Musil's novel both in regard to its narratological implications and to the prominent role it plays as Ulrich's utopian vision in the novel's first section. To my knowledge, only Ulf Eisele has discussed its connection to Ulrich's program of a 'literary existence' articulated at various points in the narration; Eisele 160–203. Hans Jost Frey has perceptively articulated the tensions inherent in the fluidity and simultaneous need for formal closure of the essayistic perspective; Frey, 230–61. See also Harrison's discussion of essayism as a principle structuring Musil's narration, 148–88. For a discussion of Musil's essayism against the background of the Western essayistic tradition, see Geoffrey Howes, "Ein Genre ohne Eigenschaften: Musil, Montaigne, Sterne und die essayistische Tradition," in *Robert Musil: Essayismus und Ironie,* ed. Gudrun Brokoph-Mauch (Tübingen: Francke, 1992), 1–11, and Dietmar Goltschnigg, "Zur Poetik des Essays und des Essayismus bei Robert Musil und Hermann Broch," in *Poetik und Geschichte,* ed. Dieter Borchmeyer (Tübingen: Niemeyer, 1989), 412–24.

30. See the parallels to Musil's treatment of the Other Condition in the essays, especially "Toward a New Aesthetic" (*P* 201–2) and "The German as a Symptom" (*P* 187–92). Essayism forms the counterpart to Musil's notion of aesthetic imagination. The essay, the narrator maintains, inhabits a space "between religion and knowledge, between example and doctrine" (*MwQ* I, 273), which is also the domain of aesthetic cognition. Hence essayism corresponds to the ideal of an aesthetic imagination that incessantly devises new models for being human, which remain exemplary even as they uphold the utter singularity of experience.

31. In this regard, see Friedrich Schlegel's programmatic *Gespräch über die Poesie* in *Kritische Friedrich-Schlegel Ausgabe,* vol. 2, ed. Ernst Behler (München: Schöningh, 1967), especially the idea of a new mythology as "das künstlichste aller Kunstwerke" (312) advanced by the character impersonating the philosopher Schelling and the program outlined for the modern novel in "Brief über den Roman" (329–39) by the character who represents a spokesperson for Schlegel himself.

32. Compare Peter Bürger's thesis in *Theory of the Avant-Garde,* trans. Michael Shaw (Minneapolis: University of Minnesota Press, 1984). According to Bürger,

the historical avant-garde sought to lead art back into life as a result of its rejection of art's autonomous status and lack of social impact in the modern period.

33. Significantly, it is the problematic Nietzscheanism of Clarisse, Ulrich's childhood friend, that helps bring into sharper relief the flawed utopian visions articulated by the man without qualities. Clarisse finds in Nietzsche's thought the path for a gradual descent into the unhealthy spell of lyrical moods and exalted visions. These produce increasingly deluded, indeed demented, plans—for instance, to free the sexual murderer Moosbrugger, in which she sees the obscure anticipation of the unbounded humanity announced by Nietzsche; or to give birth to the redeemer of humankind, for which she plans to seduce Ulrich himself. Clarisse's visions are driven by longing to eradicate ordinary existence and replace it with a redeemed, alternative world. Their apocalyptic and messianic character forms a strident contrast to the historical reality of the Habsburg monarchy in the year preceding the Great War. In many ways Clarisse's undertakings provide a distorted mirror for Ulrich's utopias, casting a disturbing light on his conceptually weightier, if no less unreal, visions.

34. From this point on various events contribute to precipitating Ulrich's crisis. After a traumatic sexual encounter with Gerda, the daughter of the bank director Leo Fischel (chapter 119), Ulrich has an equally unsettling conversation with his antagonist Arnheim, who, also attracted to and repelled by Ulrich, forces him to confront the menacing consequences of his visions (chapter 121).

35. In what was meant to be a comprehensive outline for the novel's second volume, Musil summarized its central theme as follows: ". . . the major problem of the second volume is the search for what is definitely signified, or to use another expression, the search for the ethically complete action or, as I might call it ironically, the search for 100 percent being and acting" (*MwQ* II, 1745–46). The phrases "ethically complete action" and "hundred-percent being and acting" capture Ulrich's demand that existence unfold within an all-encompassing ethical framework and that human conduct be entirely grounded in this horizon.

36. The affinity between the siblings is symbolically underscored already on their first encounter, on which they wear similar house robes. This makes them look like twins in spite of their age difference. Upon seeing his sister for the second time, Ulrich is overcome by the idea "that his sister was a dreamlike repetition and variant of himself" (*MwQ* II, 754).

37. A brief dreamlike experience of love with her first, prematurely deceased husband only contributes to deepening Agathe's self-hatred, inducing her to marry the pompous pedagogue Hagauer in a pointedly masochistic act. The death of her father and the encounter with her estranged brother shake her from her lethargy, prompting her to break loose from her husband. For Agathe's self-denigration and suicidal fantasies, see chapter 21 in volume 2, "Cast all thou hast into the fire, even unto thy shoes."

38. As though Ulrich's reflections had freed her from her last inhibitions, Agathe engages in conduct that appears improper from a conventional standpoint.

For instance she exchanges the medals on her father's breast, in patent violation of the old man's directives, and secretly places one of her garters into his casket as a last, unseemly keepsake. She also refuses to grant her husband an explanation for her abrupt decision to abandon him. When she decides to forge her father's will in order to prevent her husband from claiming part of her inheritance, she crosses a line Ulrich is unable to define. The man without qualities is forced to acknowledge that his sister's behavior displays an erratic quality that makes it appear frankly wrong. Cf. the following chapters of the second volume: Chapter 5, "They do wrong"; Chapter 6, "The old gentleman is finally left in peace"; Chapter 15, "The testament."

39. For a detailed description of this condition, see chapter 12, "Holy discourse: Erratic progress."

40. "Toward a New Aesthetic" (*P* 193–208).

41. Ulrich unequivocally portrays this condition as an aberration: "I'd have to say, rather, that being 'at the inner core' of things, in a state of unmarred 'inwardness'. . . is apparently not a demand that can be satisfied by rational thinking. . . . Human nature is probably averse to it . . . all we really know is that we feel a painful need for it!" (*MwQ* II, 985).

42. These developments involve the following "galley" chapters: Chapter 45, "Beginning of a series of wondrous experiences"; Chapter 46, "Moonbeams by sunlight"; and Chapter 47, "Wanderings among people."

43. Compare the characterization of Arnheim's falling in love with Diotima in the first volume. Here "soul," the elusive core of the individual, is defined as "this half that is always missing even when everything is a whole" (*MwQ* I, 196). In this respect love appears as the force that can fill the gap called 'soul': "Only love has a special position in this; in this exceptional case the missing half grows back: the beloved seems to stand where ordinarily something was always missing" (*MwQ* I, 197).

44. Pure love is a sentiment devoid of both "moral conviction" and "sensual desire" (*MoE* II, 1217) that announces itself in the yearning for "love without a partner" or "without sex" (*MwQ* II, 952). That is, it represents the possibility of a relation to the beloved object that is not informed by the interest sustained by lust, desire, or moral considerations. In it one can easily recognize the main traits of the Other Condition as discussed in Musil's film essay (*P* 193–208).

45. Agathe addresses precisely this paradox as she expresses the wish that her brother would explicitly state his feelings toward her: "How fine it would be if he would only say: 'I want to love you as myself, and I can love you that way better than any other woman because you are my sister!'" (*MwQ* II, 1150).

46. Hörisch discusses this mechanism of reflection within the framework of social role playing. His analysis revolves around a parallel between Ulrich and Agathe and Julius and Lucinde in Friedrich Schlegel's *Lucinde.* Jochen Hörisch, "Selbstbeziehung und ästhetische Autonomie. Versuch über ein Thema der

frühromantischen Poetologie und Musils *Mann ohne Eigenschaften,*" *Euphorion* 69 (1975): 350–61, here 356.

47. In exploring Musil's indebtedness to early Romanticism, Manfred Frank points to parallels in Novalis's notions of love and of a higher self, concluding that the unity promised by the siblings' love is ultimately the unity of the subject of Western metaphysics. Frank thereby assumes that the novel's references to early Romanticism authorize the conclusion that Musil shared the same ideological horizon as the Romantics. To be sure, Musil drew on early Romantic tropes in his portrayal of the siblings' relation. Yet his understanding of subjectivity and selfhood is not framed by the metaphysical premises of idealism but rather by his studies in experimental psychology. Manfred Frank, "Auf der Suche nach einem Grund. Über den Umschlag von Erkenntniskritik in Mythologie bei Musil," in *Mythos und Moderne,* ed. Karl Heinz Bohrer (Frankfurt a.M.: Suhrkamp, 1983), 318–62, here 332–36. For a discussion of Musil's debt to the Romantics, see also Klaus Laermann, *Eigenschaftslosigkeit: Reflexionen zu Musils Roman "Der Mann ohne Eigenschaften"* (Stuttgart: Metzler, 1970), and Maximilan Aue, "Musil und die Romantik. Einige grundsätzliche Überlegungen," in *Sprachästhetische Sinnvermittlung,* eds. Dieter P. Farda and Ulrich Karthaus (Frankfurt: Lang, 1982), 125–34.

48. This connection is explicitly stated in a sketch written after 1934 (*MoE* II, 1898), which presents the siblings' consummation of incest as symbolically collapsing two poles, namely, their biologically different bodies. This union, aimed at undoing the siblings' reciprocal otherness, destroys their love by annihilating their ability to converse. As Musil notes, such dialogical incapacitation results from that "obliteration of the opposition" produced by the siblings' union. One can conclude that realizing unity does not engender the bliss one glimpses in the exchange staged by love but rather annihilates the difference that nurtures love and makes the perception of bliss possible. Thus the siblings' endeavor to make the Other Condition permanent appears grounded in flawed premises from the onset. As in *Törless,* here too sexual intercourse seems to at first promise the attainment of an 'other' condition. In the end, however, this promise reveals itself as a delusion.

49. From here on my analysis focuses on unauthorized texts from the unpublished materials. The 1995 translation of *MwQ* offers a selection of these materials, translated by Burton Pike. Where parenthetical references point to the German edition, translations are mine.

50. This section encompasses the following "galley" chapters: Chapter 52, "To her displeasure, Agathe is confronted with a historical synopsis of the psychology of the emotions"; Chapter 54, "Naïve description of how an emotion originates"; and Chapter 55, "Feeling and behavior. The precariousness of emotion." The numerous variants revolving around the siblings' investigation reflect Musil's difficulties and hesitations. In the galley chapters (authorized for publication in 1937 and withdrawn the following year), this investigation unfolds in long essayistic passages

couched in diary notes written by Ulrich. In later drafts Musil did away with the fiction of the diaries, curtailing Ulrich's reflection on feeling and dramatically embedding it in conversations with Agathe. Musil's debt to contemporary studies on the psychology of feeling is documented in Renate Heydebrand, *Die Reflexionen Ulrichs in Robert Musils Roman "Der Mann ohne Eigenschaften"* (Münster: Aschendorff, 1966), 117–56.

51. Irmgard Honnef-Becker has examined the different levels of self-referential thematization of the novel within the novel. Her notion of a self-referential narrative is indebted to early Romantic aesthetics, which she sees as providing the frame for the novel's own enactment of self-referential structures. According to her definition, a self-referential narrative does not present, or refer to, an object 'outside' itself but rather thematizes its own inadequacy in the very task of presentation. In other words, the literary medium stages its own limitations in the self-imposed task of presenting reality, rather than presenting reality itself. Honnef-Becker's study limits itself to illustrating the different levels on which self-referentiality operates in the novel; it does not endeavor to situate this phenomenon within the broader horizon of Musil's aesthetic and ethical inquiry. Irmgard Honnef-Becker, "Selbstreferentielle Strukturen in Robert Musils Roman *Der Mann ohne Eigenschaften,*" *Wirkendes Wort* 44 (1994): 72–88.

52. For a discussion of Musil's documented or presumed debt to contemporary inquiries in the psychology and sociology of religion and their impact on his portrayal of the siblings's dialogs, see Heydebrand, 143–71.

53. In a planned sequel to this scene Ulrich argues that what is at stake are "Two *images* of the world! But only one reality! Perhaps one can nonetheless live in it one way or the other" (*MoE* I, 1279).

54. According to Musil's plans, this chapter was to mark a turning point in the siblings' relation (*MoE* II, 1281). It was to introduce their attempt at plunging ordinary experience into the Other Condition, possibly by means of their erotic union. Its centrality in the economy of the narration is underscored by the existence of five different drafts, to which Musil dedicated the last two years of his life. The drafts at issue here comprise (in the order in which they appear in the 1978 edition of *MoE*): 52, "Atemzüge eines Sommertags," Reinschrift ("Breaths of a Summer Day," fair copy; 1232–39); 52, "Atemzüge eines Sommertags" [Letzte Vorstufe zur Reinschrift] ("Breaths of a Summer Day," last draft before the fair copy; 1240–49); earlier drafts: 6.., "Atemzüge eines Sommertags" (1306–24); 61, "Atemzüge eines Sommertags" (1324–37); 63, "Versuche, ein Scheusal zu lieben" ("Attempts to Love a Monster," 1349–56). Due to Musil's practice of leaving texts undated, coupled with his habit of working on different drafts simultaneously, it is hard to determine with certainty the chronology and degree of legitimacy of the alternate drafts, though Musil reportedly expressed his satisfaction with one of these texts, whose fair copy (Reinschrift) he completed on the day of his death. See Karl Dinklage, "Ende der *Schwärmer,* Ende des *Mann ohne Eigenschaften,*" in

Robert Musil: Theater, Bildung, Kritik, eds. Josef Strutz and Johann Strutz (München: Fink, 1985), 228–29. This version, like the draft that seems to have immediately preceded it, ends somewhat abruptly with a discussion of feeling that appears to be a shortened version of the analogous section in the superseded diary chapters. The symbolic description of the garden, which forms the focus of my reading, is found only in the three longer versions predating the Reinschrift draft. Given Musil's proclivity for rearranging materials between different chapters, the absence of the allusive garden description from the Reinschrift version does not entail that the passage was to be dropped altogether.

55. The undertaking adumbrated in the siblings' relation is portrayed as a patent delusion from the onset. Though consumed by desire to realize an ideal love, Ulrich cannot help but suspect in the relation to his sister a self-deceived adventure driven by a "protest against life" (*MwQ* II, 1022), more specifically, against the fundamental human condition of self-division. As he had previously acknowledged, ". . . there was no doubt that what brought them together was not so much love for each other as a repelling of the rest of the world" (*MwQ* II, 951). Though less prone than Ulrich to indulge in self-analysis, Agathe also surmises the delusory character of their common enterprise: ". . . for if she summed things up quite honestly, this enchanted garden in which she found herself together with Ulrich was also, of course, more desire than reality. She did not really believe that the Millennium could have begun . . ." (*MwQ* II, 1191). According to some notes Musil jotted down in 1932, the siblings were to fully acknowledge their delusion after a symbolic trip into the "Millennium": "So the idea of the twins [is] an illusion. The illusion. The counter-illusion of ordinary integration. It collapses: end of the trip or dissipation" (*MoE* II, 1851).

56. This has been unconvincingly argued by Karl Dinklage, who pieced together anecdotal information and a number of conjectures to maintain that Musil decided to end the novel with the "summer day" chapter due to the increasing duress of his exile in Geneva. Dinklage, 228–29. Dinklage's claim is contradicted by several statements made by Musil himself shortly before his death, which document his plans for a sequel to the "summer day" complex. For a discussion of Musil's plans in the last months of his life, see Frisé's, 79–104.

57. See Musil's comments in this regard in *MwQ* II, 1747 and 1752.

Postscript

1. See the sketch titled "Concluding Section" (Schlußteil), most likely drafted after 1934 (*MoE* II, 1902).

2. See in this regard the comprehensive section on the "inductive way of thinking" found in Musil's *Nachlaß* (*MoE* II, 1882–84).

3. In this respect Musil argues, quite cryptically, for a "reduction of morality to moments of genius" (*MoE* II, 1882). The ensuing suggestion that genuine ethical

experience remains consigned to the private realm of 'genius morality' does little to specify this vision. Musil was planning on dedicating an important section of the second volume to this discussion, as demonstrated by the drafts of the so-called genius chapters from his unpublished materials. Written between 1939 and 1941, these chapters include 48, "A mentality directed toward the significant, and the beginning of a conversation on the subject" (*MwQ* II, 1335–41); 49, "General von Stumm on genius" (*MwQ* II, 1341–49); and 50, "Genius as a problem" (*MwQ* II, 1349–52). The main obstacles with which Musil was wrestling in this line of reflection are highlighted by his self-critical question, "What about the objection concerning the criterion of creation, of genius, of spirit [*des Geistes*]?" (*MoE* II, 1883). Musil realized that in defining true ethical experience as 'genius' he was simply reframing the problem without providing a solution. In fact, he was merely shifting the crucial issue of articulating a criterion for identifying the elusive realm of genuine morality from the domain of the ethical to the 'aesthetic' horizon of spontaneous creativity and prodigious illuminations that make up 'genius.'

Works Cited

Abrams, Meyer H. *The Mirror and the Lamp: Romantic Theory and the Critical Tradition.* New York: Oxford University Press, 1953.

Adorno, Theodor W. "Standort des Erzählers im zeitgenössischen Roman." 1954. *Noten zur Literatur. Gesammelte Schriften.* Vol. 11. Ed. Rolf Tiedemann. Frankfurt a.M.: Suhrkamp, 1974. 41–48

———. "The Essay as Form." Trans. Bob Hullot-Kentor and Frederic Will. *New German Critique* 32 (1984): 151–71.

Adorno, Theodor W., and Max Horkheimer. *Dialectic of Enlightenment.* Trans. John Cumming. New York: Herder and Herder, 1972.

Agamben, Giorgio. *Stanzas: Word and Phantasm in Western Culture.* Trans. Ronald L. Martinez. Minneapolis: University of Minnesota Press, 1993.

Anderson, Mark M. *Kafka's Clothes: Ornament and Aestheticism in the Habsburg Fin de Siècle.* Oxford, U.K.: Oxford University Press, 1992.

Arens, Katherine. *Functionalism and Fin de Siècle: Fritz Mauthner's Critique of Language.* New York: Lang, 1984.

———. *Structures of Knowing: Psychologies of the Nineteenth Century.* Dordrecht: Kluwer, 1989.

Arntzen, Helmut. "Ulrich und Agathe. Heilige Gespräche." *Sprachästhetische Sinnvermittlung.* Lang: Frankfurt a.M.: 1982. 117–24.

Ashheim, Steven E. *The Nietzsche Legacy in Germany, 1890–1990.* Berkeley: University of California Press, 1992.

Aue, Maximilan. "Musil und die Romantik. Einige grundsätzliche Überlegungen." In *Sprachästhetische Sinnvermittlung.* Eds. Dieter P. Farda and Ulrich Karthaus. Frankfurt: Lang, 1982. 125–34.

Bahr, Hermann. *Dialog vom Tragischen.* Berlin: Fischer, 1904.

———. *Zur Überwindung des Naturalismus. Theoretische Schriften 1887–1904.* Ed. Gotthard Wunberg. Stuttgart: Kohlhammer, 1968.

Bakhtin, Mikhail. *The Dialogical Imagination: Four Essays.* Ed. Michael Holquist. Trans. Caryl Emerson and Michael Holquist. Austin: University of Texas Press, 1981.

Balázs, Béla. *Der sichtbare Mensch oder die Kultur des Films.* Wien: Deutsch-Österreichischer Verlag, 1924.

Baltz-Balzberg, Regina. "Antidekadenzmoral bei Musil und Nietzsche." In *Robert Musil. Theater, Bildung, Kritik.* Eds. Josef Strutz and Johann Strutz. Munich: Fink, 1985. 204–26.

Bambach, Charles R. *Heidegger, Dilthey, and the Crisis of Historicism.* Ithaca, N.Y.: Cornell University Press, 1995.

Barnouw, Dagmar. *Weimar Intellectuals and the Threat of Modernity*. Bloomington: Indiana University Press, 1988.

Bathrick, David, and Andreas Huyssen, eds. *Modernity and the Text: Revisions of German Modernism*. New York: Columbia University Press, 1989.

Bauman, Zygmunt. *Legislators and Interpreters: On Modernity, Postmodernity, and Intellectuals*. Ithaca, N.Y.: Cornell University Press, 1987.

———. *Modernity and Ambivalence*. Ithaca, N.Y.: Cornell University Press, 1991.

Beard, Philip. "'Beginn einer Reihe wundersamer Erlebnisse': Prüfstein einer Umwandlung in Musils Gebrauch von Essayismus und Ironie." In *Robert Musil. Essayismus und Ironie*. Ed. Gudrun Brokoph-Mauch. Tübingen: Francke, 1992. 105–14.

Beiser, Frederick C. *The Fate of Reason: German Philosophy from Kant to Fichte*. Cambridge, Mass.: Harvard University Press, 1987.

Beller, Steven. *Vienna and the Jews, 1867–1938: A Cultural History*. Cambridge, U.K.: Cambridge University Press, 1989.

Beller, Steven, ed. *Rethinking Vienna 1900*. New York: Berghahn, 2001.

Benjamin, Walter. *Der Begriff der Kunstkritik in der deutschen Romantik*. 1920. *Abhandlungen. Gesammelte Schriften*. Ed. Rolf Tiedemann and Hermann Schweppenhäuser. Vol. I-1. Frankfurt a.M.: Suhrkamp, 1974. 7–122

———. *The Concept of Criticism in German Romanticism*. 1920. *Selected Writings*. Vol. 1: 1913–1926. Ed. Michael W. Jennings. Cambridge, Mass.: Harvard University Press, 1996. 116–200.

Berghahn, Volker. *Imperial Germany 1871–1914*. Providence: Berghahn, 1994.

Berman, Art. *Preface to Modernism*. Urbana: University of Illinois Press, 1994.

Bey, Gesine. "'Bei mir laudabile.' Zu Robert Musils Berliner Studienjahre." *Wissenschaftliche Zeitschrift der Humboldt Universität zu Berlin* 38.6 (1989): 655–66.

Blanchot, Maurice. *Le livre á venir*. Paris: Gallimard, 1959.

Blasberg, Cornelia. *Krise und Utopie der Intellektuellen. Kulturkritische Aspekte in Robert Musils Roman "Der Mann ohne Eigenschaften."* Stuttgart: Heinz Akademischer Verlag, 1984.

Böhme, Hartmut. *Anomie und Entfremdung: Literatursoziologische Untersuchungen zu den Essays Robert Musils und seinem Roman "Der Mann ohne Eigenschaften."* Kronberg: Scriptor, 1974.

———. "Die 'Zeit ohne Eigenschaften' und die 'neue Unübersichtlichkeit.' Robert Musil und die Posthistoire." In *Kunst, Wissenschaft und Politik von Robert Musil bis Ingeborg Bachmann*. Ed. Josef Strutz. München: Fink, 1986. 9–33.

———. "Theoretische Probleme der Interpretation von Robert Musils Roman 'Der Mann ohne Eigenschaften.'" 1976. Reprinted in *Robert Musil*. Ed. Renate von Heydebrand. Darmstadt: Wissenschaftliche Buchgesellschaft, 1982. 120–59.

Böhme, Hartmut, and Gernot Böhme. *Das Andere der Vernunft: Zur Entwicklung von Rationalitätsstrukturen am Beispiel Kants*. Frankfurt a.M.: Suhrkamp, 1983.

Bohrer, Karl Heinz. *Suddenness: On the Moment of Aesthetic Appearance*. 1981. Trans. Ruth Crowley, New York: Columbia University Press, 1994.

Bolterauer, Alice. *Rahmen und Riss. Robert Musil und die Moderne*. Wien: Praesens, 1999.

Bolz, Norbert. *Auszug aus der entzauberten Welt: philosophischer Extremismus zwischen den Weltkriegen*. München: Fink, 1989.

Bonacchi, Silvia. *Die Gestalt der Dichtung: Der Einfluss der Gestalttheorie auf das Werk Robert Musils*. Bern: Peter Lang, 1998.

Braun, Wilhelm. "Musil's Siamese Twins." *The Germanic Review* 33 (1958): 41–52.

———. "The Confusions of Törless." *The Germanic Review* 40 (1965): 116–31.

———. "The Temptation of Ulrich: The Problem of True and False Unity in Musil's 'Der Mann ohne Eigenschaften.'" *The German Quarterly* 29 (1956): 29–37.

Brokoph-Mauch, Gudrun, ed. *Robert Musil. Essayismus und Ironie*. Tübingen: Francke, 1992.

Buber, Martin. *Ecstatic Confessions*. 1909. Ed. Paul Mendes-Flohr. Trans. Esther Cameron. San Francisco: Harper & Row, 1985.

Bürger, Peter. "Literarische Form als Denkform: Musils 'Der Mann ohne Eigenschaften.'" In *Prosa der Moderne*. Peter Bürger and Christa Bürger. Frankfurt a.M.: Suhrkamp, 1988. 422–37.

———. "Literary Institution and Modernization." First published in *Poetics*, 12 (1983). In *The Decline of Modernism*. Trans. Nicholas Walker. University Park, Penn.: Pennsylvania State University Press, 1992. 3–18.

———. *Theory of the Avant-Garde*. Trans. Michael Shaw. Minneapolis: University of Minnesota Press, 1984.

Calinescu, Matei. *Five Faces of Modernity: Modernism, Avant-Garde, Decadence, Kitsch, Postmodernism*. Second, revised edition. Durham, N.C.: Duke University Press, 1987.

Chamberlain, Houston Stewart. *Foundations of the Nineteenth Century*. 1899. Trans. John Lee. New York: Fertig, 1968.

Chamberlin, Edward, and Sander Gilman, eds. *Degeneration: The Dark Side of Progress*. New York: Columbia University Press, 1985.

Classen, Albrecht. "Robert Musil, *Der Mann ohne Eigenschaften:* Der antizipatorische Charakter des ersten Buches." *Carleton Germanic Papers* 15 (1987): 1–16.

Connolly, William E. *Political Theory and Modernity*. Ithaca, N.Y.: Cornell University Press, 1993.

Corino, Karl. *Robert Musil. Leben und Werk in Bildern und Texten*. Reinbek bei Hamburg: Rowohlt, 1988.

———. *Robert Musil: Eine Biographie*. Reinbek bei Hamburg: Rowohlt, 2004.

———. "Robert Musil und Alfred Kerr. Der Dichter und sein Kritiker." In *Robert Musil. Studien zu seinem Werk*. Eds. Karl Dinklage, Elisabeth Albertsen, and Karl Corino. Reinbek bei Hamburg: Rowohlt, 1970. 236–83.

Corngold, Stanley. *Complex Pleasure: Forms of Feeling in German Literature*. Stanford, Calif.: Stanford University Press, 1998.

Daigger, Annette. "Musils politische Haltung in seinen frühen Essays." In *Robert Musil. Essayismus und Ironie*. Ed. Gudrun Brokoph-Mauch. Tübingen: Francke, 1992. 75–89.

Dawidowski, Christian. *Die geschwächte Moderne: Robert Musils episches Frühwerk im Spiegel der Epochendebatte*. Frankfurt a.M.: Lang, 2000.

Diersch, Manfred. *Empiriokritizismus und Impressionismus: Über Beziehungen zwischen Philosophie, Ästhetik und Literatur um 1900 in Wien*. Berlin: Rütten & Loening, 1973.

Dinklage, Karl. "Ende der *Schwärmer*, Ende des *Mann ohne Eigenschaften*." In *Robert Musil: Theater, Bildung, Kritik*. Ed. Josef Strutz and Johann Strutz. München: Fink, 1985. 227–43.

Ehrenfels, Christian von. "Über Gestaltqualitäten." 1890. *Psychologie, Ethik, Erkenntnistheorie. Philosophische Schriften*. Vol 3. Ed. Reinhard Fabian. München / Wien: Philosophia, 1988. 128–167.

Eisele, Ulf. "Ulrich's Mutter ist *doch* ein Tintenfaß. Zur Literaturproblematik in Musils 'Mann ohne Eigenschaften.'" In *Robert Musil*. Ed. Renate von Heydebrand. Darmstadt: Wissenschaftliche Buchgesellschaft, 1982. 160–203.

Eksteins, Modris. *Rites of Spring: The Great War and the Birth of the Modern Age*. New York: Houghton Mifflin, 1989.

Everdell, William R. *The First Moderns: Profiles in the Origin of Twentieth-Century Thought*. Chicago: University of Chicago Press, 1997.

Fanta, Walter. *Die Entstehungsgeschichte des "Mann ohne Eigenschaften" von Robert Musil*. Wien: Böhlau, 2000.

Finlay, Marike. *The Potential of Modern Discourse: Musil, Peirce, and Perturbation*. Bloomington: Indiana University Press, 1990.

Frank, Manfred. "Auf der Suche nach einem Grund. Über den Umschlag von Erkenntniskritik in Mythologie bei Musil." In *Mythos und Moderne*. Ed. Karl Heinz Bohrer. Frankfurt a.M.: Suhrkamp, 1983. 318–62.

Frey, Hans Jost. *Der unendliche Text*. Frankfurt a.M.: Suhrkamp, 1990.

Frisé, Adolf. "Unvollendet—Unvollendbar? Überlegungen zum Torso des *Mann ohne Eigenschaften*." *Musil-Forum* 6(1):79–104.

Gay, Peter. *Weimar Culture: The Outsider as Insider*. New York: Harper & Row, 1968.

Gilman, Sander L. *Freud, Race, and Gender*. Princeton, N.J.: Princeton University Press, 1993.

———. *The Case of Sigmund Freud: Medicine and Identity at the Fin de Siècle*. Baltimore, Md.: Johns Hopkins University Press, 1993.

Gnam, Andrea. "Referenzverlust als narratives Problem." *Wirkendes Wort* 43 (1993): 90–98.

Goltschnigg, Dietmar. *Mystische Tradition im Roman Robert Musils.* Heidelberg: Stiehm, 1974.

———. "Zur Poetik des Essays und des Essayismus bei Robert Musil und Hermann Broch." In *Poetik und Geschichte.* Ed. Dieter Borchmeyer. Tübingen: Niemeyer, 1989. 412–24.

Guyer, Paul. *Kant and the Claims of Taste.* Second edition. Cambridge, New York: Cambridge University Press, 1997.

———. *Kant and the Experience of Freedom: Essays on Aesthetics and Morality.* Cambridge, U.K.: Cambridge University Press, 1993.

Habermas, Jürgen. "Modernity versus Postmodernity." 1979. *New German Critique* 22 (Winter 1981): 3–14.

———. *The Philosophical Discourse of Modernity: Twelve Lectures.* Trans. Frederick G. Lawrence. Cambridge, Mass.: MIT Press, 1987.

———. *The Structural Transformation of the Public Sphere.* Trans. Thomas Burger. Cambridge, Mass.: MIT Press, 1989.

———. *The Theory of Communicative Action.* 1981. Trans. Thomas McCarthy. Boston: Beacon, 1984.

Hamlyn, D. W. *The Psychology of Perception: A Philosophical Examination of Gestalt Theory and Derivative Theories of Perception.* London: Routledge & Paul, 1957.

Harrington, Anne H. *Reenchanted Science: Holism in German Culture from Wilhelm II to Hitler.* Princeton, N.J.: Princeton University Press, 1996.

Harrison, Thomas. *Essayism: Conrad, Musil, and Pirandello.* Baltimore, Md.: Johns Hopkins University Press, 1992.

Henderson, Linda Dalrymple. "Die moderne Kunst und das Unsichtbare: Die verborgenen Wellen und Dimensionen des Okkultismus und der Wissenschaften." In *Okkultismus und Avantgarde. Von Munch bis Mondrian 1900–1915.* Ed. Hellmut Seemann and Veit Loers. Frankfurt: Tertium, 1995. 13–31.

———. *The Fourth Dimension and Non-Euclidean Geometry in Modern Art.* Princeton, N.J.: Princeton University Press, 1983.

Henninger, Peter. *Der Buchstabe und der Geist: Unberwußte Determinierung im Schreiben Robert Musils.* Frankfurt a.M.: Lang, 1980.

Herf, Jeffrey. *Reactionary Modernism: Technology, Culture, and Politics in Weimar and the Third Reich.* Cambridge/New York: Cambridge University Press, 1984.

Heydebrand, Renate von. *Die Reflexionen Ulrichs in Robert Musils Roman "Der Mann ohne Eigenschaften."* Münster: Aschendorff, 1966.

Hickman, Hannah. *Robert Musil and the Culture of Vienna.* LaSalle, Ill.: Open Court, 1984.

Hofmannsthal, Hugo von. *Reden und Aufsätze I, 1891–1913*. Ed. Bernd Schoeller. Frankfurt a.M.: Fischer, 1979.

———. *The Lord Chandos Letter*. Trans. Russel Stockman. Marlboro, Vt.: The Marlboro Press, 1986.

Hohendahl, Peter Uwe. "The Scholar, the Intellectual, and the Essay: Weber, Lukács, Adorno, and Postwar Germany." *The German Quarterly* 70.3 (Summer 1997): 217–32.

Honnef-Becker, Irmgard. "Selbstreferentielle Strukturen in Robert Musils Roman *Der Mann ohne Eigenschaften*." *Wirkendes Wort* 44 (1994): 72–88.

Hörisch, Jochen. "Selbstbeziehung und ästhetische Autonomie. Versuch über ein Thema der frühromantischen Poetologie und Musils *Mann ohne Eigenschaften*." *Euphorion* 69 (1975): 350–61.

Howes, Geoffrey. "Ein Genre ohne Eigenschaften: Musil, Montaigne, Sterne und die essayistische Tradition." In *Robert Musil. Essayismus und Ironie*. Ed. Gudrun Brokoph-Mauch. Tübingen: Francke, 1992. 1–11.

Huch, Ricarda *Die Blütezeit der Romantik*. Leipzig: Haessel, 1905.

Hüppauf, Bernd. "Musil in Paris. Robert Musils Rede auf dem Kongreß zur Verteidigung der Kultur (1935) im Zusammenhang seines Werkes." *Zeitschrift für Germanistik* I:1 (1991): 55–69.

———. "Von Wien durch den Krieg nach irgendwo: Nation und utopisches Denken bei Musil und im Austromarxismus." In *Text + Kritik: Zeitschrift für Literatur*, 21–21, third ed. (November 1983): 1–28.

Jakob, Michael. "'Möglichkeitssinn' und Philosophie der Möglichkeit." In *Robert Musil. Essayismus und Ironie*, ed. Gudrun Brokoph-Mauch. Tübingen: Francke, 1992. 13–24.

Janik, Allan. *Wittgenstein's Vienna Revisited*. New Brunswick, N.J.: Transaction Publishers, 2001.

Janik, Allan, and Stephen Toulmin. *Wittgenstein's Vienna*. New York: Simon & Schuster, 1973.

Johnston, William M. *The Austrian Mind: An Intellectual and Social History, 1848–1938*. Berkeley: University of California Press, 1972.

Jonsson, Stefan. *Subject without Nation: Robert Musil and the History of Modern Identity*. Durham, N.C.: Duke University Press, 2000.

Kandinsky, Wassily. *Concerning the Spiritual in Art*. Trans. M.T.H. Sadler. New York: Dover, 1977.

Kandinsky, Wassily, and Franz Marc. *The Blaue Reiter Almanach*. 1912. Second edition. Ed. Klaus Lankheit. New York: DaCapo, 1989.

Kant, Immanuel. *Critique of Judgment*. Trans. John Henry Bernard. New York: Hafner, 1951.

———. *Critique of Pure Reason*. Trans. and ed. Paul Guyer and Allen W. Wood. Cambridge, U.K.: Cambridge University Press, 1999.

———. *Werkausgabe*. Ed. Wilhelm Weischedel. Frankfurt a.M.: Suhrkamp, 1974.

———. "What Is Orientation in Thinking?" 1786. *Kant: Political Writings*. Trans. H. B. Nisbet. Ed. Hans Reiss. Cambridge, U.K.: Cambridge University Press, 1970.

Karthaus, Ulrich. *Der andere Zustand. Zeitstrukturen im Werke Robert Musils*. Berlin: Schmidt, 1965.

———. "Der Mann ohne Eigenschaften und die Phantasie. Überlegungen im Anschluß an Kant." *Musil-Forum* 7 (1981): 111–17.

Kassner, Rudolf. *Die Moral der Musik*. München: Bruckmann, 1905.

Key, Ellen. *Century of the Child*. New York: Putnam, 1909.

———. "Die Entfaltung der Seele durch Lebenskunst." *Die Neue Rundschau* 1(1905): 641–86.

Klages, Ludwig. *Vom kosmogonischen Eros*. München: Georg Müller, 1922.

Koffka, Kurt. *Principles of Gestalt Psychology*. New York: Harcourt, Brace and Company, 1935.

Köhler, Wolfgang. *Die physikalischen gestalten in ruhe und im stationären zustand*. Erlangen: Philosophische Akademie, 1924.

Köhnke, Klaus. *The Rise of Neo-Kantianism: German Academic Philosophy between Idealism and Positivism*. 1986. Trans. R.J. Hollingdale. Cambridge, U.K.: Cambridge University Press, 1991.

Kretschmer, Ernst. *Medizinische Psychologie*. Leipzig: Thieme, 1922.

LaCapra, Dominick. "Trauma, Absence, Loss." *Critical Inquiry* 25 (1999): 696–727.

Laermann, Klaus. *Eigenschaftslosigkeit: Reflexionen zu Musils Roman "Der Mann ohne Eigenschaften."* Stuttgart: Metzler, 1970.

Landauer, Gustav. *Skepsis und Mystik. Versuche im Anschluß an Mauthners Sprachkritik*. Berlin: Fontane, 1903.

Large, Duncan. "Experimenting with Experience: Robert Musil, *Der Mann ohne Eigenschaften*. " In *The German Novel in the 20th Century*. Ed. David Midgley. Edinburgh: Edinburgh University Press, 1993, 110–27.

Lepenies, Wolf. *Between Literature and Science: The Rise of Sociology*. 1985. Trans. R. J. Hollingdale. Cambridge, U.K.: Cambridge University Press, 1988.

LeRider, Jacques. *Modernity and Crises of Identity: Culture and Society in Fin-de-Siècle Vienna*. Trans. Rosemary Morris. New York: Continuum, 1993.

Lethen, Helmut. *Cool Conduct: The Culture of Distance in Weimar Germany*. 1994. Trans. Don Reneau. Berkeley: University of California Press, 2002.

Lévy-Bruhl, Lucien. *Les fonctions mentales dans les sociétés inférieures*. Paris: Alcan, 1910.

Lindner, Martin. *Leben in der Krise. Zeitromane der neuen Sachlichkeit und die intellektuelle Mentalität der klassischen Moderne*. Stuttgart: Metzler, 1994.

Luft, David S. *Robert Musil and the Crisis of European Culture, 1880–1942*. Berkeley: University of California Press, 1980.

Lukács, Georg. "On the Nature and Form of the Essay." *Soul and Form*. 1910. Trans. Anna Bostock. Cambridge, Mass.: MIT Press, 1974. 1–18.

———. *The Theory of the Novel.* 1920. Trans. Anna Bostock. Cambridge, Mass.: MIT Press, 1971.

Luserke, Matthias. *Robert Musil.* Stuttgart: Metzler, 1995.

Lyotard, Jean-François. *Lessons on the Analytic of the Sublime.* 1991. Trans. Elisabeth Rottenberg. Stanford, Calif.: Stanford University Press, 1994.

———. *The Postmodern Condition: A Report on Knowledge.* Trans. Brian Massumi. Minneapolis: University of Minnesota Press, 1984.

Mach, Ernst. *Popular Scientific Lectures.* Trans. Thomas J. McCormack. LaSalle, Ill.: Open Court, 1986.

———. *The Analysis of Sensations and the Relation of the Physical to the Psychical.* Trans. C. M. Williams. New York: Dover, 1959.

Maeterlinck, Maurice. *The Treasure of the Humble.* Trans. Alfred Sutro. London: Allen, 1897.

Magris, Claudio. *Der habsburgische Mythos in der österreichischen Literatur.* Trans. Madeleine von Pásztory. Salzburg: Otto Müller, 1966.

———. *Der Ring der Clarisse. Großer Stil und Nihilismus in der modernen Literatur.* 1984. Trans. Christine Wolter. Frankfurt a.M.: Suhrkamp, 1987.

Maier-Solgk, Frank. "Musil und die problematische Politik: Zum Verhältnis von Literatur und Politik bei Robert Musil, insbesondere zu einer Auseinadersetzung mit Carl Schmitt." *Orbis Literarum* 46.6 (1991): 340–63.

Mann, Thomas. *Reflections of a Non-Political Man.* Trans. Walter Morris. New York: Ungar 1983.

Mannheim, Karl. *Ideology and Utopia.* New York: Harcourt, Brace & World, 1936.

Mauthner, Fritz. *Beiträge zu einer Kritik der Sprache.* 1901–2. Hildesheim: Olms, 1967.

———. *Gottlose Mystik.* Dresden: Carl Reissner, 1924.

McBride, Patrizia C. "On the Utility of Art for Politics: Musil's 'Armed Truce of Ideas.'" *The German Quarterly* (Fall 2000): 366–86.

McCarthy, John A. *Crossing Boundaries: A Theory and History of Essay Writing in German, 1680–1815.* Philadelphia: University of Pennsylvania Press, 1989.

Mehigan, Tim. *Critical Responses to Robert Musil's* The Man without Qualities. Rochester, NY: Camden, 2003.

Midgley, David R. "'Das hilflose Europa': Eine Aufforderung, die politischen Essays von Robert Musil neu zu lesen." *The German Quarterly* 67.1 (1994): 16–26.

Mommsen, Wolfgang J. *Bürgerliche Kultur und künstlerische Avantgarde. Kultur und Politik im deutschen Kaiserreich, 1870 bis 1918.* Berlin: Propyläen, 1994.

———. *Imperial Germany 1867–1918: Politics, Culture, and Society in an Authoritarian State.* Trans. Richard Deveson. London: Arnold, 1995.

Monti, Claudia. *Musil. La metafora della scienza.* Napoli: Pironti, 1983.

Moser, Manfred. "Erinnerung, blitzartiger Einfall und—natürlich—die Ironie." In *Robert Musil. Theater, Bildung, Kritik.* Ed. Johann Strutz and Josef Strutz. Munich: Fink, 1985. 110–42.

Moser, Walter. "Diskursexperimente im Romantext zu Musils *Der Mann ohne Eigenschaften*." In *Robert Musils: Untersuchungen*. Ed. Uwe Baur and Elisabeth Castex. Königstein/Taunus: Athenäum, 1980. 170–97.

Mosse, George L. *The Crisis of German Ideology: Intellectual Origins of the Third Reich*. New York, Grosset & Dunlap, 1964.

Müller-Funk, Wolfgang. *Erfahrung und Experiment. Studien zu Theorie und Geschichte des Essayismus*. Berlin: Akademie, 1995.

Münsterberg, Hugo. *Grundzüge der Psychotechnik*. Leipzig: Barth, 1914.

Musil, Robert. *Beitrag zur Beurteilung der Lehren Machs*. 1908. Ed. Adolf Frisé. Reinbek bei Hamburg: Rowohlt, 1980.

———. *Briefe 1901–1942*. 2 vols. Ed. Adolf Frisé. Reinbek bei Hamburg: Rowohlt, 1981.

———. *Der literarische Nachlaß*. CD-ROM. Ed. Friedbert Aspetsberger, Karl Eibl, and Adolf Frisé. Reinbek bei Hamburg: Rowohlt, 1992.

———. *Diaries 1899–1941*. Trans. Philip Payne. Ed. Mark Mirsky. New York: Basic Books, 1998.

———. *The Enthusiasts*. Trans. Andrea Simon. New York: Performing Arts Journal Publications, 1983.

———. *Gesammelte Werke in neun Bänden*. Ed. Adolf Frisé. 9 vols. Reinbek bei Hamburg: Rowohlt, 1978.

———. *On Mach's Theories*. Trans. Kevin Mulligan. Washington, D.C.: Catholic University of America Press, 1982.

———. *Precision and Soul: Essays and Addresses*. Ed. and trans. Burton Pike and David S. Luft. Chicago: University of Chicago Press, 1990.

———. *Selected Writings*. Ed. Burton Pike. Trans. Ernst Kaiser, Burton Pike, and Eithne Wilkins. New York: Continuum, 1986.

———. *Tagebücher*. Ed. Adolf Frisé. 2 vols. Second, revised edition. Reinbek bei Hamburg: Rowohlt, 1983.

———. *The Confusions of Young Törless*. Trans. Shaun Whiteside. New York: Penguin, 2001.

———. *The Man without Qualities*. Trans. Sophie Wilkins and Burton Pike. 2 vols. New York: Knopf, 1995.

Nietzsche, Friedrich. *Kritische Studienausgabe*. 15 vols. Eds. Giorgio Colli and Mazzino Montinari. Second edition. München: dtv/de Gruyter, 1988.

———. *Basic Writings of Nietzsche*. Trans. and ed. Walter Kaufmann. New York: Modern Library, 1968.

———. *Human, All Too Human*. Trans. R. J. Hollingdale. Cambridge, UK: Cambridge University Press, 1986.

———. *The Gay Science*. Trans. Walter Kaufmann. New York: Vintage, 1974.

———. *On the Genealogy of Morals*. Trans. Walter Kaufmann. New York: Vintage, 1989.

———. *Unfashionable Observations*. Trans. Richard T. Gray. Stanford, Calif.: Stanford University Press, 1995.

Nordau, Max. *Degeneration*. 1895. Lincoln: University of Nebraska Press, 1993.

Pike, Burton. *Robert Musil: An Introduction to His Work*. Ithaca, N.Y.: Cornell University Press, 1961.

Pott, Hans-Georg. *Robert Musil*. Munich: Fink, 1984.

Rabinbach, Anson. *In the Shadow of Catastrophe: German Intellectuals Between Apocalypse and Enlightenment*. Berkeley: University of California Press, 1997.

Rasch, Wolfdietrich. "Musil. *Der Mann ohne Eigenschaften*." In *Der deutsche Roman. Vom Barock bis zur Gegenwart*. Ed. Benno von Wiese. Düsseldorf: Bagel, 1965. vol. 2. 361–419.

Rathenau, Walther. *Zur Mechanik des Geistes oder Vom Reich des Seele* (1913). *Hauptwerke und Gespräche. Walter Rathenau-Gesamtausgabe* II, ed. Ernst Schulin. Munich: Gotthold Müller, 1977. 105–295.

Rentsch, Thomas. "Wie ist ein Mann ohne Eigenschaften überhaupt möglich? Philosophische Bemerkungen zu Musil." In *Paradigmen der Moderne*, ed. Helmut Bachmaier. Amsterdam: Benjamins, 1990. 50–76.

Rieckmann, Jens. *Aufbruch in die Moderne. Die Anfänge des Jungen Wien*. Königstein / Taunus: Athenäum, 1985.

Rogowski, Christian. *Distinguished Outsider: Robert Musil and His Critics*. Columbia, S.C.: Camden, 1994.

———. *Implied Dramaturgy: Robert Musil and the Crisis of Modern Drama*. Riverside, Calif.: Ariadne Press, 1993.

Ronell, Avital. *Stupidity*. Urbana: University of Illinois Press, 2002.

Roth, Marie-Louise. *Robert Musil. Ethik und Ästhetik. Zum theoretischen Werk des Dichters*. München: List, 1972.

Russegger, Arno. *Kinema Mundi. Studien zur Theorie des "Bildes" bei Robert Musil*. Vienna: Böhlau, 1996.

Ryan, Judith. *The Vanishing Subject: Early Psychology and Literary Modernism*. Chicago: University of Chicago Press, 1991.

Schärf, Christian. *Geschichte des Essays. Von Montaigne bis Adorno*. Göttingen: Vandenhoeck & Ruprecht, 1999.

Scheler, Max. *Wesen und Formen der Sympathie*. Second ed. Bonn: F. Cohen, 1923.

Schiller, Dieter. "'Die Grenze der Kultur gegen die Politik.' Zu Robert Musils Rede auf dem Pariser Kongreß 1935 (mit Dokumenten.)" *Zeitschrift für Germanistik* 3 (1988): 274–90.

Schlegel, Friedrich. *Kritische Friedrich-Schlegel-Ausgabe*. Ed. Ernst Behler. München: Schoningh, 1967.

Schneiders, Werner. *Deutsche Philosophie im 20. Jahrhundert*. München: Beck, 1998.

Schorske, Carl. *Fin-de-siècle Vienna: Politics and Culture*. New York: Knopf, 1980.

Schulte-Sasse, Jochen. "Foreword: Theory of Modernism Versus Theory of the

Avant-Garde." In Peter Bürger, *Theory of the Avant-Garde*. Trans. Michael Shaw. Minneapolis: University of Minnesota Press, 1984. vii–xlvii.

———. "Imagination and Modernity: Or the Taming of the Human Mind." *Cultural Critique* 5 (Winter 1987): 23–48.

———. "Modernity and Modernism, Postmodernity and Postmodernism: Framing the Issue." *Cultural Critique* 5 (Winter 1987): 5–22.

Simon, Walter B. *Die verirrte Erste Republik: eine Korrektur österreichischer Geschichtsbilder*. Innsbruck: Multiplex, 1988.

Söder, Thomas. *Untersuchungen zu Robert Musils "Verwirrungen des Zöglings Törless."* Rheinfelden: Schäuble, 1988.

Spengler, Oswald. *The Decline of the West*. 1918–22. Trans. Charles F. Atkinson. New York: Knopf, 1926–28.

Spörl, Uwe. *Gottlose Mystik in der deutschen Literatur um die Jahrhundertwende*. Paderborn: Schöningh, 1997.

Sprengel, Peter. *Literatur im Kaiserreich: Studien zur Moderne*. Berlin: Schmidt, 1993.

Sprengel, Peter, and Gregor Streim. *Berliner und Wiener Moderne: Vermittlungen und Abgrenzungen in Literatur, Theater, Publizistik*. Wien: Böhlau, 1998.

Stadler, Friedrich. *Studien zum Wiener Kreis: Ursprung, Entwicklung und Wirkung des logischen Empirismus im Kontext*. Frankfurt a.M.: Suhrkamp, 1997.

Steinberg, Michael P. *Austria as Theater and Ideology: The Meaning of the Salzburg Festival*. Second edition. Ithaca, N.Y.: Cornell University Press, 2000.

Stern, Fritz. *Einstein's German World*. Princeton, N.J.: Princeton University Press, 1999.

———. *The Politics of Cultural Despair: A Study in the Rise of the Germanic Ideology*. Berkeley: University of California Press, 1961.

Tewilt, Gerd-Theo. *Zustand der Dichtung. Interpretationen zur Sprachlichkeit des "anderen Zustands" in Robert Musils "Mann ohne Eigenschaften."* Münster: Aschendorff, 1990.

Todorov, Tzvetan. *Theories of the Symbol*. 1977. Trans. Catherine Porter. Ithaca, N.Y.: Cornell University Press, 1982.

Varsava, Jerry A. "Törless at the Limits of Language: A Revised Reading." *Seminar: A Journal of Germanic Studies* 20.3 (September 1984): 188–204.

Vogt, Guntram. "Robert Musil: Politik als Methode. Zum Kontext von Kunst, Wissenschaft, Politik." In *Kunst, Wissenschaft, und Politik von Robert Musil bis Ingeborg Bachmann*. Ed. Josef Strutz. München: Fink, 1986. 146–64.

Webber, Andrew. "Sense and Sensuality in Musil's *Törless*." *German Life and Letters* 41.2 (1988): 106–30.

Weber, Max. *From Max Weber: Essays in Sociology*. Trans. and ed. H. H. Gerth and C. Wright Mills. New York: Oxford University Press, 1946.

———. *The Protestant Ethic and the Spirit of Capitalism*. Trans. Talcott Parsons. Los Angeles: Roxbury, 1998.

Weininger, Otto. *Geschlecht und Charakter: Eine prinzipielle Untersuchung*. 1903. München: Matthes & Seitz, 1980.

Weissensteiner, Friedrich. *Der ungeliebte Staat: Österreich zwischen 1918 und 1938*. Vienna: Österreichischer Bundesverlag, 1990.

Willemsen, Roger. *Das Existenzrecht der Dichtung. Zur Rekonstruktion einer systematischen Literaturtheorie im Werk Robert Musils*. München: Fink, 1984.

———. *Robert Musil. Vom intellektuellen Eros*. München: Piper, 1985.

Willey, Thomas. *Back to Kant: The Revival of Kantianism in German Social and Historical Thought, 1860–1914*. Detroit, Mich.: Wayne State University Press, 1978.

Williams, Cedric E. *The Broken Eagle: The Politics of Austrian Literature from Empire to Anschluss*. London: Elek, 1974.

Wittgenstein, Ludwig. *Tractatus Logico-Philosophicus*. Trans. C. K. Ogden. London: Routledge and Kegan Paul, 1933.

Wohl, Robert. *The Generation of 1914*. Cambridge, Mass.: Harvard University Press, 1979.

Zima, Peter V. "Robert Musils Sprachkritik. Ambivalenz, Polyphonie und Dekonstruktion." In *Robert Musil. Theater, Bildung, Kritik*. Eds. Josef Strutz and Johann Strutz. München: Fink, 1985. 185–203.

Zweig, Stefan. *The World of Yesterday: An Autobiography*. New York: Viking, 1943.

Index

About the Author

Patrizia C. McBride is an associate professor of German in the Department of German, Scandinavian, and Dutch at the University of Minnesota.

Avant-Garde & Modernism Studies